SHIRLEY STACKHOUSE'S GARDENING YEAR

SHIRLEY STACKHOUSE'S GARDENING YEAR

ANGUS & ROBERTSON PUBLISHERS

ANGUS & ROBERTSON PUBLISHERS

Unit 4, Eden Park, 31 Waterloo Road,
North Ryde, NSW, Australia 2113;
94 Newton Road, Auckland 1,
New Zealand; and
16 Golden Square, London W1R 4BN,
United Kingdom

First published in Australia
by Angus & Robertson Publishers in 1980
Paperbound edition 1981
Reprinted 1985, 1986, 1989

National Library of Australia
Cataloguing-in-publication data.

Stackhouse, Shirley.
Shirley Stackhouse's gardening year.

Index
ISBN 0 207 14817 1

1. Gardening. I. Title.

635

Typeset in 10pt Paladium by
Graphicraft Typesetters
Printed in Singapore

CONTENTS

INTRODUCTION

THIS book is based on the gardening column I have written for the *Sydney Morning Herald* over the past twelve years. Though considerably changed from their original form I hope that readers may find some of their favourite "bits" and that those of you who have been clipping and saving columns over the years may at last be able to discard them in favour of the book.

As Australia is a big country with many different climatic zones, the times generally given for planting and flowering have a bias towards the temperate region where the majority of Australian gardeners are to be found. Gardeners in hot or very cold climates will need to adjust the times a month to six weeks either way depending on their particular area.

Lists of plants given in the "Flowering Now" pages are not meant to be complete — long lists are boring — but hopefully enough to be helpful in planning a garden.

The book is intended to be read for enjoyment as well as for gardening information — perhaps it will provide just that bumper book of bedside reading you have been looking for.

Shirley J. Stackhouse.

Grevilleas are rapid-growing, hardy plants and flower over a long period.

CHECKLIST

It is usually too hot in January to undertake anything too strenuous in the garden but routine weeding, watering and spraying must be maintained. Try to do as much as possible early in the morning or in the late afternoon when you can take advantage of daylight saving.

Skin cancer is a real hazard, so wear a hat and sun screen lotion while gardening in the sun.

Flowering now

Trees and shrubs:
Abelia,
Abutilon,
Acalypha hispida (Chenille Plant),
Beloperone (Shrimp Plant),
Calodendron capense (Cape Chestnut),
Cassia fistula,
Ceratostigma willmottianum (Skybush),
Clerodendron ugandense (Butterfly Bush)
Cuphea,
Delonix regia (Poinciana),
Duranta,
Fuchsia,
Gardenia,
Hebe,
Hibiscus,
Hydrangea,
Lagerstroemia (Crepe Myrtle),
Lavender,
Malvaviscus,
Murraya,
Mussaenda,
Nerium (Oleander),
Pentas,
Plumbago,
Plumeria (Frangipani),
Punica (Pomegranate),
Roses,
Russelia,
Tecomaria,
Tibouchina (Lasiandra),
Vitex.

Annuals and perennials:
Alyssum,
Aster,
Begonia,
Daisy (Marguerite, Shasta, Pyrethrum),
Felicia,
Geranium,
Impatiens (Busy Lizzie),
Perennial Phlox,
Petunia,
Marigold,
Stokesia (Stoke's Aster),
Verbena,
Zinnia.

Bulbs:
Agapanthus,
Canna,
Crinum,
Dahlia,
Gladiolus,
Gloriosa Lily,
Hemerocallis (Day Lily),
Ismene (Spider Lily),
Lilium species.

Climbers:
Allamanda,
Antigonon,
Beaumontia,
Bougainvillea,
Campsis,
Clerodendron,
Doxantha,
Lonicera (Honeysuckle),

White and blue Agapanthus flowering now make good clump plantings and low hedges.

JANUARY

Plant

Mandevilla,
Maurandya,
Solandra (Cup of Gold),
Thunbergia.

Natives:
Acacia elata (Cedar wattle),
A. implexa (Hickory Wattle),
A. longissima,
A. maidenii,
Brachychiton populneus (Kurrajong),
Buckinghamia (Ivory Curl Tree),
Ceratopetalum gummiferum (New South Wales Xmas Bush),
Craspedia (Billy Buttons),
Crotalaria (Bird Flower),
Gossypium (Sturt's Desert Rose),
Grevillea spp.,
Hibbertia scandens,
Hibiscus splendens,
Hibiscus tileaceus (Cotton Tree),
Omalanthus populinifolius (Bleeding Heart Tree).

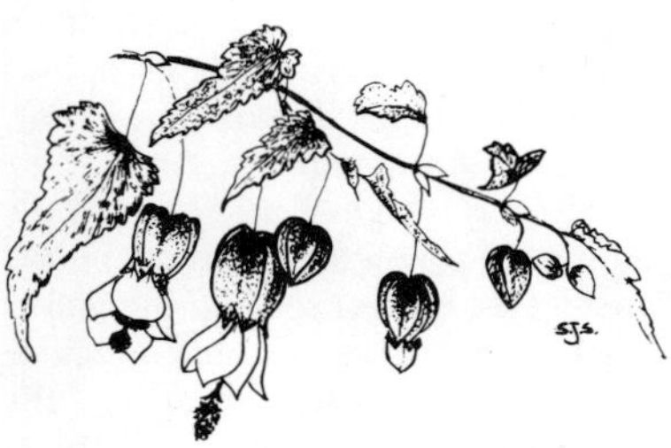

Summer-flowering Abutilon megapotanicum — *a good plant for a ground cover or basket. It has prostrate growth, variegated leaves and red and yellow bells.*

Trees, shrubs and climbers:
Plant out Christmas gift potted plants (in the garden or repot for balcony or patio use). Plant Hydrangeas in the shade. Expose other container plants to the sun gradually to harden them off. If your flower display has been spoiled by bad weather, add extra colour with plantings of small-foliage plants such as Coleus, Iresine, *Vinca major* "Variegata" and silvery Artemesia, Santolina, Senecio and Nepeta (Catmint). Climbing plants such as Allamanda, Antigonon, Bougainvillea and many other summer/autumn flowering creepers are available now, some in flower.

Annuals: Seedlings of annuals like Marigolds and Snapdragons can still be planted to give flowers through to autumn. Seeds of winter/spring flowering annuals can be started in seed boxes and kept in a cool semi-shade position.

Bulbs:
Brunsvigia,
Clivia,
Colchicum,
Crinum,
Liriope,
Nerine,
Sternbergia,
Zephyranthes (Storm Lily).
(See also p. 16.)

Vegetables:
Late summer plantings of beans (butter and French),
beetroot,
broccoli,
cabbage,
carrot,
Chinese cabbage,
lettuce (summer varieties only),
radish,
silver beet,
sweet corn,
tomato.

Cool-temperate areas only:
Brussels sprouts,
peas,
turnip,

Coast and inland:
Cauliflower,
celery,
cucumber,
leek.

Fertilise

Gardens can be fertilised now with an all-purpose fertiliser broadcast evenly. Azaleas, Camellias and Daphne can be fertilised with special Camellia and Azalea fertiliser. Water before and after applying the fertiliser, to prevent burning and ensure absorption.

Roses should be watered regularly and fertilised with an all-purpose fertiliser or a mulch of cow or fowl manure in preparation for the autumn flush. (See also p. 16.)

Keep leafy vegetables growing quickly with regular watering and fortnightly applications of foliar fertiliser. Lettuce can quickly run to seed in hot weather if not forced. Give passionfruit dressings of complete fertiliser and give fruiting tomatoes side dressings of sulphate of ammonia.

Prune

This is not a big pruning period, but regular pruning of spent flower heads will maintain compact growth and good flowering, particularly with Roses now. Berries are now set on Cotoneasters and long summer canes (without fruit) can be trimmed so the berry crop is not hidden when it begins to colour.

New South Wales Christmas Bush (*Ceratopetalum gummiferum*) can be pruned as soon as the display of red bracts has finished. Prune flowering wood only, do not cut into old or hard wood. Water and fertilise with animal manure or blood and bone.

Pests and Diseases

Spray Azaleas for lace bug with Rogor 40.

Ripening fruit including tomatoes, capsicum and all citrus should be sprayed for fruit fly with Rogor 40 or Lebaycid. Crab-apples grown for their flowers and decorative fruit may also provide a home for fruit fly.

All citrus, Gardenias, Japonica, Lillypilly, Pittosporum and Persimmon need spraying for white wax scale with white oil (5 ml in 2 L water).

Brown scale accompanied by sooty mould may also be a problem on many ornamentals. Spray with white oil as above. Malathion may also be added to the mixture.

Watch for fungus diseases on vegetables, fruit trees and ornamentals. Spray with a fungicide.

Roses particularly may need regular attention during the summer months to protect them from insect pests such as aphids and the fungus disease black spot.

Chrysanthemums could be showing signs of nematode damage (browning and dying off of lower leaves) so keep the plants growing strongly with regular feeding and keep ahead of the nematodes. Pick off and burn badly infected leaves and spray with a systemic spray or sprinkle Nemacur granules and water them in.

Thrips are a pest on Gladiolus — continue to spray emerging flower spikes with Malathion, or flower buds will open brown and withered.

Codlin moth may be a problem in apples — spray with Carbaryl. Spray citrus scale (red, brown or black scales on branches, leaves and fruit) with white oil. Spray red spider (silvery leaves with red spots beneath) on Azaleas, beans, Fuchsia, apples, etc. with Kelthane.

Apply sprays in the late afternoon, when heat has gone from the sun and when the wind has dropped. White cedar moth larvae can be trapped by "bagging" trunks. Treat termites with Dieldrin or call in a pest control expert.

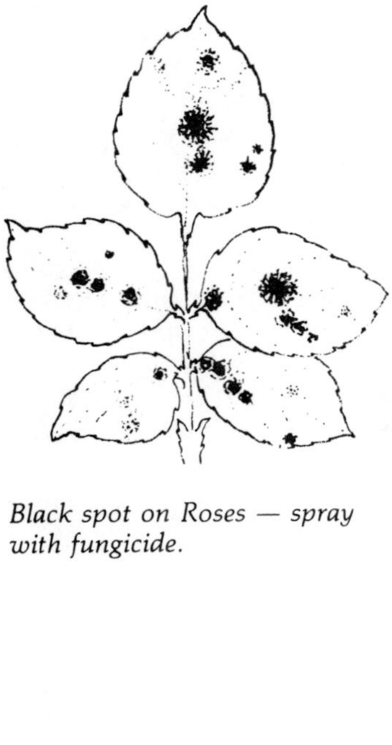

Black spot on Roses — spray with fungicide.

Garden Care

Take cuttings of Azaleas, Camellias, Daphne, Hypericum and Fuchsia now, using the ripened spring growth. Take short cuttings with a heel, strip surplus leaves from the stem, dip in a hormone rooting powder and plant two-thirds of the cutting's length in a mixture of sharp sand and potting mix.

Take cuttings early in the day, while the stems are full of sap, and plant them immediately. Cuttings should be kept moist but not too wet and should be put in a cool, partially shaded position out of the direct sun.

Geranium cuttings can also be taken at this time. They strike so readily that there is no need to use rooting powder on them.

Another summer task is dividing up clumps of the Tall Bearded Iris. After the old centre plant is discarded, the leaves of plump healthy plants should be trimmed into a pointed fan shape and replanted with the top of the rhizomes showing above the ground. Water well, and firm the soil.

THE JANUARY GARDEN

January is traditionally a time to survey your life and make some new resolutions. The garden can share in this stock-taking too and though our new year starts in mid-summer rather than towards the end of winter, which is a more natural time to think about new beginnings, it is a good time to look at the garden to see just how it can be improved.

Australian gardens need summer shade on the hot north and western aspects. Deciduous trees, climbers growing over pergolas or trellis-work will help to cool both house and garden. Perhaps you feel the need for a swimming pool to help you cool down, or better surface drains to carry off the water from sudden summer storms, or mulch on garden beds to cut down on the need for watering and weeding.

It may be too hot to do much about these things now but you can sit in the shade and make plans. If you haven't got a cool, shady spot in the garden to sit in, that's the first thing to plan.

Summer gardens can be a riot of brilliant colour filled with Hibiscus, Bougainvillea, hybrid Cannas and showy annuals like Petunias, Marigolds and Zinnias or they can be cool and restful with blue and white flowers against green lawns and shrubbery.

If you like the idea of a cool blue and white colour scheme for summer, there are plenty of plants to choose from. Blue and white Hydrangeas for the shady beds, clumps of blue and white Agapanthus and fringes of white Shasta Daisies for sunny spots will give you a basic planting combined with green grass and shady trees. These plants also have the advantage of requiring little maintenance during the hot weather, when they need only regular watering.

Other plants that will give you true blue flowers through summer are the blue Skybush (*Ceratostigma willmottianum*), a dwarf shrub of the Plumbago family, Plumbago itself with china blue flowers and light green foliage and Felicia, a sub-shrub bearing bright blue Daisy flowers with yellow centres. These can be bought in flower ready to plant out. Plumbago may be difficult to find but some nurseries are carrying it because it has become popular with landscape gardeners.

Geum — a summer-flowering perennial for the rockery — brightest orange flowers and strawberry-like foliage. Suitable for sun or part-shade.

GARDENKEEPING

Compost

January is a month which has good composting weather and it is an ideal time to start a compost heap if you don't already have one. As well as being good for the garden, a compost heap will solve the problem of what to do with the piles of grass you mow each week, as well as your fruit and vegetable peelings, eggshells, tea leaves, coffee grounds and the nutshells left after Christmas.

In most home compost heaps, lawn clippings probably make up the bulk of the material added to the heap. But there are other things that will supply bulk to build up a newly-started heap. If you live near the beach, seaweed is a marvellous source of compost. It is a good fertiliser and rots down quickly into the soil. It is easy to gather and has the advantage of being free.

Seaweed has been used as a fertiliser for centuries in some parts of the world and it is surprising that more people don't take advantage of the amount that can be picked up from the beach. All you need to do with seaweed is rinse some of the surplus salt off it by playing the hose over it before adding it to the compost heap or spreading it on the garden (if you are using it for mulch).

Seaweed will help build up the sandy soil in beach areas, too, so when you go down for your daily swim take a plastic garbage bag and bring some home. Gather the dry stuff from the high tide line — it's a lot easier to carry and doesn't smell.

If you don't have a beach handy buy a bale of straw from a produce store and add that to your compost heap, it works just as well. Or, if you have a timber factory or mill in your area, you will be able to get a load of sawdust. Whatever you use in your compost heap, lawn clippings, seaweed, sawdust or straw, it must be put down in layers with a thin layer of soil and a sprinkle of fertiliser like sulphate of ammonia and lime or dolomite spread between each layer.

Each layer should be dampened as the heap is built up and a sheet of black polythene should be spread over the top of the heap to build up heat and keep the rain off during wet weather.

Turn the heap over with a fork once a week to make sure you get an even compost. After a few weeks you will begin to see the composting materials starting to resemble good, rich soil and it will be full of earth worms. If you keep fowls on deep litter you can add the litter to the compost heap for very good results. Any manure added will improve the compost, but old-fashioned cow manure is not as easily come by as it once was.

The compost can be added to the garden bed as a mulch or dug in before planting. You will need to add more as it decomposes (after about three months). Whether you have sandy or heavy soil you will find that regular additions of compost will soon make it good and friable and you won't have the expense of buying loads of soil, which often turn out to be full of weeds.

Once you have a compost heap you never have any shortage of potting mix. I use a mixture of half compost and half peat moss for striking cuttings and seed raising and find it provides a good rooting medium which does not dry out as quickly as sand. You do need to pick out the earth worms though

— they are good in the compost heap but you don't want them in your pots.

People sometimes complain that they don't have a compost heap because they smell. A well-managed heap should not have an unpleasant smell. If it does it may be because it is too wet. The heap should be damp without being soggy.

If your heap does develop an odour a good handful of lime sprinkled over it plus a few spades of soil to cover any rotting vegetable matter will quickly solve the problem.

Watering

The most extraordinary myths persist among gardeners in spite of the efforts of gardening writers to spread the light. During heatwaves, for instance, people let their gardens burn and shrivel in the hot, dry winds because they believe the plants should not be watered until the sun has gone down.

Common sense tells us that when we are hot and thirsty we have a drink or take a shower — if we did not we could become dehydrated and collapse from heat exhaustion. The same thing happens to all living things whether humans, animals or plants.

As soon as the hot winds start we should turn on the sprinkler, adjust it to fine spray and point it so that it throws a fine spray in the air. As that scorching wind howls through the spray it becomes a moist wind that does not dry or burn the garden. In effect, we create a micro-climate that drops the temperature, cooling us as well.

There are valid reasons — under normal conditions — for watering after the sun has gone down. The water will stay in the soil longer at night and be available to the plants overnight instead of being evaporated by the sun. But a plant that has collapsed at noon from heat and lack of water is not going to thank you for a drink at bedtime. It will be dead.

The best way to combat the deadly effects of hot winds is with a system of fixed sprinklers on 2 m (6 ft) standpipes which spray a fine mist, maintaining the air's moisture content. This system works well as long as there are no water restrictions in your area.

Failing the ideal, turn your sprinkler to fine spray and move it about the garden to give an all-over cover. Where water is short the garden can be refreshed with your bathwater, providing it's not too soapy!

All gardens benefit from mulching but it is a necessity in areas where every drop of water counts. A layer of 6-8 cm (3 in) of leaf litter, pebbles, lawn clippings or newspaper will provide a satisfactory mulch.

Those who fail to spray their gardens in the big heat will have a lot of sorry-looking specimens in the garden.

Some plants are more tender than others — Fuchsias, Hydrangeas and Maples are susceptible. They can be kept looking beautiful through a hot summer if they are planted on the south-east side of the house where they will have some protection from the sun and those hot north-westerlies.

Under heat wave conditions Willows turn yellow, as if autumn had arrived overnight. Even the massive root systems of these water-hungry plants cannot keep pace with the transpiration of water from the leaves in the heat. However, they will begin to grow new leaves as soon as there is a good fall of rain.

Oak trees showing yellow, burnt leaves are mostly yellowed on the windward side, the dense canopy of leaves being enough to protect the rest of the tree from burning. Scorched looking leaves on Oaks can also be caused by the Oak blotch miner, an insect pest which is active from December to April and can cause premature leaf fall.

TREES AND SHRUBS

Shrubs for Sunny Positions

Warm, humid weather makes everything grow madly; even my Liliput Zinnias are twice the size they should be. I have had to give the Cotoneasters a haircut. Cotoneasters put out long canes in summer which occupy a lot of room and, later on, obscure the berries. The berries are already well developed and shearing off the surplus summer growth keeps the bushes under control without disturbing the berries.

Gardeners often ask about shrubs which are suitable for hot, sunny positions — Oleanders, Hibiscus, Abelia and Tibouchina all thrive under a blazing sun. Planted as a mixed summer flowering border instead of or beside a fence, they will keep your garden vivid with colour well into autumn.

A newly planted border of young shrubs will not look very interesting unless the gaps are filled with quick-growing summer annuals. Dahlias can be grown very successfully among these shrubs for a couple of years and provide both bulk and colour.

Clumps of perennials can be used among the shrubs for more permanent plantings. Perennial Phlox and Stokesia make attractive borders for additional summer colour. Perennial Phlox blends particularly well with Crepe Myrtle (Lagerstroemia) and both flower for months in summer. Crepe Myrtle can be grown with Hibiscus and Oleander as a shrub if it is heavily pruned after flowering. It also makes a charming small tree for the garden or footpath.

All the shrubs mentioned do well in seaside gardens too — they will stand up to sun, wind and a certain amount of neglect, which makes them suitable for holiday homes where not too much work is wanted.

Summer-flowering perennials like Shasta Daisies, Stoke's Aster and perennial Phlox are also ideal companions for flowering sub-shrubs like *Gardenia radicans*, the dwarf Gardenia, *Cuphea ignea* (commonly called Cigar Plant), Beloperone (*Drejerella guttata*, the Shrimp Plant which comes in two varieties, the pinky-brown and the much showier lime green and yellow), Felicia with bright blue Daisies, Geraniums, Thousand Wonders

*Shrimp Plant (*Drejerella guttata*)—a small shrubby plant for the garden. Hardy, free-flowering in hot, dry weather.*

Begonia and Pentas. If you don't have them you will find most of these on sale in pots and a single plant will soon form a good clump. All are suitable for use in garden beds combined with summer annuals or roses, or they can be used in rockeries.

All need a sunny position in normal garden conditions and need very little attention other than the usual watering, fertilising and removal of spent blooms. The Shrimp Plant does need regular cutting back to keep it a good shape, otherwise it becomes rather straggly.

Geraniums are particularly good in summer. Zonal Geraniums (upright type) will begin to suffer from rust in humid weather and should be sprayed with Captan or a similar fungicide. Ivy Geraniums are undoubtedly the most rewarding of the Pelargonium family to grow in humid coastal gardens. Even so they are more spectacular in dry-summer areas.

Shrubs and Groundcovers for the Shaded Garden

Impatiens are among the brightest and most easily grown plants for partial shade and make excellent potted plants for balconies or cool patios. Some of the newer dwarf varieties can be grown in hanging baskets, in a position sheltered from the wind.

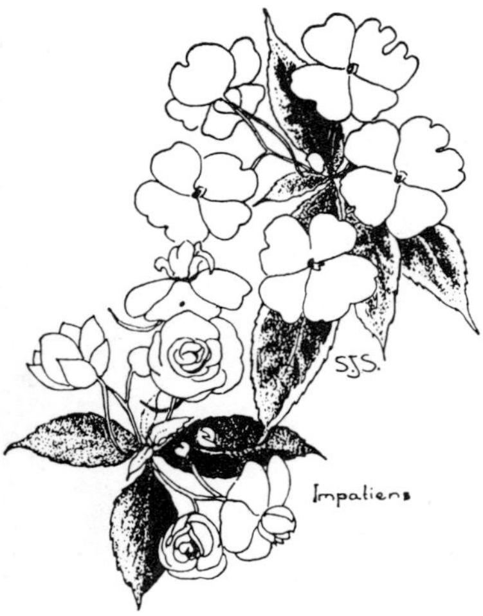

Impatiens — a useful groundcover for a shady spot.

The New Guinea hybrids with brightly variegated foliage and vivid flowers need slightly different treatment because they lose their leaf colour if planted in shade. However, if they get too much sun they wilt dramatically and a little shifting around is sometimes necessary to find the right spot. Morning sun or filtered sunlight is suitable and frequent watering is necessary if it is being grown in a container.

The Impatiens varieties with variegated flowers, usually in the form of a white cross across the petals, also lose their markings if they are in too much shade. Moved to a slightly sunnier spot, they quickly regain their stripes. They can be brought indoors for short periods and placed in a well-lit position while they are in full bloom.

If you long for colour but have only a shady balcony, try some *Impatiens sultanii* (commonly called Busy Lizzie). They grow readily from seed sown at all but the coldest time of the year and strike from cuttings in a flash. They are also useful for those shady spots under trees where the grass won't grow, and have no objection to dampish spots. Left to themselves, they will have some flowers at most times of the year. However, if they grow a bit tall and lush during summer they can be cut back in March (try to cut just above a leaf joint).

I once planted Impatiens in a shady, sloping, part of the garden that turned into a miniature stream in wet weather and was usually a little bit damp. The Busy Lizzies got busy and naturalised themselves so that, looking down from the house, they formed a rivulet of flowers running away down the slope.

If you are looking for a suitable planting for a shady courtyard or similar small garden area try combining tree ferns with *Fuchsia magellanica* (often known as *F. gracilis*), a weeping Fuchsia with small, slender bells in red and purple along the stems.

This Fuchsia grows to about 2 m (7 ft) and the arching canes can be trained along a fence if necessary, rather like a creeper. Underplant with smaller Fuchsias and Impatiens and, for winter colour, add a Camellia and a couple of long-flowering Azaleas in tubs or planted in the ground. This will give you a fairly low-maintenance planting with year-round colour and a good contrast of foliage form as well.

Lawn should never be attempted in this sort of small, cool garden. Instead, try a combination of paving, pebbles or pine bark and mossy ground-covers like club moss (Selaginella), Baby's Tears (Helxine) or Native Violet (*Viola hederacea*).

Holly Fern, Maidenhair and creeping Club Moss — all suitable for a shady spot.

Fuchsia gracilis is a rather neglected landscaping plant. It has a naturally graceful form and is almost constantly covered in tiny but colourful flowers. It does not seem to be troubled by pests or diseases, even those that worry other, more tender, Fuchsias. In my garden it does not even seem to be attacked by the vine moth caterpillar which often defoliates Fuchsias at this time of year. It is also popular with birds like small honeyeaters, which delicately insert their long bills into the slender bells. This Fuchsia is often seen in old gardens — it was more popular fifty years ago than it is now — but can be found in nurseries. It also grows readily from cuttings taken at any time.

Those shady areas where the grass won't grow vigorously enough to choke out weeds are the places to plant ground-covers. There are a number of good ground-cover plants which thrive in shaded areas. One which flowers in autumn is *Plectranthus oertendahlii,* a fast-growing, prostrate plant with broad, serrated leaves, dull green on top and purple beneath and spikes of white flowers.

This plant is a shade lover, and wilts in full sun. It will choke out weeds and forms a cover about 20 cm (8 in) high. The flowers last for several weeks and can be picked. *P. oertendahlii* also makes a good basket plant, the soft stems gracefully cascading over the sides. There is also a variety, *P. eckloni,* which flowers in March. It is a shrub with violet-blue flowers.

Hibiscus

People everywhere habitually grumble about the weather, but gardeners on the temperate east coast enjoy the best of all possible worlds. In January it is warm enough for our gardens to be almost tropical — vivid with Hibiscus and Oleander and fragrant with Frangipani. While winters are cool enough for the cold climate pleasures of autumn foliage and spring-flowering blossoms and bulbs.

Many gardeners tend to concentrate all their energies towards the spring flush and miss out on a lot of summer colour. But even the most spring-oriented garden should find room for a splash of summer.

Hibiscus, which give constant colour for months, come in the most brilliant reds, hot pinks, golds and orangy colours. There are some beautiful varieties in flower including the herbaceous perennial type "Southern Belle" which is available in eight varieties. Some of these are late season flowerers and start

Hibiscus rosa-sinensis — *for summer and autumn flowers.*

coming into bloom in March. The evergreen Hibiscus, *H. rosa-sinensis,* is at its best in autumn when most of those pesky little black hibiscus beetles have gone and flowers are not faded so quickly by the sun.

There are many new varieties available with large flowers, some with ruffled edges and in two colour combinations. The newer hybrids, the Hawaiian Hibiscus, are truly spectacular and it is well worth visiting a nursery which specialises in these to see the wonderful variety of colour available. Three Hawaiian varieties to look out for are "Tango", an unusual orange with a grey centre, "Peggy Walton", a single lavender bloom with a wine centre and "Ivy's Idol", a large single gold.

"Ann Miller" is a showy rose pink with white splashes, and "Fiesta" has orange flowers with a white throat. Two that have been around for a while and have good large blooms are "Crown of Bohemia", a double gold, and "Prince of Japan", a large single velvet red. "Orange Triumph", a Hawaiian type, has huge orange and yellow flowers which seem to start out to be single but have a prominent central cluster of petals. I don't know whether to describe them as semi-double or double but they are unusual. Another unusual Hibiscus is a climbing variety with sulphur-yellow flowers with a dark brown eye.

The deciduous Hibiscus, *H. syriacus,* is not as flamboyant as the *rosa-sinensis* type but it is worth considering where frost is a problem because it can withstand cold weather. The colours are not so vivid and the flowers are somewhat smaller than the more commonly grown *H. rosa-sinensis* but they are still very attractive and there are single and double forms. Gardeners in frost areas who have trouble with Hibiscus could try growing *H. syriacus* instead. The best known is probably the single mauve. There is also a very good double white. *H. syriacus* is not just for frosty areas, it does very well on the coast and in sub-tropical areas.

Hibiscus planted out from containers now will make plenty of growth before the cold weather slows them up and, in flower, Hibiscus is one of the plants that is at its best in autumn.

All varieties need well-drained, sunny conditions and a fairly rich soil. Sandy soil will need liberal additions of humus to improve the texture or the Hibiscus will not grow well, developing yellow leaves and flowers that fail to open. I am often asked the reason for their buds dropping and the answer is very dry weather. Hibiscus should be given a deep soaking once a week when the weather is hot and dry.

Another cause of trouble is the hibiscus beetle, a small black beetle which gets right inside the buds before they open. The only way to deal with it is to spray regularly, and even then it is hard to get at beetles inside the buds. Chemspray has a specific spray for them called simply "Hibiscus Spray". (Incidentally, Malathion should not be used on Hibiscus.)

Hibiscus can be grown as a hedge or in a mixed shrub border. It also makes a good small tree for the footpath, particularly if it is grown as a standard. In Brisbane Hibiscus is commonly used in this way for street planting and looks very

Hibiscus *"Southern Belle" — the huge flowers are snowy-white with a dark red eye and white stamen.*

effective. It could be used more on footpaths because it is ideal in situations where overhead wires are a problem. Standard Hibiscus is also the answer in inner suburbs where dense growths on footpaths are not wanted "because someone might be hiding behind it".

It is important to choose a vigorous, quick-growing variety to grow as a standard. "Wilder's White", a single white bloom with a red eye, makes a good standard. You must also start with a plant which has a good straight trunk if you want a tree-like result. All side shoots must be removed and any subsequent shoots should be rubbed off with the thumb.

It is always best to stake anything being grown as a standard. If the position is windy, as it often is on a footpath, use a 2 m (6 ft) length of water pipe as a stake and drive it in firmly before you put the tree in position. You will then be able to get the trunk as close as possible to the stake and the roots can be arranged without damage.

PERENNIALS AND ANNUALS

Columbines

Aquilegias, popularly (and much more prettily) called Columbines, are perennials that flower in early summer. The little old-fashioned ones are called "Granny's Bonnets" and are charming enough to have a spot in any garden where the climate is suited. The big hybrid varieties are really good garden flowers, with a range of pastel colours in blue, cream, pink, yellow and red. The leaves are like large Maidenhair fern and are attractive background for the flowers.

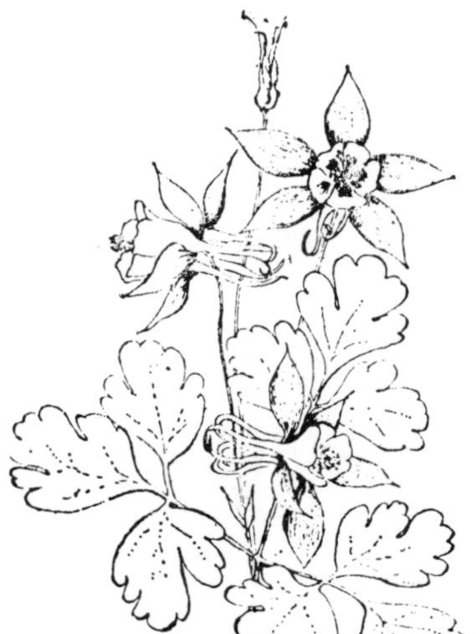

Columbine (Aquilegia) — seeds sown now will flower next summer.

Columbines are old traditional flowers which are rather neglected these days. I have had Columbines for a number of years — large-flowered hybrids like McKana Giants. However, after seeing species Columbines growing overseas I planted some local seed which produced a mixed bag of charming flowers. Some are double in pale pink or white and look like little ballerinas in layers of frilly skirts. Others are single red, yellow and deep blue. The only species description in my RHS dictionary that fits them is *Aquilegia caryophylloides,* of garden origin, usually mixed, some double.

Whatever they are, they are a lot of fun and I can recommend trying Columbines from mixed seed to anyone interested in growing less commonly known perennials.

Columbines thrive in semi-shade and like to be kept fairly moist during the growing season in early spring to summer. They are members of the Ranunculaceae family and originate in several countries from Europe to the US. There are also several species from South Africa. The rosettes of bluish-green foliage are attractive even when the plants are not flowering, though they die down for a time in autumn and winter. Seeds are available from specialist nurseries. The plants set seed freely, so if you see any growing in a friend's garden ask them to save you some seed.

Seed sown in January will flower next summer, though, like all perennials, they do better in the second year when the plants have become established.

Clytostoma, a summer-flowering climber with lilac bells and bright-green, glossy foliage.

CLIMBERS AND CREEPERS

Trumpet Creepers

Summer-flowering creepers give a lavish display of flowers for months (even in the rain). Fast growing, they are ideal for quick cover to give privacy for outdoor living areas or to beautify a fence, trellis, carport or shed.

A number of these summer-flowering vines have showy trumpet-shaped flowers. Among them, two of the Bignonia family, Clytostoma, with delicate masses of lavender flowers, and Campsis, with its brilliant orange-red flowers, are the most spectacular. Note that Campsis is deciduous and is useful where winter sun is desirable.

Doxantha (the Cat's Claw creeper) is another of the Bignonia family and the most rampant of the trumpets. The gorgeous golden flowers appear in late spring and continue into summer. It is a marvellous cover-up and can be combined with Clytostoma for extra effect.

Solandra, the Hawaiian Lily, is another rampant vine and has the largest trumpet — 23 cm (9 in) across. It is particularly useful in seaside areas because it is resistant to salt spray. Solandra has yellow flowers and needs a particularly strong support. Send it up a sturdy trellis or over a tall dead stump.

Two Thunbergias have lovely trumpets. *T. gibsonii* has large orange flowers and *T. grandiflora* is pale blue. These are for frost-free positions, being tropical plants.

Phaedranthus (Mexican Blood-trumpet) is another spectacular member of the Bignonia family, with blood-red flowers which turn magenta-crimson with age and yellow inside.

Probably the best known of the Bignoniaceae is Pyrostegia, formerly known as *Bignonia venusta.*

Though it is not a summer flowerer (it flowers from July to October), a discussion of trumpet vines hardly seems complete without giving it a mention. It can be mingled with one of the other trumpets to provide about nine months of colour.

All the creepers I have mentioned are easily grown in any ordinary garden situation provided they get almost full sun. Though they are all vigorous growers they are easily kept under control.

Even Doxantha, though it attaches itself to brick and timber surfaces, is easily removed and does not disfigure the surfaces as Virginia Creeper and Boston Ivy do.

Cardiospermum (Balloon Vine)

Bleeding-hearts

Bleeding-heart is the common name of *Clerodendron thomsonae,* which is a lovely plant for warm climates. There are several

Clerodendrons which I would like to recommend to readers in warm climates — they are really colourful and have everything going for them except perfume.

Clerodendron speciosissimum (Glory Bower) is a gorgeous, red-flowered climber with shiny leaves and *C. ugandense* is a shrub with charming blue flowers like a cloud of butterflies (hence the popular name of Butterfly Bush). *C. thomsonae* is a dainty climber with hanging white bracts, each with a tiny red blossom and stamens dangling from it (hence "Bleeding-Heart").

The other Bleeding-Heart, *Dicentra spectabilis,* is only suitable for cool climates. It is a delicate, old-fashioned plant for a shady border and has a number of charming names: Lady-in-a-bath (held upside down it does look like a tiny lady in a bath, too), Lady's Locket, Dutchman's Breeches, Lyre Plant and Seal Flower. Whatever name you call it, it is a little pet. But don't try to grow it unless you live in a cold winter area.

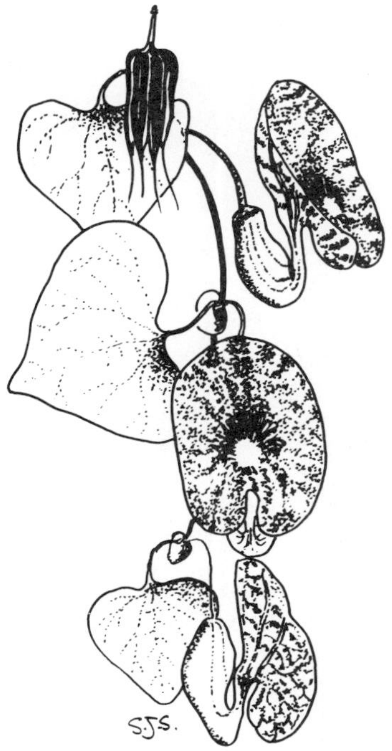
Dutchman's Pipe (Aristolochia elegans), *an unusual and easily grown, summer-flowering climber for warm climates.*

ROSES

Ensuring the Best Results

Roses are hard-working garden shrubs. They flower through warm weather (in warm climates they flower all year) with fragrant blossoms, ideal for cutting. Although they always seem to have a few flowers out, Roses do have distinct flushes of bloom — in spring, summer and autumn — unless they are Roses that flower in spring only, like the Banksia Roses.

Autumn is often the loveliest season for Roses. Much of the fungus disease that troubles them through the summer subsides with the onset of cooler, less humid weather and the flower colours are not faded so quickly by the sun.

If you want to get the best results from your Roses in autumn, now is the time to give them a little extra care. Fungus disease like mildew and black spot infect the leaves. Apart from spoiling the appearance of the bush, these diseases damage the leaves so that they are unable to manufacture enough sugars and starch to keep the plant healthy. Badly infected leaves die and the whole plant can be defoliated if you do not spray it.

You will recognise mildew if the Rose leaves (and sometimes the buds) become dusted over with a white powdery substance. Leaves affected by black spot develop rings of yellow or red tissue. Eventually the whole leaf yellows and falls off. Both these diseases should be sprayed with a fungicide such as Captan or Zineb, or you can use a rose spray which includes an insecticide.

Insect pests are always active during the summer months and you may need to be on the lookout for aphids (on new growth), leaf hoppers and small caterpillars. Insect pests can be controlled with Malathion or sprays based on pyrethrum, which is not toxic to the environment.

Roses should be watered regularly during summer and fertilised with an all-purpose fertiliser or a mulch of cow or fowl manure.

Summer pruning is important and is done simply by cutting back spent blooms. Spent heads left on bushes will result in the plant using its energy to develop seed pods instead of flowers.

If you are in doubt about how much to prune, just cut as though you were picking a bunch of Roses. Trim up any die-back that has developed on the ends of stems, too. In a few weeks you will see new growth beginning to produce your autumn Rose flush.

The main Rose planting time is from May to August, when the plants are dormant, but container grown Roses can be planted at any time during the year. If your nurseryman stocks them don't hesitate to add to your Rose garden in January. Container-grown Roses will grow well provided you avoid planting on excessively hot or windy days and take care not to let them dry out.

Miniature Roses are always sold in pots and make a bright addition to a sunny patio or balcony in summer.

BULBS

Lilies

Liliums do best in a cool climate and gardeners in hilly districts may be interested in some exquisite species available from Victorian Lilium nurseries.

L. nepalense has large trumpet-shaped flowers of greeny-yellow with deep purple centres and green stamens. Another species (*L. wardii*) has a mass of small dainty pink spotted flowers and is easier to grow.

Gardeners will find very rewarding the old Tiger Lily (*L. tigrinum*) and the Speciosum and Parkman hybrids. Try Tiger Lilies in a pot. I have seen some growing up the fluted columns of a patio, where they had morning sun and protection from the wind. Dried Lily pods look good in flower arrangements.

The Gloriosa Lily is in flower this month. The flowers are spectacular bright yellow with red or flame-tipped petals which curve back so it resembles a Tiger Lily. The Gloriosa Lily (*Gloriosa superba*) dies back after flowering and regrows from a new tuber formed after flowering. It needs well-drained conditions because the tubers tend to rot during wet winters. I have mine growing in a pot to control soil wetness during the dormant period. Apart from its fascinating flowers, its climbing habit is interesting as it clings by tendrils on the ends of each leaf. In a warm, frost-free climate, the Gloriosa Lily grown on a trellis makes a beautiful display.

The pods of Liliums and Iris that have flowered and set seed should be picked out and placed in a brown paper bag when nearly ripe. In this way the seed does not scatter and get lost when the pod bursts. Liliums and Iris, like the Pacific Coast hybrids, are worth growing from seed. They will not necessarily be true to the parent, but will give healthy, virus-free plants.

Bulbs to Plant Now

A number of bulbs can be planted out now. Cyclamen, Brunsvigia, Crinum, Clivea, Nerine and Amaryllis can all be put in the ground or in pots. Also look for the autumn flowering bulbs of *Sternbergia lutea* (the Autumn Crocus) and Colchicums, which make good pot subjects or can be planted round the base of deciduous trees like Japanese Maples. Sternbergias are delightful little bulbs, the golden flowers being much more like true Crocus than other bulbs given this name, for example the Zephyranthes.

Some of these bulbs, Cyclamen and Nerines for instance, are not suitable for warm climates but the Zephyranthes (commonly called Rain Lilies or Autumn Crocus) grow very well in warm areas, naturalising in lawns and even paths where they find a congenial spot. White, pink and yellow species are available.

Gloriosa Lily, a showy Lily with climbing habit — flowering now.

Colchicums can be enjoyed anywhere if they are raised in a dish filled with pebbles and a little water. Placed on a window sill they will flower happily.

Another autumn flowering bulb is a member of the Lily family. This is Liriope, the Turf-lily which is suitable for most climates. In autumn Liriope has spikes of blue flowers like Grape Hyacinth which rise from a grass-like clump of leaves. The attractive, variegated-leaf Turf-lily makes a showy potted plant while the green forms make good ground cover plants that are able to tolerate shady and dry conditions.

NATIVES

Bleeding Heart Tree

There is a native tree flowering now which I am often asked to identify. It is *Omalanthus populifolius* (also called Homalanthus, sometimes called Bleeding Heart tree). It is an erect, shrubby tree with distinctive poplar-like leaves, mainly dark green but often with several bright scarlet leaves scattered through them. The leaf-stems are also red and the flowers are cream terminal racemes, like tassels, which cover the tree in summer. They are not particularly showy but the tree does look very attractive in flower.

I don't know whether anyone ever actually plants this tree. I think it is more often a volunteer, springing up in the garden uninvited, and people are often surprised to find that it is a native plant.

It comes up nearly as freely as Privet in my garden and I have to pull a lot out, though a few make a good contribution to a native area. Homalanthus is native to a wide area of coastal Australia and belongs to the Euphorbiaceae family. I'm sure many will recognise this as the mystery tree in their gardens.

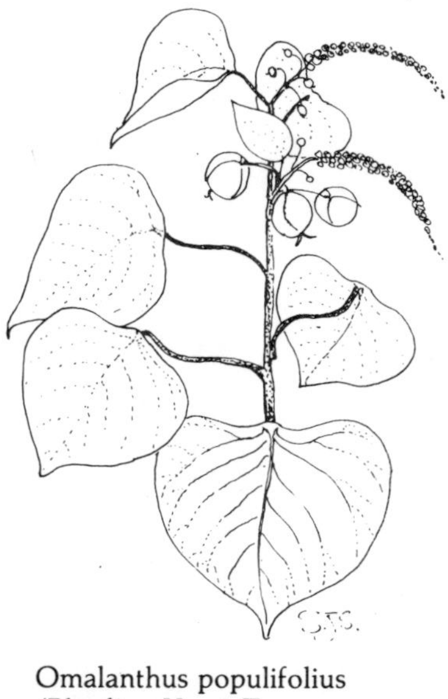

Omalanthus populifolius *(Bleeding Heart Tree or Homalanthus)*

Transplanting Kangaroo Paws

What to do when a splendid clump of Kangaroo Paws in full bloom has to be moved because of alterations? It is possible to move Kangaroo Paw after flowering. Being a perennial, it becomes fairly dormant in the autumn, which would be the best time to find a new home for it.

The clump should be thoroughly soaked by leaving a dripping hose on it overnight to soften the soil. When the new position is prepared, the clump can be lifted carefully with a large fork to avoid breaking the roots.

If the old clump is too big, young plants around the edges can be teased out, as with any perennial. Surplus plants may be potted for gifts and the rest replanted immediately. It should not be planted deeper than before.

EDIBLES

Vegetables to Plant and Pick

Gardeners who planted Patio-pik cucumbers earlier in the season should be picking them now and enjoying them. There is still time to plant a few of these. They will grow quickly in the warm weather. Other vegetables that can be planted now include beetroot, carrots, lettuce, radish and silver beet.

Fruit fly may be attacking tomatoes and capsicums and they should be sprayed with Rogor. Take care not to eat the fruit for seven days after spraying. The spray will also protect tomatoes against the aphids that carry the virus yellow top. This disease is common in coastal areas and infected plants are stunted with yellowing of the foliage, which tends to curl down and inwards.

Tomato Apollo a new tomato hybrid on the market, is resistant to wilt. Fungal wilts cause wilting of the plants from the bottom up, followed by yellowing and browning of the leaves. The wilting diseases are soil-borne, so if you have lost tomatoes from wilt in previous years Apollo is good news.

Tomatoes also suffer from virus wilt which is carried from plant to plant by thrips. This disease can be controlled by keeping the thrips down by spraying with Malathion, clearing weeds and culling infected plants.

A common cause of poor growth and losses of tomato plants is the tomato root nematode which is often present in the soil. Nemacur can be sprinkled and watered into the soil either before planting or round plants already growing.

Herbs

Herbs are an important part of the garden and if you are visiting a nursery look around for some small, established herb plants if you haven't already got herbs growing.

Basil is a member of the mint family and really adds flavour to summer salads and any tomato dishes cooked or raw.

Chives are easily grown and look attractive in a small pot on a balcony. Oregano (which is wild Marjoram) and Marjoram are both good perennial herbs which can be grown as rockery, border or container plants. Thyme and Sage can also be grown this way, though Sage is larger and spreads more than the neat Thymes and Marjoram.

Two herb plants which are much larger than the usual herbs are Rosemary and Bay. The Bay will grow into a tree in time, but is slow-growing and makes a useful tub plant for a balcony, patio or on either side of an entrance.

Rosemary is a delightful shrub which should have a place in any garden. I grow it in a rockery and use it in cooking, not just with lamb but in chicken and beef dishes as well and find it gives a very pleasant flavour to roasted or casseroled meats. Rosemary can be used as a tub plant. Frequent nipping off of sprigs to pop into the pot will keep it nice and compact. Most herbs need a fairly sunny position in well-drained soil to grow well. Rosemary will tolerate a hot, sunny and even fairly windy situation if you want to use it on a balcony.

INDOORS

Unit Gardens

Flowering pot-plants are a boon to people in flats or units who crave a few flowers. There is something for each season, starting with Chrysanthemums in January, then Cyclamen, Poinsettia, Cineraria, African Violets and others distributed throughout the year.

For indoor colour now there are also good supplies of fancy-leaf Caladium and Gloxinia, with their large bells of glowing colour.

Gloxinias make splendid indoor plants and colourful additions to a shade house. They must have good drainage and be kept out of direct sunlight. A little liquid fertiliser every three weeks will keep the plant growing through summer.

Tuberous Begonias also make glamorous-growing indoor plants. Give them a well-lighted position as they drop their flower buds if they are put in a dim corner. Keep these plants moist and don't get water on the flowers or crown of the plant. Give them a fortnightly feed with half-strength Aquasol, Thrive or Zest.

CHECKLIST

February is usually the most humid month and may be very wet, making it a period of rampant growth and an increase in weeds, fungus diseases and insect pests.

Flowering now

Trees and shrubs:
Abelia,
Begonia coccinea,
Buddleia,
Ceratostigma (Skybush),
Clerodendron,
Cuphea,
Fuchsia,
Gardenia,
Heliotrope,
Hibiscus,
Lagerstroemia (Crepe Myrtle),
Lantana hybrids,
Malvaviscus,
Nerium (Oleander),
Pentas,
Plumbago,
Pomegranate,
Roses,
Thevetia,
Tibouchina (Lasiandra).

Perennials and annuals:
Alyssum,
Amaranthus,
Aster,
Balsam,
Begonia,
Brachycome (Swan River Daisy),
Calliopsis,
Celosia,
Cosmos,
Eschscholtzia (Californian Poppy),
Geranium,
Gomphrena,
Impatiens,
Marigold,
Petunia,
Phlox (annual and perennial),
Portulaca,
Salvia,
Torenia,
Verbena,
Zinnia.

Bulbs:
Amaryllis,
Canna,
Crinum,
Dahlia,
Dietes,
Hemerocallis (Day Lily),
Tigridia,
Zephyranthes.

Climbers:
Allamanda,
Antigonon,
Aristolochia,
Bougainvillea,
Cobaea scandens,
Mandevilla,
Maurandya,
Mina lobata,
Morning Glory,
Quisqualis (Rangoon Creeper),
Solandra.

Natives:
Buckinghamia (Ivory Curl Tree),
Craspedia (Billy Buttons),
Crotalaria (Bird Flower),
Epacris (native Heath),
Grevillea hybrids,
Hakea,
Helichrysum,
Hibbertia,
Indigofera,
Melastoma,
Pavonia,
Rhododendron lochae,
Scaevola,
Senecio (Groundsel Daisy),
Tristania.

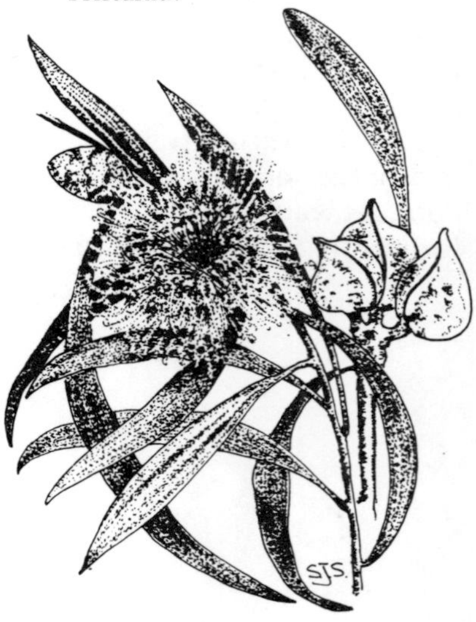

Hakea laurina—*pincushion flowers of cream and crimson.*

FEBRUARY

Plant

Trees, shrubs and climbers:
Plant out all container-grown trees, shrubs and climbers and stake pre-planting in windy or exposed areas to prevent storm losses. Avoid excessively hot periods — plant in cool of evening and provide temporary shade in very hot districts. Keep watered.

Perennials and Annuals:
Seed or seedlings of Ageratum,
Alyssum,
Anemone,
Aquilegia,
Aubrieta,
Bellis perennis,
Calendula,
Candytuft,
Canterbury Bell,
Carnation,
Cheiranthus (Wallflower),
Cineraria,
Cornflower,
Dianthus,
Forget-me-not,
Gypsophila,
Honesty,
Larkspur,
Linaria,
Livingstone Daisy,
Lupin,
Marigold,
Mignonette,
Nasturtium,
Nemesia,
Nemophila,
Nigella,
Pansy,
Penstemon,
Polyanthus,
Poppy (Iceland),
Primula,
Scabiosa,
Schizanthus,
Snapdragon,
Stocks,
Sweet Pea,
Sweet William,
Viola,
Virginian Stock.

In warm, humid climates delay planting until March.

Bulbs:
Bearded Iris,
Cyclamen.

In temperate and cool zones start planting all spring-flowering bulbs:
Babiana,
Daffodil,
Dutch Iris,
Freesia,
Hyacinth,
Ixia,
Lachenalia,
Leucojum (Snowflake),
Muscari (Grape Hyacinth),
Narcissus,
Ranunculus,
Scilla,
Sparaxis,
Triteleia.

Vegetables:
Beans,
beetroot,
cabbage,
carrots,
cauliflower,
celery,
cress,
lettuce,
onions,
parsley,
parsnip,
peas,
potatoes,
radish,
shallots,
silver beet,
swedes,
turnip.

Fertilise

Feed Roses and Hydrangeas with complete fertiliser or rotted manure after pruning.

Give Hibiscus complete fertiliser and water well.

Side dressings of fertiliser on vegetables and annuals should be used to keep up growth and fortnightly, half-strength foliar feeding will be needed on indoor plants, ferns, Azaleas and leafy vegetables such as lettuce. Water over the foliage for maximum effect.

Fertilise trees attacked by longicorn beetle with Osmocote or Shirley's Popular Special.

Prune

Hydrangeas can be pruned now, cutting to two plump buds and removing spindly and old wood at the base of the plant. (See also p. 26.)

Trim Cotoneasters and Abelias carrying long summer growth that will obscure the berry display already developing.

Trim long unwanted summer canes on rampant creepers like Wistaria, Jasmine, etc. to keep under control.

New South Wales Christmas Bush will have finished and should be pruned, cutting only new wood to produce compact flowering wood next season.

Towards the end of the month, lightly prune Roses for the autumn flush by removing spent flowering sprays and any dieback on twigs. (See also p. 32.)

Ceratostigma (Blue Skybush) a small blue-flowered shrub blooming now.

Pests and Diseases

Fungus diseases (leaf spots, mildew, rot) on vegetables and ornamentals should be sprayed with fungicide such as Captan, Mancozeb or dusting sulphur. (The last should not be used on cucurbits.) To prevent damping off of seedlings caused by soil-borne fungus attacking germinating seeds, dust all seeds with Captan before sowing.

Fruit fly in ripening fruit, tomatoes, capsicum etc., can be controlled by picking off all diseased fruit and gathering and burning fallen fruit. Plants should be sprayed with Rogor or Lebaycid — follow directions on the pack.

Spray for sucking and chewing insects on vegetables, Roses and other ornamentals when necessary using pyrethrum spray, Derris, or Malathion.

Lemon scab (warty, scabbed fruit and scabby areas on leaves and twigs) should be sprayed with Zineb in white oil.

Virus diseases in tomatoes (wilt, yellow top, blight) should be sprayed with Malathion to control insect pests which spread the virus. Keep beds weeded and cull badly infected plants.

Spray red spider mite on ornamentals (Azaleas, Fuchsias,

etc.), tomatoes and beans with Kelthane. (See also p. 26.)

Scale on ornamentals and indoor plants should be sprayed with white oil plus Malathion or a systemic spray. Wipe off indoor plants with a cotton bud dipped in soapy water.

For dollar spot fungus in lawns try TMTD.

Various caterpillars, snails and slugs are also on the rampage this month. For protective action see p. 27.

Garden Care

Prepare vegetable beds for planting — dig over, add compost and fertiliser, plus lime in heavy soils.

Stake Dahlias and Chrysanthemums to prevent wind and storm damage. (See also p. 27.)

Mulch garden beds, Camellias and Azaleas to conserve moisture and keep down weeds but keep mulch from direct contact with stems.

A thought for St Valentine's Day — time to plant Pansies.

Blossom end rot of tomatoes caused by calcium deficiency.

THE FEBRUARY GARDEN

Grey, damp days at this time of year make the garden very subdued. The brash summer flowers that glow so brightly in the sun droop or close in the rainy weather, but the grey-leaved plants, usually just a foil for the others, come into their own and shine like old silver.

While the shrubs and flowers are bent with the weight of raindrops, the silver-leaved plants remain unbowed. This is not because they like damp weather but because their leaves have a felted surface of fine hair which sheds water.

The felted surface, which in some plants — like *Stachys lanata* commonly called Lamb's Ears — has become a woolly covering, evolved as a protection from hot sun. Silver-leaved plants come from hot, dry areas. Many of our silvery garden plants originated in Mediterranean areas where they exist on harsh and stony ground, often in mountain screes. Others come from hot desert areas of America and Africa. Many Australian natives have also developed this protection.

Whatever the country of origin, silver-leaved plants need full sun to grow successfully because the felty covering screens the sunlight and the plant has to work hard to manufacture chlorophyl. They also need fast drainage. If water lies round them they quickly rot. Plant them in rockeries or let them spill over stone walls.

Silver plants are invaluable in the garden for providing a backdrop for brightly coloured flowers. They are often fragrant, like Lavender, or pungent, like Artemesia, which gives them added interest.

Our sloping garden is right in the current fashion with the "layered look" and the silvery clumps of Lavender, Artemesia, Senecio (Dusty Miller) and a ground-cover of *Cerastium tomentosum* provide a background that pulls it all together and makes it flow.

Some readily grown silver-leaved plants are Dusty Miller (*Senecio cineraria*), with yellow daisy flowers in summer; Lamb's Ears (*Stachys lanata*), suitable for a border or ground cover and has uninteresting purplish spikes but is grown for the leaves. *Cerastium tomentosum* makes a spreading, fast-growing, silvery mat and is a useful ground-cover or rockery plant. The white flowers in early summer give it the rather fanciful name of Snow-in-summer.

Catmint (*Nepeta faassenii*) is a delightful foliage plant, grey, tinged with green, with lavender spikes of flowers all summer. Like many silver-leaved plants, Nepeta is aromatic and is traditionally supposed to be irresistible to cats. Our cats can take it or leave it but it is worth growing in the rockery or border because of its small, neat and pretty habit.

One of the Thymes — *Thymus lanuginosus* — has silver-grey, woolly leaves and will stand up to traffic. It is suitable for use between stepping stones in a path or on a partially paved courtyard area. Pinks make silvery clumps, too, and though the foliage is not fragrant the flowers make up for it by filling the garden with fragrance in early summer.

Silver-leaved Lamb's Tongue, Cerastium, Artemesia, Senecio and Lavender.

A most intriguing native silver plant is *Calocephalus brownii*, which grows in a tangle of silvery twigs. It will stand exposed seaside conditions and, given regular watering and very good drainage, it will form a broad, spreading mound. At our place it hangs over a low wall among Pelargoniums, in a windy position, and is looking very handsome.

Lavendula dentata makes the best hedge plant. It is the strongest growing with woody stems and rounded, compact growth. *L. stoechas*, variously called Italian or true French Lavender, is a low dense shrub with darker purple flowers than *L. dentata* and makes a good rockery plant.

Wormwood (Artemesia) is one of the bitter herbs (Tansy and Rue are the others) and is strongly aromatic. The divided leaves have almost a lacy appearance, making it a good accent plant among other shrubs. Rosemary Hemphill, in her book *Herbs for All Seasons*, suggests making a "tea" from the leaves and rubbing it into animals' coats as a flea repellent. The name Wormwood comes from its old use as a moth repellent — the worms being the moth larvae.

There are silver trees as well as the smaller plants I have mentioned. What could be more silvery than Queensland Silver Wattle *(Acacia podalyriifolia)* with its silver grey phyllodes (not true leaves) that look as if they had been cut out of felt.

Eucalyptus cineria — the Argyle Apple — is another native with silvery-grey leaves which looks best grouped with trees of contrasting foliage. There is also a lovely South African native called Silver Tree (*Leucadendron argenteum*) which shines in the sun so much that it barely looks real.

Gather Lavender heads and dry for sachets or potpourri.

GARDENKEEPING

Pruning Hydrangeas

Hydrangeas can be pruned during February. Some people prefer to prune (or are in the habit of pruning) in late winter but there are some advantages to summer pruning. The new growth has longer to mature and summer pruning reduces the size of the bush, freeing garden space that can be used for plantings of spring annuals or bulbs that flower in late summer and autumn — Crinums and Amaryllis, for instance.

This double use of space is important in small gardens where space is precious. Hydrangeas are often taken out because they occupy so much space for so much of the year when all that is necessary is better management.

In cooler areas Hydrangea flower heads remain on the plant turning first lime green and then developing rich red and purple colouring. If your bushes retain the flower heads right through winter in this way it would be wrong to prune in summer and deprive yourself of their beauty on the bush and in flower arrangements.

When pruning, cut to a node carrying two fat growth buds. Don't prune young plants too drastically or the plant will use all its energies in growth rather than the production of flower heads. Cut out dead wood at the base of the plant and remove old wood bearing spindly canes. Sprinkle fertiliser (either blood and bone or an all-purpose fertiliser) round the bushes after pruning and water well.

Hydrangeas are sometimes infected with mildew during a wet steamy February. This first shows as a yellowish spot or blotch on the leaves which blossoms into a white, powdery mass. A lot of mildewed leaves will be removed with pruning and should be burnt rather than introduced to the compost heap. The plants can then be sprayed with Captan or a similar fungicide.

Hydrangeas are sometimes attacked by white scale. Spray this with white oil (85 ml in 5 L of water with 10 ml Malathion added). Repeat spray in about ten days.

Care of Azaleas

Azaleas will need attention now. Red spider is the villain this time and the indication of red spider attack is a silvered appearance on top of the leaves. Underneath, the leaves are spotted with excreta and nymph casts, giving them a reddish, speckled look. Kelthane is the only thing that seems to destroy red spider and you must make sure that you spray under the foliage as well as on top. Don't inhale this spray and take care to wash thoroughly afterwards. Some Azalea leaves may still be disfigured from last year's infestation of red spider and no amount of spraying will improve the appearance of the damaged leaves. However it will get rid of any new infestation so that new leaf growth is protected from disfigurement.

Azaleas respond well to the liquid nitrogen type fertilisers and these are safe to use on potted Azaleas. Apply at half the recommended strength for three consecutive weekly doses, rather than in one big dose.

Ground covers can be kitten high—Orange Sherbet in the back garden summer shade.

Summer formal: A charming combination of a trimmed Privet, French Lavender and heads of Garlic.

Summer informal: Daylilies, Crucifix Orchids, Hydrangea and Wormwood run riot in a small section of my garden.

Trimming Agapanthus

Most Agapanthus have finished blooming now and are developing large seed heads. These should be cut off down at the base of the clump before they scatter seed through the garden. These seed heads can be used in flower arrangements and you might like to select a few of the best for this.

If you want to increase your plants, leave some heads to ripen and when they are dry and almost ready to start splitting open tie a paper bag over the heads, fastening it firmly round the stem. Seed caught in the bag can be planted in a seedling box and will grow readily. Plants grown from seed will take three years to flower but the plants develop fairly quickly and can be planted out to build up a border or low hedge after about eighteen months.

Agapanthus are useful plants, being marvellous soil-holders for a bank, ideal for a narrow driveway or for a footpath planting against a fence. They flower best in full sun but will tolerate filtered sunlight and even grow well in shady conditions, although they won't flower if they become too shaded.

When you prune off the flower heads clean up any dead leaves caught in the clumps and give the plants a handful of blood and bone or all-purpose fertiliser. Always water after fertilising so that plants don't suffer leaf burn and to help dissolve the fertiliser.

Staking Dahlias and Chrysanthemums

This is a good time to stake Dahlias and Chrysanthemums. Use the light green-painted cane stakes available at most nurseries — they blend in with the foliage and you won't have to worry about splinters.

Long, unwanted canes on creepers and shrubs like Abelia and Cotoneaster should be cut back. And if you have a hedge that has grown to monster proportions you might like to invest in one of the new cordless electric shears. Though expensive they are a worthwhile investment considering the mileage involved in hand-clipping round a boundary.

Caterpillars, Snails and Slugs

If your Fuchsias are being mysteriously defoliated, look for vine moth caterpillars. They are pretty, striped creatures with greeny-yellow bodies marked with black stripes and red spots.

Fully grown they can be 5 cm (2 in) long, and half a dozen will strip a Fuchsia bare in a flash. Don't waste time spraying them – pick them off and stamp on them.

Every kind of caterpillar and snail, slug and assorted creepy-crawly appears now so keep a sharp eye on Dahlias and the tender young buds forming on Roses for the autumn flush – spray with Malathion, a non-toxic spray like Clensil or garlic spray, or the biological control for caterpillars – Dipel.

For plant-climbing snails try a sawdust mulch. Snails do not care for sawdust at all. It clings to their sticky "foot" and stops them from gliding along. A protective ring of sawdust around seedlings should keep the snails at bay, but the garden will need an extra ration of nitrogen to counteract the sawdust in the soil.

Inspect citrus and other ornamental trees, like Gardenias, for ants. Their presence indicates scale infestation — the ants feed on the "honey dew" excreted by the scale insects. Spray with white oil, and add Malathion if the infestation is heavy.

Weeds

There are plenty of weeds that are troublesome in February. Summer Grass (*Sagitaria sanguinalis*) is a bad pest of lawns and gardens, mainly because of its rapid growth. It spreads rapidly and roots at every node which touches the soil. It also seeds quickly and freely so you may get two or three generations in a summer. If you can get it out before it seeds it is fairly easy to control in gardens. Regular close cutting of lawns will prevent it from seeding and, as it is an annual, it will die off at the end of the season.

Paspalum is another perennial pest which keeps coming up each year in bigger and stronger clumps. If Paspalum invades your lawn it is probably best to let it take over, and settle for a Paspalum lawn. It should be dug out of gandens with a hoe but in paths it can be poisoned with a weedicide to avoid damage to the path.

Another perennial pest is Curled Dock (*Rumex crispus*), which has a deep, tough root resistant to herbicides though Zero is worth trying. The only way to eradicate Dock is by digging it right out, using something like an old chisel as a tool.

One of the reasons for the spread of noxious weeds is that many people don't recognise them when they see them. I have known people to cultivate Crofton Weed, Prickly Pear, Lantana and other pests without realising that they were noxious weeds.

Sydney's suburban Ku-ring-gai Council usually has a potted Privet on display at the council chambers so that people can recognise it if they have it growing. Perhaps someone could expand this idea into a display of noxious weeds in a place where people could see them easily.

Leaves and seeds of the Plane tree used extensively in footpath plantings.

TREES AND SHRUBS

Trees for Sun Protection

One result of a very hot summer is that many people discover that their houses do not have enough protection from the afternoon sun and become so hot that sleep is impossible at night in stifling bedrooms.

Curtains on the inside will give some protection from direct sun but curtains of greenery on the outside will deflect and absorb a lot of the sunlight that would otherwise fall directly on walls and roofs. By using trees to cast shade from some distance and creepers growing on the walls, you can have a double line of defence.

Before you take the plunge and festoon your house with jungle-like growth, remember that the same sun that is your enemy during a heatwave is your best friend in the depths of winter. Plan your planting so that some of the key shade trees and creepers are deciduous.

A low, single-storey house can be sheltered by small, 8 m (26 ft), trees and tall shrubs like Abelia and Oleander. They revel in a hot aspect, provide summer flowers, and will insulate western walls — particularly glass walls which make modern buildings look glamorous but transmit heat very quickly.

To shade a split-level or double-storey house you will need tall, fast-growing trees, and Eucalyptus is a good solution here. Though not deciduous, their shade is not dense enough to make a house noticeably darker or colder in winter.

E. citriodora (the Lemon-scented Gum) is suitable for gardens. It is a handsome tree growing to 15 m (50 ft) with scented leaves, creamy-white new bark in summer and white flowers in winter. If a smaller tree is needed, the narrow-leafed Willow Peppermint (*E. nicholii*) grows to 8 m (26 ft) with a graceful willowy habit and will stand up to wind-swept conditions.

Scribbly Gum (*E. haemastoma*), which usually seems to have three trunks, is the landscape gardener's dream. It grows naturally into artistic curves and survives in poor sandstone soils, growing to a moderate size.

These three Eucalypts are suitable for almost any garden but one of the most popular Gums, the Tasmanian Blue Gum, is most unsuitable for suburban gardens. It is planted for its attractive rounded, grey-white juvenile foliage, but quick as a flash it will sky-rocket up 30 m (100 ft) — 60 m (200 ft) in Tasmania — and develop adult foliage which is deep green with no low branches — telegraph poles with tufts on top.

Dedicuous trees are a good choice for shading kitchen or bedroom windows where both sun and light are desirable in winter. Any of the flowering Prunus varieties will provide summer shade and are lovely to look at when they are in bloom. Prunus are small trees which will fit into the smallest garden. But use the purple-leaved varieties with caution near the house because they tend to be a bit dark and brooding viewed from, say, a kitchen window.

Crepe Myrtle (Lagerstroemia) makes a delightful small tree if it is not pruned back heavily every year. It is a mass of flowers for months during the summer, turns a rich colour in autumn and the silvery branches are attractive, particularly on unpruned trees whose branches have not been mutilated.

The Box Elder (*Acer negundo*) is a useful deciduous tree which will provide some shade for a hot house without engulfing it. If you like variegated leaves try one of the variegated Box Elders. The variety "Variegatum" has leaves that are margined white, grows to 6 m (20 ft) and is a fast grower. Another variety, "Aureo-marginatum" is similar except for gold margins.

Whichever of these trees you plant, be careful not to place them too close to the house. Trees planted under the eaves develop bent trunks as they reach out for more light, and rub

Variegated foliage of Box Elder (Acer negundo aurea-marginata) *in its spring beauty.*

Leaves and seeds of the Alder (Alnus cordata) *— a beautiful addition in cool-temperate zone gardens.*

against walls and guttering in stormy weather, damaging paintwork and making irritating scratching noises. They will also grow more slowly, particularly on a westerly aspect, because they never get the benefit of rain and roots searching for water will cause cracks in foundations.

Crepe Myrtle

Lagerstroemia (the Crepe Myrtle) is in its glory now and is particularly useful in a small garden because it will provide autumn colour and is deciduous. It can be grown as a small tree or pruned back in winter to produce a compact shrub.

The colours range from white through pink and mauve to red and are the summer equivalent of the spring-blossoming Prunus varieties.

Tibouchina

Tibouchina (commonly misnamed Lasiandra) is a must for brilliant colour throughout summer. The masses of purple flowers open from furry red buds and the velvet green leaves provide a rich background colour all year.

Tibouchina — rich purple flowers with prominent stamens and sickle-shaped leaves.

Ours grows against a neighbour's clump of orange Cannas and that corner of the garden vibrates with colour when the sun shines. Unlike Hibiscus and Lagerstroemia, Tibouchina is a soft shrub with brittle stems and should be pruned twice — after flowering and again when spring growth starts — to keep the shrub compact.

If you have never bothered to look closely at the flowers of Tibouchina, take a minute to examine them. The stamens are worth looking at — notice the sickle-shaped anthers — a fascinating bit of design. There are several different Tibouchinas available — all worth growing. Perhaps the best is *T. granulosa,* which develops into a small tree with glorious sprays of rich purple flowers lasting over a long period right through autumn. *T. alstonville* flowers profusely from February through autumn. Other improved Tibouchinas will be available from time to time — pink, white and multi-colours (white, lavender and purple on single sprays).

Miniature Pomegranates

Miniature Pomegranate (*Punica granatum* "Nana") is a pet of a plant for the rockery. It is a small deciduous shrub with dainty foliage and bright orange flowers, followed by small, edible and very decorative fruit. They are making a gay splash in chain stores and nurseries and as Persephone found, they are hard to resist.

It will stand cold weather and enjoys full sun and rich, well-drained soil. *P. granatum* grows to 1.5 m (5 ft) and is also a hardy and showy shrub.

PERENNIALS AND ANNUALS

Begonias

That most elegant and unassuming of plants, the tree Begonia (*B. coccinea*) — also called Angelwing Begonia — is brightening shady gardens with its cascades of red, pink or white flowers. This tall, slender plant is tree-like only by comparison with the other members of the Begonia family. Its smooth, succulent stems rise to about 2 m (6 ft). The leaves are either green or strikingly coloured with red markings and silvery spots, and the flowers hang in male or female clusters.

You may not have noticed that this plant bears two different flowers, but the male flowers are small and almost heart-shaped while the female flower is much larger with a large winged ovary which remains on the plant after the flowers have fallen, prolonging its colourful stage in the same way that coloured bracts do.

The tree Begonia is a native of Brazil and flowers from October to May. It should have a shady position sheltered from the west and north and is best grown against a wall where it is protected from strong winds.

The Begonia family is diverse and all are attractive in a garden rockery, or containers.

The fibrous Begonias (*Begonia semperflorens*) such as the pink, red or white "Thousand Wonders" are available in a number of free-flowering hybrid forms with green, purple and variegated foliage. These are small and compact and flower in sun or partial shade.

The decorative-foliage Begonias (*B. rex* hybrids and others such as *B. masonian*, the Iron-cross Begonia) make good container plants for the shade house or partly shaded verandahs, balconies and patios while the elegant tuberous Begonias have exquisite Rose-like flowers that put them into the top class of decorative flowering plants for indoor use.

Recently the Elatior Begonia — a hybrid between the fibrous and tuberous rooted Begonias — has been introduced. The Elatior is a beauty with hanging clusters of large semi-double blooms and has been very popular in some countries. Unfortunately in Australia it seems to be very prone to mildew in humid weather. I have heard that it does well as an indoor plant in air-conditioned rooms and in areas where humidity is naturally low it should be a joy.

I am fond of a dainty Begonia commonly called Ivy-leaf Begonia (*B. richmondensis*). It is an upright grower and constantly bears clusters of pink flowers in the shady rockery sections of my Sydney garden. Another one somewhat similar though smaller and daintier is the Fuchsia Begonia (*B. fuchsiodes*).

If you are looking for a plant to collect which has a seemingly infinite variety of interesting foliage and flowers and, except for the temperamental tuberous varieties, is easy to grow — you couldn't choose better than the Begonias.

The Tree Begonia (Begonia coccinea) *brightens a shady position in the garden with flowers of red, pink or white.*

For sheltered spots, a new flowering potted plant — the Elatior Begonia.

ROSES

Pruning

Roses should be trimmed for their autumn flush. Cut all spent flower heads back to a fat bud — in the same way as in cutting a bunch of flowers. Sprinkle a handful of fertiliser round the root area and water in well, and you will be rewarded by an autumn flush which connoisseurs regard as the best Roses.

Summer Pests and Diseases

If you are looking for a hobby that will keep you busy, take up Rose growing. Roses in humid climates always seem to need attention. In the throes of a humid summer, fungus diseases are rampant: mildew and black spot are part of the summer Rose scene and aphids lurk on every tender shoot.

I planted chives round all my Roses and the decrease in the aphid population was remarkable — the aphids may possibly have transferred their attention to something that hasn't been planted with chives, but they are certainly leaving the Roses alone.

There are a couple of other friends of Roses in the garden. Ladybirds and praying mantis are both valuable aids against aphids. Don't confuse the praying mantis with the stick insect, which is a plant eater. Stick insects are long and thin and resemble a dried twig, which is a perfect camouflage. The mantis is smaller, a delicate green colour, has a triangular head and bulging eyes. Take care not to destroy these friendly insects and, together with plantings of garlic or chives, you will find aphids much less of a problem.

Unfortunately I don't know of anything that fancies mildew or black spot for dinner, but regular spraying with a suitable fungicide will keep these diseases under control.

There can be a lot of white scale on Roses in summer. White scales cluster on the shaded side of branches and infestations will be worse where Roses are being grown in shaded conditions or where the branches are shaded by other growth. Scales must be scrubbed off or sealed to prevent the animals from breathing. Most sprays do not penetrate the protective scale to attack the animal beneath. Paint the branches with white oil or scrub with a toothbrush dipped in soapy water if the patches are small. Wear gardening gloves to protect your hands from the thorns. A systemic spray like Metasystox is also effective. Garden sprays are poisonous to people, birds and family pets as well as the pests they are directed at. Please use sprays with care and read the directions on the label.

Rosa rugosa scabrosa *flowering now despite the siege of summer pests and diseases.*

BULBS

Iris

In areas where they grow well, Tall Bearded Iris can be planted at this time and old clumps that have not been disturbed for three or more years can be broken up and replanted.

Tall Bearded Iris need a sunny position that is protected from strong winds which will damage the fragile flowers. They need good drainage and grow best in loam that has had plenty of compost added. In very acid soil a little lime is necessary and a little superphosphate or complete fertiliser can be added as well.

Rhizomes should be firm and healthy — rotted portions can be cut away and burnt but rhizome rot is a sign of poor drainage or overuse of nitrogenous fertilisers. Where clumps show signs of this rot they should be dug and transplanted to a better position.

The rhizomes should be planted so that only half of it is covered and the top surface shows above the soil. Trim leaves back to a fan shape.

Beautiful new varieties of these Iris can be bought from specialist Iris nurseries. They stock as well Beardless Iris — all the fascinating Louisianas, Stylosas, Evansias, plus Iris-like plants.

Iris are one of the most exquisite of flowering plants and though the tall beardeds flower in spring, there are others which flower in other seasons making them an interesting and beautiful addition to the garden.

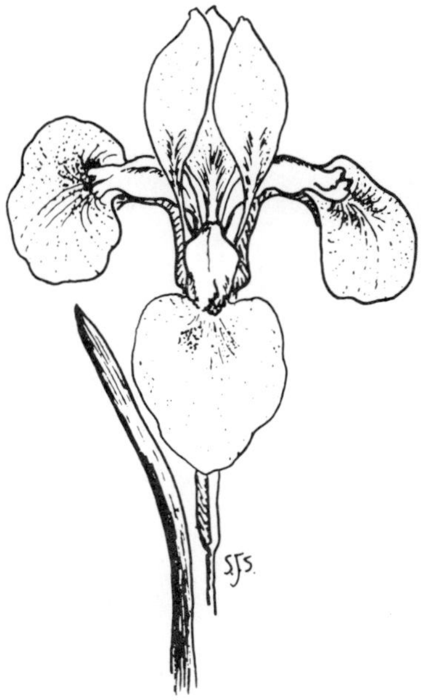

Delicately veined blue Pacific Coast hybrid Iris — one of the many spring-flowering Iris.

Flowering Ginger

Flowering Ginger is growing strongly and you should keep a look out for signs of the stem-boring caterpillar that infests this plant when the flower stems begin to develop. If not noticed, the whole flower display can be ruined by this pest. The caterpillar bores into the stem at the leaf axils and later, when the flowering stems develop, into the base of bud stems so that the flowering heads break off without opening. Spray with a systemic insecticide to control this pest.

The Ginger Lily (*Hedychium gardnerianum*) grows well here. It is not a tropical plant though most people regard Ginger blossoms as synonymous with the tropics. However, it is possible to grow some of the more tropical Gingers here. The lovely White Ginger (*Hedychium coronarium*) and the Shell Ginger (*Alpinia speciosa*) can be grown in a warm position protected from the cold winds and frosts. I found some Shell Ginger flowering this week in a local garden. Not for everyone, but interesting if you have a yen for the romantic tropical plants.

Shell Ginger — waxy, white and shell-like with deep red throats and yellow edged petals.

Cyclamen in the Garden

A potted Cyclamen is one of the most spectacular of the indoor flowering plants. The showy florist's Cyclamen has been specially bred for indoor use but the Cyclamen species, like everything else, grow outdoors in their native habitat in the Mediterranean region.

They are not often grown as garden plants but, given suitable conditions, species Cyclamen will grow outdoors. I visited a garden where these plants had been naturalised under a big Liquidamber. The Liquidamber provides just the right woodland conditions that Cyclamen need, and the original plants have hybridised themselves and seeded until the ground under the tree is a carpet of tiny pink and white flowers.

If you have the right conditions under a deciduous tree you might like to try growing these small Cyclamen from seed. Not for everyone, but good if you're looking for something a bit different. Specialist seedsmen usually advertise Cyclamen seed for sale around February.

If you live in a warm climate you will be able to buy Cyclamen in flower for indoor decoration during the winter months. It should be discarded after flowering because it will not survive the humid hot summer.

The popular florist's Cyclamen with the large, vividly coloured flowers is not a garden plant but it can be raised from seed, provided it is given some sort of shelter in a bush house or shade house. If no bush house is available a partly enclosed verandah would be suitable and, of course, once they have reached the flowering stage they are ideal indoor plants.

To raise Cyclamen from seed, a seed box filled with a mixture of loam, leaf mould and sharp sand in equal parts should be used. Buying a bag of seedling raising mixture from a nursery, garden department or store may cost a little more but has the advantage of being sterile, properly balanced and weed-free.

Wet the soil mixture thoroughly and allow surplus moisture to drain away, then sprinkle the seed evenly over the surface.

A layer of soil mixture should be sprinkled over the seeds and the whole lot firmed down. The best way is with a board cut to the size of the inside of the box, with a handle in the centre.

A point to remember is that Cyclamen seeds germinate unevenly. Some may come up fairly quickly, and then there will be a gap of two or three weeks before the next lot emerges.

The eastern coastal summer climate is notoriously humid. Seedlings planted at this time of year are prone to fungus disease, particularly damping-off. Cyclamen is more susceptible than other seedlings because of its soft, fleshy stem — a fungicide like Thiram (Arasan) may be applied as a protective soil drench against damping-off.

Two forms of Holly-leaved Grevillea. Top: G. steiglitziana *which has bronze-green foliage and red flowers. Bottom:* G. gaudichaudii *bearing burgundy toothbrush flowers amid bronze-tipped foliage.*

NATIVES

Suggested Plants for a Native Garden

Home gardeners have a lot more interest in growing native plants in gardens these days. A native garden blends well with a lot of modern architecture — particularly in suburban areas which still retain a bushland atmosphere. The soft greyish colours and weeping foliage of many natives provides a good foil for the glass and concrete boxes and, with the addition of mulches and the use of ground covers, add up to low maintenance gardens which suit busy people. Native trees and shrubs also attract birds to the garden and birds will help to keep insect pests under control, so they are useful as well as decorative to have around.

I have visited several interesting native gardens belonging to members of the Society for Growing Australian Plants (S.G.A.P.) and the approach to creating a native or partly native garden was different in every garden visited though all had combined natural materials with native plants to create a total environment.

Ideally a native garden should not have any lawn. Mulches of gravel, bark chips or leaf litter combined with stepping stones of natural sandstone or timber rounds plus some paved areas — again using natural materials — and ground-cover plants provide a suitable substitute for conventional lawns. If there are young children to consider, a sunny area could be grassed and service areas such as clothes lines could be included in this area and screened by plantings of native shrubs.

Two plants to consider for a native garden: 1. Wonga Vine (Pandorea pandoreana) *which has creamy flowers with a purple throat; 2. Grevillea "Rondo" with ruby-red flowers.*

In one garden I visited railway sleepers had been used to edge planted areas where the soil level had been raised and the driveway was cobbled with basalt rocks pushed into a concrete foundation. Trailing plants grew over the railway sleepers to soften the effect.

Native Violets (*Viola hederacea*) are good trailing and ground-cover plants for partial shade or filtered sunlight and are very attractive when planted under tree ferns which are also shade lovers. Other trailing and ground-cover plants for sunny positions include purple-flowered False Sarsparilla (*Hardenbergia violacea*), and Scarlet Running Postman (*Kennedia rubicunda* and *K. prostrata*). When using these ground-covers it is always best to mulch the ground first, then plant the trailers to grow over the mulch. In this way weeds are suppressed and soil is held in position while the plants are growing.

Grevillea biternata is nature's gift to the gardener looking for a good, bright green, dense cover. The narrow green leaves carpet the ground, flowing over rocks, walls or flat ground. In spring it sends up flowering stems of creamy flowers. Blue-flowered Scaevolas (the Fan Flowers) will form green mats with blue flowers in spring. The Fan Flowers look attractive on a sunny bank — they need sandy, well-drained soil.

Fan Flower and False Sarsparilla — showy natives to use as ground-covers.

When you start thinking of native shrubs you can't beat Grevilleas — there are so many different varieties, ranging from ground-covers to tall trees, that there is a Grevillea for every situation. There are also a number of hybrid Grevilleas which make good, easily grown and showy garden shrubs such as "Robyn Gordon", with bright red brushes; "Golden Sparkle", with variegated foliage; "Ivanhoe", which has bronze-tipped foliage; and the many "Poorinda" hybrids, particularly "Royal Carpet" and "Royal Mantle".

One of my favourite Grevilleas is the Grey Spider Flower (*G. buxifolia*) a subtle and charming flower which, along with the Red Spider Flower (*G. speciosa* formerly *punicea*), is seen flowering in profusion in bushland round the Sydney area in spring. The Queensland Grevillea (*G. banksii*) is an excellent garden shrub which grows to around 3 m (10 ft) with red or sometimes white flowers.

I find the holly-leaved forms fascinating and they might not be as well known as some. *G. ramosissima, G. steiglitziana* and *G. gaudichaudii* are spreading low growers with bronze-green foliage while *G. ilicifolia* has bluish holly-like leaves. They are all good ground-cover plants and can also be used in tubs.

Other easy to grow native shrubs are the Wax Flowers (Eriostemon), Thryptomene, Mint Bush (Prostanthera), Pimelea, Melaleuca, Leptospermum, Hovea, native Hibiscus, Geraldton Wax (*Chamaelaucium uncinatum*) and many others.

*Scribbly Gum (*Eucalyptus haemastoma*). This small tree is a good choice for sandstone areas.*

Every native garden needs at least one gum tree even if it is only to supply barbecue wood. But in suburban gardens – particularly on sandstone, where there is no great depth of soil – the very tall growing trees should be avoided. One very attractive smaller Eucalypt is *E. cinerea,* which has oval silvery leaves. These remain silvery, unlike the Tasmanian Blue Gum, which is often planted for the beautiful silvery blue of the juvenile foliage. These blue juvenile leaves are rapidly replaced by the green sickle-shaped leaves of the adult tree. The Scribbly Gum (*E. haemastoma*) is a good choice for sandstone areas, being a small tree up to 8 m (26 ft) high and native to the Sydney area. The mallees make attractive garden trees and *E. speedmanii* (which has red or yellow flowers in summer) grows only to 5 m (16 ft) while *E. forrestiana* has showy red fruits and grows only to around 4 m (13 ft).

But don't just plant a Gum. Other native trees are equally suitable. The She Oak (Casuarina), for example, includes small species such as *C. distyla* (3 m — 10 ft), *C. littoralis* (7 m — 23 ft), *C. stricta* (8 m — 26 ft) and *C. torulosa* (7 m — 23 ft). These are graceful conifer-like trees which don't cast a dense shade.

Melaleuca linarifolia forms a small tree up to 7 m (23 ft) with fine lemon-scented leaves and white flowers and would be a valuable addition to any garden. Another good tree is *Agonis flexuosa,* which has weeping branches, white flowers and is also aromatic. There is a variegated form which has ornamental green, cream and pink foliage and can be grown in the garden or in a large tub.

Banksia ericifolia is an easily grown large bushy shrub with large orange "candles" in autumn and winter. *B. serrata* has a gnarled trunk and branches which make it look ancient — good for the garden or a bonsai subject.

There are also many beautiful flowering native trees which are not too big for the home garden. Think of *Backhousia citriodora,* Brachychiton (Flame Tree), Elaeocarpus (Blueberry Ash), *Hymenosporum flavum* (native Frangipani), Barklya, Buckinghamia, Acacia and, for a damp spot, Callicoma (Black Wattle).

Native gardens need annuals and perennials beneath the trees and shrubs and there are many suitable flowering plants: Everlasting Daisies (Helichrysum), Australian Bluebells (Wahlenbergia), Swan River Daisy (Brachycome), Flannel

Flowers (Actinotus), wild Iris (Patersonia) and Kangaroo Paw (Anigozanthus), to name a few.

Many of these are small shrubby or prostrate natives and make good rockery plants. Many are also free flowering and colourful. For a rockery situation look for plants like *Calocephalus brownii* (a silvery foliage shrub), Chorizema, Helichrysum, Baxteri, Dampiera, *Hibbertia stellaris,* Patersonia, *Pelargonium rodneyanum* (a purple-flowered native Geranium), Scaevola (Fanflower), *Mazus pumilio, Pratia pedunculata,* Viola and Wahlenbergia.

There are also showy native creepers like Golden Twining Guinea Flower (*Hibbertia scandens*), Bower Plant (*Pandorea jasminoides*), Wonga Wonga Vine (*P. pandoreana*), *Clematis aristata,* Bluebell Creeper (Sollya) and, for shady areas, Cissus.

These are just a few of the many easily-grown natives you will find either at native plant nurseries or even at most retail nurseries. There is a rich treasure trove of fascinating plants to be discovered.

If you need a fence round your native garden brush fences, old-fashioned post and rail and dry-stone walls will blend with the surroundings.

Basic care for natives is simple — good drainage, regular watering until established, no digging around roots, no chemical fertilisers and plenty of mulch to suppress weeds and keep soil from drying out. Add a little TLC (tender loving care) and wait for the flowers.

EDIBLES

Greek Vegetables

I recently visited a Greek neighbour who is famous locally for his vegetable garden. When I got round to the sunny backyard I found it was not just an ordinary vegetable garden but a Greek one. A grape vine on a trellis was hung with grapes and another trellis was waiting for the vines to grow big enough to form an arbour. Capsicums, aubergine (egg plant) and tomatoes grew in neat, raised beds edged with basil and parsley. Glossy purple onions had just been hung to dry — Greek salad on the hoof!

If you are growing these ingredients, here is a recipe for them. Slice and gently fry all of the above vegetables in a little olive oil. Season. Cover and cook until tender. Serve cold with roast lamb or any cold meat.

This is gardening at its most enjoyable. If you are growing vegetables try to grow things you will enjoy eating. There is more incentive to look after your plants when you are looking forward to eating them.

CHECKLIST

Autumn is one of the most important and exciting periods of the gardener's year. The planning and planting done over the next few weeks will produce quick dividends in spring. In the spring, the seasonal plantings of vegetables, annuals and bulbs reach their peak and foundations can be laid for long-term developments by planting trees and shrubs for future shade and privacy.

Perennial Phlox, Abelia and Michaelmas Daisies — flowers for autumn.

Flowering now

Trees and Shrubs:
Abelia,
Azaleas (early varieties),
Bauhinia galpinii,
Begonia coccinea,
Camellia sasanqua,
Cassia,
Ceratostigma (Skybush),
Clerodendron ugandense (Butterfly Bush),
Cuphea,
Frangipani,
Fuchsia,
Gordonia,
Hibiscus,
Holmskoldia,
Lagerstroemia,
Plumbago,
Roses,
Tecomaria,
Tibouchina granulosa (Brazilian Glory Tree).

Early berries on Arbutus,
Contoneaster,
Crataegus,
Pyracantha.

Annuals and Perennials:
Aster (perennial Michaelmas Daisy),
Chrysanthemum,
Dahlia,
Hedychium (yellow Ginger),
Helianthus,
Impatiens,
Marigold,
Petunia,
Phlox (perennial),
Physostegia (Mock Erica),
Plectranthus,
Roses,
Rudbeckia.

Bulbs:
Belladonna Lily,
Canna,
Colchicum,
Day Lily (autumn-flowering),
Liriope,
Nerine,
Sternbergia,
Zephyranthes.

Climbers and creepers:
Antigonon,
Podranea,
Quisqualis (Rangoon Creeper),
Solandra,
Thunbergia.

Natives:
Acacia terminalis (Sunshine Wattle),
Banksia,
Epacris,
Stenocarpus (Queensland Firewheel Tree).

MARCH

Plant

Trees, shrubs and climbers:
All container-grown plants.

Annuals:
Seedlings of Aquilegia (Columbine),
Canterbury Bell,
Penstemon,
Polyanthus Primrose,
Stock.

Seed or seedlings of Ageratum,
Antirrhinum (Snapdragon),
Bellis perennis,
Calendula,
Carnation,
Cineraria,
Cornflower,
Delphinium,
Dianthus,
Foxglove,
Honesty,
Iceland Poppy,
Larkspur,
Leptosyne,
Linaria,
Livingstone Daisy,
Lobelia,
Lupin,
Marigold,
Mignonette,
Nemesia,
Pansy,
Pinks,
Primula,
Schizanthus,
Sweet Alice,
Sweet Pea,
Verbena,
Viola. (See also p. 48.)

Bulbs:
Anemone,
Babiana,
Daffodil,
Dutch Iris,
Freesia,
Hyacinth,
Ixia,
Lachenalia,
Leucojum (Snowflake),
Muscari (Grape Hyacinth),
Narcissus,
Ranunculus,
Sparaxis,
Scilla (Bluebells),
Tritonia. (See also p. 53.)

Vegetables:
Seed or seedlings of broad beans,
beetroot,
cabbage,
carrot,
lettuce,
onion,
parsley,
parsnip,
peas,
radish,
silver beet,
turnip

"Paradise"—a lovely Rose with mauve and cherry splashes.

Fertilise

Azaleas, Camellias and Rhododendrons can be fertilised with one of the soluble foliar fertilisers this month. (These plants will not need fertilising again until after flowering.)

Broadcast complete fertiliser or blood and bone in beds where vegetables or annuals are to be planted and round trees and shrubs. Water before and after.

Available now, hybrid Begonias for instant and long-lasting colour.

Prune

Fuchsias and Geraniums can be pruned and healthy prunings will make good cuttings. (See also p. 45.)

Trim spent heads on Roses, Lavender and Murraya.

Disbud Chrysanthemums and *Camellia japonica* if larger but fewer flowers are preferred.

A dainty summer rarity which flowers well — Bauhinia corymbosa *(syn.* scandens*) is a true climbing Bauhinia with small pink flowers and red stems.*

Pests and Diseases

Black aphids on Roses and Chrysanthemums should be sprayed with pyrethrum or Malathion.

Pests on vegetables (green vegetable bug, tomato mite, bean fly) may be in evidence. Spray green vegetable bug on ripening fruit and ornamentals with Malathion if not controlled by a parasite which causes the bugs to turn grey-black in colour instead of yellow-red. Dusting sulphur will control tomato mite and Malathion or Diazinon will control bean fly. Pull out and burn diseased vegetables at the end of their season.

Watch out for late season caterpillars including tomato caterpillar, false looper, the vine moth caterpillar on grape vines and Fuchsias and the light brown apple moth (leaf rolling caterpillars) on fruit and ornamentals — spray with Carbaryl or Malathion.

Sawflies are active now: (paperbark, cypress pine, tea-tree and steelblue). Paperbark sawfly attacks Bracelet Honey Myrtle (*Melaleuca armillaris*) and can defoliate trees. The larvae also pupate in bark (heavy infestations may kill trees) and in paling fences, soft weather-boards and floorboards in houses. Spray with Malathion or inject trunks with Rogor.

The white cedar moth defoliates White Cedars (Melia) in autumn. Banding, spraying with Malathion or injection with Rogor are all effective.

Snails and slugs are active, particularly on damp or dewy evenings — protect all plantings of seedlings and bulbs with snail bait.

Fungus diseases such as mildew, black spot, dollar spot in lawns and Geranium rust are still present — spray with fungicide.

Lemon scab causes worry now when fruit develops warty growths and scabs. No treatment to be carried out now but spray with Bordeaux in spring. The fruit quality will not be affected.

Garden Care

All spent summer annuals and vegetables that are coming to the end of their season should be removed. Don't hang on to weak, diseased and unproductive plants. If you have not already done so, add compost or rotted manure, peat moss or spent mushroom compost to garden beds before making new plantings.

Put up trellis for Sweet Peas in a sunny position.

Lawns that are thin (often caused by mowing too close) or tend to brown in winter can be rejuvenated by oversowing now with a grass seed mixture of rye, bent and fescues. Mow and rake lawn, broadcast seed over the lawn area and water gently to wash seed down to the soil.

Dollar spot (round brown spots in lawns) can be watered with a fungicide.

If you do not have time to pull them out at least cut the seed heads off weeds such as Canadian Fleabane to stop them spreading and infesting the garden the following summer.

Cassia bicapsularis — *bright yellow flowers now.*

THE MARCH GARDEN

March is a particularly colourful time for gardens. Brilliantly coloured flowering shrubs like Cassia, Hibiscus, Tibouchina, Plectranthus and Roses are all at their best. The berry bushes, Cotoneaster, Pyracantha and Crataegus, are adding bright red and orange to the autumn scene. The more delicate flowers of *Camellia sasanqua* have also joined the parade with many of the single pink varieties in bloom, providing scent as well as colour.

You need to be a financial wizard to follow the ups and downs of the money market, but in warm coastal gardens you can count on gold being steady for March.

The main source of the golden glow is the humble *Cassia bicapsularis,* which grows so quickly and easily in any soil or situation. Like all quick-growing trees and shrubs it tends to be short-lived. But in any case it is always most beautiful while young.

It grows readily from seed, rather too readily sometimes. I am always pulling up surplus young ones but, by leaving one or two healthy young plants occasionally, I always have a new bush coming on as a replacement for older and shabbier Cassias.

More sources of gold are the yellow daisy-flowered hardy perennials Helianthus (Autumn Glory) and Rudbeckia (the Gloriosa Daisy). These showy flowers are a valuable source of colour in the autumn garden, when annuals are between seasons.

Helianthus is the perennial form of the big, tough, showy annual sunflower but, unlike its sturdy summer relative, the stems and golden flowers are fine and graceful. The best way of adding this plant to your garden is to see if your friends are growing it. They will have plants to give away later in the year when they are sub-dividing clumps. Otherwise, look for it in the plant lists of nurseries specialising in perennial plants. Local nurseries rarely carry it.

Sunshine Wattle (*Acacia terminalis*) is doing its bit to brighten up the stony hillsides around bushland remaining at the edges of suburban sprawl. This dainty Wattle has fairly large, pale yellow balls of flowers which are not quite the bright golden splash you would expect from the "sunshine" name. But the native part of our garden is its natural habitat and, looking down from the house to where it grows among gums and rock ledges, it really does look like dappled sunlight on sandstone.

Camellia sasanqua *hybrids which bloom even if neglected.*

Exotic tropical colour is provided by the creepers Allamanda and Bougainvillea.

A perennial border in summer splendour with Agapanthus, Bergamot (Monarda), Perennial Phlox, Cannas, Gladiolus and Salvia.

Brilliant reds provided by Dahlias, Ixora and Bauhinia galpinii, *a small shrubby plant flowering throughout summer months and into autumn.*

GARDENKEEPING

Rain

Heavy rain often falls in coastal regions during March. The rain can be heavy enough to cause flooding and wash soil away from gardens on sloping sites. It softens soil around trees and shrubs, particularly newly-planted ones, making them vulnerable to wind damage.

Any plants in the garden that have not been growing long enough to establish good root systems are susceptible to being blown over in windy conditions that follow a long wet period. Tall-growing plants like Dahlias and Chrysanthemums also start to sprawl from the combined weight of the rain on foliage and the softening of the soil.

Stake any plants in need of support, tying them firmly but not tightly with plant ties or a length of old nylon stocking. Don't use string or wire as this will cut into the bark. Check recently-planted annuals and bulbs to make sure that soil has not been washed away from them. Firm up any annuals that have been loosened by the rain.

Heavy rain also tends to leach fertiliser out of the soil, so a ration of blood and bone or all-purpose fertiliser should be spread round the garden. It will be readily taken up by plant roots while the soil is thoroughly damp. Even though it has been so wet, the garden should still be given a quick hosing after fertiliser has been spread to wash off any granules on stems and leaves, where it will burn, unless it is still raining.

When the weather fines up again, continue planting bulbs and spring annuals so they can make good growth before the weather gets cold.

Drainage

Prolonged "wets" cause a lot of drainage problems. I have a number of inquiries about what to grow on boggy ground near septic systems. Excessively wet weather always overtaxes drainage systems which rely on the absorption ability of the soil. There are plants which don't mind this soggy situation (Cannas will thrive and give a brilliant display in full sun). Cannas are magnificent flowers and there are some wonderful hybrid varieties that are good garden plants.

If you live in an area where you can get delivery of a truckload of ashes or cinders (sometimes known as "breeze") this will help solve the absorption problem. They can be simply spread over the damp area to a depth of 8 to 10 cm (3 to 4 in) or formed into an ash-bank on sloping ground. Where an existing lawn has become waterlogged the turf can be lifted, a layer of ashes spread underneath and the turf replaced. If the area is too large for this method a series of diagonal trenches can be dug and filled with ashes.

An application of gypsum at the rate of 1 cup per square metre will help drainage on clay soils. Never try to solve your sullage problems by planting Willow trees, unless the site is a 10 ha (25 acre) paddock.

Geranium Cuttings

Geranium cuttings can be taken in March. Pick out the best pieces as you prune, cut to just below a joint and strip off all but the top two or three leaves. Cuttings should be only about 8 to 10 cm (3 to 4 in) and will root really readily in a mixture of sharp sand and compost or peat moss. Cuttings of Geraniums, Pelargoniums and Fuchsias will grow into nice little flowering pot plants by next spring and will make good patio or balcony plants.

A lot of Geraniums turn up their toes during wet weather and if you find, when you are pruning, that stems are weak and brown inside the plants should be dug out and burnt. This is the result of fungus disease. Unless you are able to replace the soil or sterilise it, don't replant Geraniums in the same spot.

Pegs for Dahlias

A gardener has hit on an idea for identifying the colours of Dahlias by labelling them with a plastic peg in the appropriate colour when she lifts the tubers — quick, easy and effective. It sounds a good idea to me, and one you may like to try.

Chrysanthemum Care

When my son took a short-cut through the Chrysanthemums on his bicycle both he and the Chrysanthemums ended up in a mangled heap. I applied sticking plaster liberally to both, and they are now fully recovered.

Brittle-stemmed plants like Chrysanthemums are often damaged by dogs, cats, kids or wind and rain. But if they are not completely snapped off they can often be saved. Press the broken edges together using matches as splints and bind firmly with sticking plaster or sticky tape (use nurserymen's binding tape if you have it). Support the damaged branch firmly with a stake, and keep your fingers crossed.

For single, spectacular Chrysanthemum blooms pinch back all side buds leaving only the bud at the end of the stem.

Chrysanthemums are budding up nicely now, and at this time every year there is always a lot of advice given about debudding. This is only really necessary if you are growing show plants. Debudding will give you larger but fewer flowers. Left alone, your Chrysanthemums will have masses of smaller flowers that give a better massed display.

Black Chrysanthemum aphids are rife at this time and a heavy infestation can ruin young buds. Spray with Clensel or a pyrethrum-based spray.

If you haven't staked your Chrysanthemums you will find them gradually leaning over with the weight of the developing flowers. By the time the flowers open they are all facing the ground and the stems are so curved that it is difficult to use them in flower arrangements. On the other hand, a garden full of stakes looks unattractive. You can overcome the problem by growing "cushion mums", which don't need support, or try an idea I noticed in a garden. Chrysanthemums growing in a bed across the front of a house were held back by a length of 2.5 cm (1 in) pine moulding nailed at either end to a stout stake. By the time the plants flowered, growth had hidden the supporting timber.

Pruning Fuchsia and Geraniums

Fuchsias and Geraniums can be pruned this month. Cut back long spindly branches but don't be tempted to prune either of these too hard or they may die.

TREES AND SHRUBS

Autumn Berries

The berries are with us again. The early berrying shrubs like *Pyracantha fortuneana* with its bright orange-red berries are outdoing themselves.

We acknowledge the arrival of autumn, and cooler weather, with a big bunch of Pyracantha on the table. (It looks great but makes it rather hard to pass the salt.) The thick clusters of scarlet berries make Pyracantha (Firethorn) a very attractive house decoration, as long as you can dodge the thorns. The berries last well when cut.

The Strawberry Tree (Arbutus) which this month has cream bells and red/yellow berries.

The popular name Firethorn is a translation of the Greek (*pyr* — fire and *acanthos* — thorn) and is a good description of the bright fruit and sharp thorns characteristic of these shrubs. The thorns are rather a drawback unless they are made to serve a purpose. Pyracanthas make a good hedge and the thorns will deter intruders in the shape of people and animals. (City folk won't be much troubled by wandering animals but country readers can find them quite a problem.)

There are several varieties available with differently coloured fruits and varied fruiting times. A planting of three different kinds will give you a supply of berries for months. The brilliant red berries belong to *Pyracantha coccinea* "Lalandei", which bears during February, March and April. *P. angustifolia* is orange during April and June. *P. rodgersiana* "Aurantiaca" has clear yellow berries in March and April.

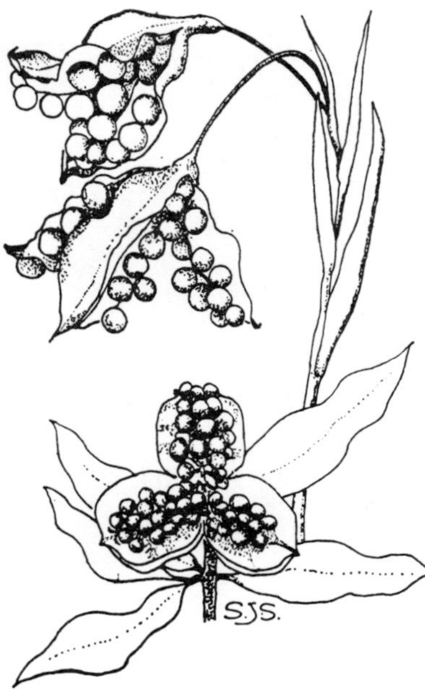

The autumn berries of Iris foetidissima *(top) and* Pittosporum revolutum.

Crataegus or Hawthorn also has bright red berries and wicked thorns but, unlike the evergreen Firethorn, it is deciduous and has pretty, perfumed flowers. *Crataegus crus-galli* (Cockspur Thorn) makes a good hedge or windbreak and has good autumn leaf colour in the hills. *C. lavallei* grows into a small tree with very large red berries lasting well into winter, and also has good autumn leaf colour. There are several good double varieties of *C. oxyacantha* (known as English May) — "Paulii" has bright scarlet flowers, "Plena" is a double white and "Rosa Plena" is a double rose pink. There are two Crataegus varieties with very large berries — *C. smithii*, about 5 m (15 ft) with red berries, and *C. mexicana*, about 10 m (30 ft) with yellow berries. *C. phaenopyrum* has small crimson berries in bunches which persist long after the bright autumn leaves have fallen.

For berries without thorns there are a number of Cotoneasters which can be grown for hedges, walling or in rock gardens. *Cotoneaster franchetti*, with silvery-grey leaves and orange-red berries, is good for walling. *C. pannosus* bears large red berries along the stems, which makes it an effective hedge subject. *C. horizontalis*, or the variety "Perpusillus", can be used in the rock garden or for walling. Its horizontally spreading branches make it adaptable for training on walls or spreading over rocks. It has small leaves and bright red berries.

If you are planning a new garden, don't forget a couple of berry bushes for bright colour in autumn.

All these berry-bearing shrubs need full sun for best results and, of course, the berries show to the best advantage in the sun too. And please do not prune them until the berries drop.

Gardens in cool climate areas are full of berries — Cotoneasters, Crataegus, Pyracantha, Holly, Berberis and Irish Strawberry (*Arbutus unedo*). In this climate the berries seem to be clustered more thickly and to shine more brightly. The Arbutus are laden with strawberry-like fruit and Lily-of-the-valley flowers. It is unusual in that it has flowers and fruit at the same time and although the fruit is far more showy, the flowers are pretty too. The fruit looks inviting but is not palatable at all. Arbutus is a decorative small tree well suited to a small garden and grows satisfactorily in temperate to cool climates.

As you might expect from its popular name of Irish Strawberry, it is native to Eire as well as southern Europe. It is evergreen and has interesting reddish, flaking bark which adds to its ornamental qualities. Arbutus can be grown from seed.

There is another strawberry tree, *Cornus capitata* (the Evergreen Dogwood), which is also covered in huge strawberry-like fruit. The flowers are inconspicuous and it has grey-green leaves covered with fine hairs. This Dogwood does not resemble the American Flowering Dogwood, *C. florida*, but is attractive in its own way. It grows to 12 m (40 ft) or more and is as wide as it is high.

An Australian native tree with rich orange autumn berries is *Pittosporum rhombifolium*, which is planted in some Sydney streets. It makes a slender pyramidal tree with shiny green leaves and a crown of berries so dense that it looks as though the tree is flowering.

Another Pittosporum, *P. revolutum*, has even more showy berries. They are a fat oblong shape in terminal clusters of three, with an orange outer husk which splits into three sections revealing bright red berries against a shiny yellow background. The leaves are sinuate, dull green and tomentose (furry) beneath. The new growth is light brown and felted, making an attractive shrub. It can be raised from seed, and I do not know why we don't see more of it.

Iris is not the sort of thing we associate with autumn berries but *I. foetidissima* has a seed capsule that splits to display large, orange-red seeds which persist for a long time. This Iris likes a moist, shady position and though the lilac-blue flowers are small and not fragrant (as well as its specific name of *foetidissima* it has the common name of Stinking Gladwyn) it is worth growing for the berries, which are good for flower arrangements. It can be grown from seed.

Cassia

When there is a warm summer quite a few plants that are usually marginal have a good season. The beautiful Golden Rain Tree (*Cassia fistula*) is one to look out for. In warm climates this tree flowers much earlier in the summer than in areas like Sydney and Melbourne and it blooms while the tree is leafless. The pendulous clusters of blossom, like yellow Wisteria, look much more dramatic than the Sydney flowering, which comes later when the tree is in leaf.

If you are tempted to try *Cassia fistula* you will only be successful if you can give it a warm, sheltered situation, totally frost-tree, in full sun and protected from cold winds. Of all the beautiful trees, I think the Golden Rain Tree is my favourite but I have never tried to grow it in Sydney. I just enjoy it when I visit my home state of Queensland and other tropical places, and make do with the humble *Cassia bicapsularis.*

One of the native Australian Cassias which makes an attractive garden shrub in cooler areas is *Cassia artemisiodies.* It has good silvery-grey foliage, flowers in September and October and can be grown in a native garden or as a specimen plant in any sunny, well-drained position.

C. brewsteri is another native with gold to orange flowers suitable for warm climates. Also for warm climates are the gorgeous pink and rainbow Cassias (*C. javanica* and hybrids).

Cassia is a fast and easy-growing small shrub with bright Buttercup flowers. It can become a weed if seedlings are not controlled.

Cupheas

I recently made the delightful discovery of a plant unfamiliar to me. It was small and bushy, with hairy leaves and brilliant cerise and red blooms. I was later able to identify it as a Cuphea called "Firefly", and have found that it is available in seeds from Yates.

Cupheas are useful small plants, free-blooming and hardy, as anyone who has grown *C. ignea* (the Cigarette Plant) will know. "Firefly" has been growing in my garden since its original owners dug up a plant in bloom for me, and I am delighted with it. It is well worth a place in the garden or rockery in a sunny position. Cupheas will grow in a shaded spot but will need pruning to prevent the plants from becoming leggy.

Camouflaged Hydrangeas

Do your Hydrangeas bother you? Some people brood about all the space they take up between seasons. I have seen a very pretty solution to this problem. One of my favourite gardens has a low Hydrangea hedge right across the front and in March luscious pink heads of Belladonna Lilies spring through the foliage. Later some other tall spikes will appear — Watsonias from the previous year. These can be planted in March for a fringe of colour round Hydrangeas in spring — and remember the Belladonnas for next year.

PERENNIALS AND ANNUALS

Spring-flowering Annuals to Plant

Spring flowering annuals are easy to grow and will reward any care given with many weeks of colour and perfume. Many gardeners today don't have the time or space for large floral borders, but even a small garden can be turned into a blaze of colour with clump plantings to create bright splashes at vantage points in the garden.

Start at the front gate or entrance. Cluster a few plants where their colour will catch the eye (your own and passers-by). Start outside on the footpath if possible with a planting by the fence-line which can flow in by the garden path. Many people have a letter-box or light standard set in a small rockery and this is a good spot for some more annual colour.

Next move to the house entrance itself. If you have steps, a patio or a landing, concentrate some annuals there in containers or in the garden if there is a suitable spot. Even if the rest of your garden is turned over to shrubs you will now give an impression of a bright, flowery garden which makes your home more attractive and more welcoming to visitors.

If you are thinking of selling your house in a few months a planting of annuals now will add to the value of the house and make it easier to sell. New homes with that just-finished, bare, or even raw look will take on a more home-like appearance very quickly with plantings of spring annuals. The idea here is to fill as much vacant space as possible. If you haven't yet decided on a landscaping scheme, or are waiting a while to afford one, beds of annuals will give colour in the meantime and can be easily swept away to make room for permanent plantings.

You may have planned a low-maintenance garden of trees and shrubs but while they are growing to an interesting size the spaces between can be filled with annuals. A rock garden can be given a lift with small or trailing annual plants like Pansies, Alyssum, Linaria, Lobelia and Nemesia which can be popped into bare spots together with a little extra compost to help them to grow.

Unit balconies, patios, window boxes — all will provide a home for a planting of spring flowers. I have troughs filled with annuals lining the top of a brick wall, where they thrive in the sun, and hanging baskets fastened to the eaves on the sunny side of the house.

Everyone can get enjoyment out of growing annuals. Young children showing an interest in gardening will enjoy the quick results, mothers at home with young children will get pleasure out of growing annuals for cut flowers and the creative satisfaction of growing pretty things, and elderly folk who find wrestling with pruning and heavy digging too much can enjoy the gentler pleasures of the annual garden.

Most annuals need plenty of sun to grow well – at least six hours a day – and well-drained soil enriched with compost, spent mushroom compost or rotted manure, and a handful of blood and bone or complete fertiliser. When you are planting have a bucket of water mixed with some Aquasol or Formula 20 and water each plant the moment you put it in. This will cut seedling losses and get your plants off to a good start.

If the soil is dry put a little water into the planting hole first so that tender young roots won't come in contact with hot, dry soil.

Try to do your planting in the cool of the day and in hot climates give newly planted seedlings some shade by pushing small leafy twigs in beside them.

Taller growing annuals for sunny positions include Anemone, Antirrhinum (Snapdragon), Carnation, Cornflower, Delphinium, Dianthus, Larkspur, Lupin, Marigold (tall varieties), Nemesia Carnival Mixed, Poppy Artists Glory, Festival and Summer Promise, Ranunculus, Stocks Austral and Newports Extra Double, Sweet Pea, Wallflower.

Lower growing annuals suitable for borders, rockeries, baskets and troughs include: Ageratum, Alyssum, Snapdragon, Floral Carpet Mixed, *Bellis perennis* (English Daisy), Livingstone Daisy, Lobelia, Marigold (dwarf varieties), *Nemesia compacta* Mixed, Pansy, Verbena, Viola and Schizanthus.

Plants suitable for semi-shade or filtered sunlight are Cineraria, Foxglove, Polyanthus, Primula. Canterbury Bells which are available as bedding plants this season will also do well in morning sun as well as full sun.

Like Foxgloves, the Canterbury Bell is tall growing, from 50 to 60 cm (20 to 24 in) and is suitable for the back of an annual planting.

Several plants that have not been readily available as bedding plants have been recently reintroduced — Canterbury Bell, Delphinium, Foxglove and Larkspur. All are delightful garden plants and it is hard to understand why they ever fell from favour. Larkspur is a particularly colourful and easily-grown plant which comes in rich, bright colours and grows on tall spikes up to 60 cm (2 ft), making it excellent for cutting for flower arrangements.

Another bedding plant is Cornflower, which can be bought in a mixture of blues, pink, mauve and white or the traditional blue (Blue Boy).

Annuals need regular attention to keep them free of weeds and fortnightly watering with one of the foliar fertilisers such as Aquasol, Bloom, Thrive or Zest to keep them growing strongly. They also require protection from snails and slugs.

Cinerarias are prone to attack by leaf miner and if this pest is noticed (it leaves a wandering track over the leaves where it has mined between the leaf surfaces) it should be sprayed with Chemspray or Rogor, following the directions on the pack.

Rust may be a problem on Calendulas and Snapdragons — spray with a fungicide such as Zineb.

Aphids are fond of Pansies and Violas and severe infestations result in Pansies not opening, deformed and twisted flowers and new growth — spray with a pyrethrum-based spray.

Caterpillars, although not a big problem in the cold weather, may attack plants, particularly in early spring — spray

Cineraria—a shade-loving plant.

or dust to control them and pick off any caterpillars as soon as they are noticed.

Mildew may attack plants that are weak or too shaded, particularly in damp or wet weather. Verbena is susceptible to mildew attack. Spray with a fungicide and pull out and burn any weak, spindly plants that are unthrifty and a source of infection to other, healthy plants.

Sweet Peas

During my Queensland childhood it was traditional for gardeners to plant Sweet Peas on St Patrick's Day, 17 March.

Time was when everyone grew Sweet Peas, but now many gardeners think twice before getting involved with them. Frankly they are a lot of trouble. They need a strong trellis and as much sunshine as possible, and this is not always convenient in today's small gardens. However, no other flower gives such a marvellous return. Well-grown Sweet Peas will flower profusely for months and are good for cutting, providing flowers in winter and spring in a wide range of colours and with a fragrance second only to the Rose.

The ideal support for Sweet Peas is a wire-netting trellis 1.8 to 2.5 m (6 to 8 ft) high, firmly supported by a timber frame and running north-south so that the plants get full sun all day. They will, however, grow quite well against a wall or fence where they can get at least six hours sun each day.

In small gardens Sweet Peas can be grown up a tripod covered with wire-netting. Three 2 m (6 ft) stakes driven firmly into the ground and lashed together at the apex will make a satisfactory tripod.

The small Bijou Sweet Pea does not need support and is well worth growing in the absence of a good trellis. It can also be used in rockeries to good effect and makes a good spill-over, or basket plant. There are several varieties available.

Sweet Peas need good drainage and rich soil with a pH of 6.5. Prepare the soil with a good sprinkle of dolomite along the row, which should be well dug to about a spade depth. Add fowl manure if available, or a complete fertiliser like Gro-Plus. Then you will be ready to plant your peas on St Patrick's Day — no deeper than 2 cm (1 in) in clay soil, but up to 5 cm (2 in) in sandy soil. When the plants have begun to grow you may have to help them to reach the wire by propping the little plants up with small twigs.

As they grow, weekly applications of weak liquid manure or monthly side dressings of superphosphate will help them along. Once they reach the flowering stage, pick them to your heart's content. The more you pick, the more flowers you'll have. Sweet Peas don't really do much for a landscaping scheme and if they don't fit into your garden plan why not grow them among your vegetables.

The revival of the tennis court in the home garden provides an ideal place to grow sweet peas as they will decorate the wire netting surround without damaging it.

CLIMBERS AND CREEPERS

Ornamental Grape

Autumn can arrive with a rush — pouring rain, chill winds and mildew. In early March I have even found the first autumn leaves on the Ornamental Grape that grows along our drive. The Ornamental Grape is usually the first thing to show colour in our area and the display is brilliant (particularly where the leaves are outlined against the sun) and long lasting.

At this time of year you will soon be noticing these colourful leaves on fences, pergolas and shining through trees and shrubs into which they have managed to escape.

The Ornamental Grape (there are several, non-fruiting "Vitis" species) is vigorous, easily grown and deciduous, making it suitable for areas where summer shade is needed. It should be pruned after the autumn display has finished to keep it under control. It can be cut back quite hard and will grow quickly in spring when the sweetly scented, though insignificant, blooms and delicate spring leaves are an added attraction. It will grow easily from hardwood cuttings taken during winter.

Another Ornamental Grape which looks attractive and interesting in March is the Chinese Grape (*Ampelopsis brevipedunculata*). This plant was formerly known as *Vitis heterophylla* and its main attraction is its clusters of small round berries which, though not edible, are very decorative. They start off green and change colour to pinkish-mauve, violet and turquoise, each spray having berries of various colours.

I find this vine less rampant than the other Ornamental Grape, the foliage smaller and the whole plant daintier. However, it too is vigorous and fast growing. Mine grew from seed given to me by a friend who grew it along the fence at the back of his Camellia garden. I don't know whether this plant is available from nurseries but, if you know anyone who has it, try growing some of the seeds.

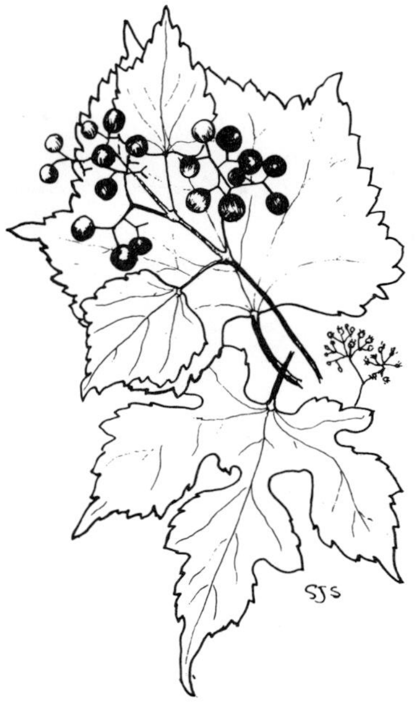

Chinese Grape (Ampelopsis) brevipedunculata) *an ornamental vine with varied foliage forms and decorative berries in autumn.*

Antigonon and Podranea

Another climber of particular interest in autumn is *Antigonon leptopus,* sometimes called Coral Vine or Love's Chain. I have never heard it called anything but Antigonon, but the common names derive from the vivid coral-pink colour of the flowers which hang in chains of heart-shaped flowers. The rather curly, green foliage is also heart-shaped.

This creeper dies back during winter, sending up new growth in spring and flowering in summer and autumn. It is at its best in humid coastal areas from mid-February to autumn and grows well on a fence or over a low wall. It is much more vigorous in tropical and warm areas and is used extensively as a ground-cover in Hawaii, where it grows and flowers well in the warm climate.

Podranea ricasoliana is another creeper that attracts attention in this season. It is a rather rampant creeper belonging to the Bignonia family. Podranea has lush compound foliage and arge trusses of very pretty pink trumpets. A hot summer

Antigonon leptopus — *a pretty pink creeper flowering now.*

promotes very vigorous growth and, because the plant flowers on the ends of new growth, a really lush display of bloom.

It is good for covering ugly fences, outhouses and anything else you want to conceal. Like all vigorous creepers, it is up to the gardener to keep it under control by pruning back unwanted growths at the end of the growing season.

Rangoon Creeper

A friend asked me if there was any such thing as a pink and red Jasmine. I was puzzled enough by this mysterious plant to go round to the place where it was growing to find out what it was, and found a *Quisqualis indica* — Rangoon Creeper — which I had only seen growing in tropical areas.

A very hot, humid summer had encouraged it to flower well enough to justify its space in the garden this year.

I would not recommend Quisqualis except in a warm to tropical area, though it obviously does grow quite successfully when planted for sentimental reasons. In more temperate zones it is planted mostly by people who have spent part of their lives in places like India, Malaysia and New Guinea. It is vigorous in a warm climate, engulfing all in its path and smothering itself with highly perfumed clusters of pink and red Jasmine-like flowers — quite fascinating.

Two long-lasting garden additions:

the Belladonna Lily (Amaryllis belladonna) — *beautiful pink, scented Lilies that bloom between February and May.*

Crucifix Orchids' delicate flower heads in orange, yellow, red, and mauve bloom from early spring right throughout summer.

BULBS

Planting for Winter and Spring

Nothing makes a spring garden look more spring-like than flowering bulbs and this is the month to plant them.

Most nurseries, garden centres and the garden sections of chain and department stores carry a good selection of bulbs at this time and special varieties can be obtained from specialist bulb nurseries in Victoria, such as Tesselaar's Bulb Nurseries, Monbulk Road, Silvan, 3793; Lake Nurseries, Broersen Seeds and Bulbs and Henk de Groot Bulb Nurseries, all of Silvan Road, Monbulk, 3793. In New South Wales Gaibor's Nursery, Great Western Highway, Wentworth Falls in the Blue Mountains has a good range of bulbs including Dutch Iris, Tulips and a good selection of Daffodil varieties suitable for cool and temperate gardens.

One of the advantages of buying from the specialist nurseries is that large quantities of bulbs can be bought quite cheaply, so that if you want to do some mass planting of, say, Daffodils, they can be bought by the hundred for less than $20. A group of friends can get together and buy in bulk economically, too. This is a good way to build up a collection of bulbs in your garden without any large initial outlay.

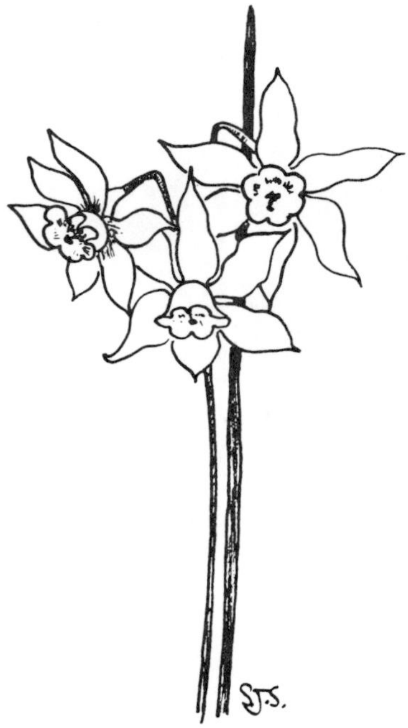

The Campernelle Jonquil — a bright golden mini suitable for a rock garden. It is a dainty contrast to the large Daffodils.

The reliable early golden Daffodil, King Alfred, is one of the best for massing, planting in clumps round the garden or naturalising under trees. As long as the soil is well drained bulbs can be left in the ground to multiply and they will come up and flower again each year. Another early Daffodil, Fortune, flowers two weeks before King Alfred, blooming in late winter to bring an early promise of spring. To have some Daffodils blooming over a long period, plant a selection of early and late-flowering varieties, so that you have a succession of blooms.

A good, late-flowering Daffodil is the Poet's Daffodil — also called Pheasant's-eye Narcissus (*Narcissus poeticus*). It flowers in late September-October when the main flush of Daffodils has vanished. The flowers are pure white with a flat red cup. The Poet's Daffodil multiplies well and forms good clumps which can be left undisturbed.

Small Daffodils are a delight for the rock garden or pots and Hoop Petticoats are among the most popular. Hoop Petticoats (*Narcissus bulbocodium*) get their name from cups shaped like a crinoline or little hoop petticoat. The petals are reduced to slender spikes. Foliage is narrow and grass-like. If you are particularly keen on Hoop Petticoats you will be interested in a new improved strain called Golden Dragon, which flowers about three weeks after the usual variety. Blooms are large, deep canary-yellow with a lime-green throat. This variety is available from Tesselaar's.

Other interesting small Daffodils include Silver Chimes which has clusters of six or more pure white flowers with small creamy trumpets; Cheerfulness, a lovely creamy white double Narcissus-type with two to four flowers per stem; and Thalia, which has up to three flowers per stem, pure white with pointed perianth and long trumpet. Among the small-cupped Narcissus types, the scented golden Jonquils, Soleil d'Or, should be included in every bulb planting. They flower freely from early winter.

Less interesting, but good value in the garden and as a cut flower, are the Paperwhites — white, bunch-flowered Narcissus which grow well in partial shade or filtered sunlight and tolerate damp though well-drained conditions. Paperwhites naturalise well and can be left undisturbed for years while they happily re-flower and multiply.

Bulbs will rot if planted in heavy soil that tends to become waterlogged and because bulbs are expensive it is well worth taking care with soil preparation before planting. Heavy soils are improved by the addition of plenty of compost, peat moss or rotted manure. Waterlogging can be overcome by providing a good drainage system and gypsum treatment.

Bulbs can be naturalised under deciduous trees and look attractive flowering against a background of fresh, green spring grasses. They will be easier to manage if any grass grown is restricted to the soft Bent or mixtures of Rye, Bent and Fescues. If preparing a naturalised area, these grasses can be sown over the area after the bulbs have been planted and left to grow unmown until the bulbs have flowered and died down. Ground-covers such as Ajuga, Cerastium and clumps of Mondo grass, Liriope or Ribbon Grass (Ophiopogon) could be used instead.

Other bulbs which are suitable for naturalising include blue Grape Hyacinth, Freesias, Ipheion (also called Triteleia and commonly known as Blue Starflower), Ixia (in sunny spots where the flowers will wave above the spring grass and foliage of the earlier-flowering bulbs), Sparaxis, blue Babiana and Snowflakes (Leucojum) for shadier areas.

Don't try to plant bulbs close up to the trunks of the trees when naturalising because the ground will be too dry and often root-filled. If the area needs to be mown, use the mower with the blades set as high as possible and don't mow after the bulbs have begun shooting, or before the foliage has begun to yellow and die off at the end of the season.

Crinum moorei — *spectacular white flowers with a faint red flush. Flowering now.*

If you garden on a sunny or partly sunny balcony, patio or window-sill you will be able to enjoy your spring-flowering bulbs in containers. Plant bulbs in pots, troughs or window-boxes large enough to allow sufficient depth of soil for root growth as well as an adequate cover of soil. Plant bulbs close together so as to get as many bulbs into the container as possible for maximum effect.

For a sunny position (six or more hours of direct sun each day), plant Ranunculus, Anemone, Daffodil, Narcissus, Jonquils, Hyacinth, Lachenalia, and Tulips. Plant each pot up with one type of bulb for impact. Bulbs can be grown on window-sills in bulb fibre. Hyacinths give the best results grown this way. Choose an attractive container, place pebbles and a piece of charcoal in the bottom, then fill with bulb fibre.

Nest the Hyacinths in the fibre with the "noses" just showing, water carefully and place the container in a cupboard or on a shelf in a dim light until the bulb begins to grow. Gradually move it into more light over the next few days and then place on a well-lighted window-sill. The bulbs will flower but should then either be discarded or planted out in the garden if there is one available because the bulbs will have exhausted themselves flowering and will not bloom the following year. Hyacinths can also be grown in a bulb glass filled with water, the bulb resting just above the water level. The roots will grow down into the water which may need to be topped up if it gets a bit low.

Crinums

Crinums flower in late summer, usually just before the *Amaryllis belladonna* (Naked Ladies) which it somewhat resembles. Crinums have nodding blooms, usually pale pink though there are white ones available. The plant is almost evergreen but the foliage dies down just before flowering. This makes the plant look rather untidy, so it is best planted behind low shrubs.

Crinums love a partly shaded position, making them useful for shady gardens, and are excellent cut flowers. They open gradually and are not as heavily perfumed as other Lilies.

The bulbs are very big and an established clump would need some moving so plant your Crinums in a permanent position so you won't be faced with the problem of trying to move them.

The necks should be well above the soil level and the only pest likely to be a problem is that old enemy the snail. Scatter a little snail bait round them at flowering time.

EDIBLES

Plant Now for Spring

Many people lose interest in their vegetable garden once the summer crops are finished. However, autumn plantings of cool-weather crops are just as rewarding and probably easier to manage because there are fewer insect pests around to cause problems.

Two important points for successful vegetable growing through the cold weather are sunlight and good drainage. Vegetable beds that were in full sun during the high summer may become shaded in winter when the sun is lower and, if drainage is not good, soil will remain cold and wet. Areas that are liable to become shaded should be left fallow and planting concentrated in beds in full sun. If soils are heavy and prone to wetness during winter, dig in plenty of spent mushroom compost, rotted manure, compost, seaweed or peat moss to raise the soil level. On sloping ground, a small surface drain dug across the top of your beds will channel off a lot of surplus water. Where seepage is a problem agricultural piping should be put down to carry the water away.

Vegetables to grow for winter and spring can be planted out now from either seed or advanced bedding plants. If you have a small garden, or are growing vegetables in containers, advanced plants will be more satisfactory than seeds in most cases.

Hyacinths will flower in glass containers.

Make sure that the plants you decide to plant are the right ones for the season. Some vegetables will run to seed (bolt) if planted out at the wrong time. Beetroot, for instance, tends to bolt in mild climates if planted out after March, carrots sown in later autumn or winter will run to seed without forming roots and the correct onion varieties must be sown for satisfactory results, depending on the season.

Care must be taken when sowing peas that the flowering period will not coincide with heavy frosts. Winter lettuce varieties should be planted now, rather than the ones that gave success during summer.

Good vegetables for the home gardener to plant in autumn include the brassicas. Plant seedlings of cabbage, broccoli, Brussels sprouts (these should be planted as soon as possible now) and cauliflower. These vegetables are fairly slow-growing and will need a fair amount of space for several months.

However, the excellent variety of small cabbage ("Superette") is quick to mature, being ready within seven weeks of planting, and Chinese cabbage (also known as Pe-tsai, Wong Bok and Chinese Great Luck) grows well and quickly from autumn sowings and plants are upright and smaller than other cabbage species.

A new mini-cauliflower (Garant) is available in seed packets from Thompson and Morgan. This is an early maturing type which can be sown direct and spaced at intervals of only 15 cm (6 in) apart. Garant is claimed to grow as easily as radish and should be a big break-through for the home gardener. Thompson and Morgan has a new vegetable called Floccoli — a cross between cauliflower and broccoli that is suitable for warmer areas.

Salad vegetables are popular even during cooler months and winter lettuce varieties for sowing or planting out now are "Mignonette", "Green Cos", "Greendale" (until the end of April) and "Winterlake" (for planting from May to July). Yates have an all-seasons variety ("Narromar") which can be sown year round.

As a change from lettuce, or for use in combination with it, try growing some of the winter salad vegetables such as corn salad (or lamb's lettuce), winter chicory ("Snowflake") or endive ("Golda"), all available in Thompson and Morgan seed packets. Corn salad is cold resistant and is popular in Europe as a salad vegetable. Winter chicory "Snowflake" produces large heads of crisp, fleshy leaves for salads and can be stored in the refrigerator for long periods without losing its freshness. Thompson and Morgan also have an asparagus chicory, a plant that sends out masses of thick shoots that can be lightly cooked or used in salads. This is apparently popular in Italy where it is preferred to real asparagus.

Shallots can be grown now from offsets or small bulbs and also from the shallot seed available in seed packets, which is the bunching type that can be sown and pulled when the stems are pencil thick.

Broad beans can be planted now if you have plenty of garden space. Broad beans take up a lot of space that could be better utilised by other vegetables, but if you like them and can provide a bed about 5 by 1.5 m (15 × 5 ft) you will be able to raise a good crop. Best varieties for the home garden are the dwarfs — Coles' Dwarf and Dwarf Prolific — but even these grow fairly tall and need trellis or similar support.

Celery seedlings and silver beet are available from nurseries throughout the year but if silver beet is planted during cold weather it may run to seed. In cooler areas spinach may be planted instead of silver beet. Spinach needs plenty of feeding to keep it growing and should be treated like lettuce in this respect. English Hybrid or Winter Hybrid are two good home-garden varieties and Thompson and Morgan have a new variety, "Monnopa", which is low in oxalic acid and will not bolt.

Homegrown peas are tender and tasty and can be sown now in most areas, except very cold zones where sowing is left until June and onwards. Peas need a support to grow properly and a trellis is a good investment for climbing varieties such as "Telephone", which is a high-yielding and space-saving pea.

An alternative to trellis or stakes is the tripod which consists of three poles lashed together in a teepee shape and spaced about 2 m (6 ft) apart so that they don't shade one another.

Sugar peas (also known as snow peas and Chinese peas) are delicious, easy to grow and different in that the entire pod is cooked and eaten. Sugar peas are climbers and will need a trellis but there are dwarf varieties. A good dwarf variety to grow is "Greenfeast", which bears plenty of pods 14 to 16 weeks after sowing. "Melbourne Market" and "Earlicrop" are early dwarf varieties ready to pick 12 to 14 weeks after sowing.

Once your vegetables are planted continue to give them regular watering (when necessary) and feeding to keep them growing well. Vegetables grow more slowly during the cold weather but should be kept moving steadily or they will be tough and bitter.

Keep weeds down by hoeing between the rows or mulching and apply side dressings of blood and bone or complete fertiliser once vegetables are growing. Foliar sprays such as Aquasol will boost leafy crops.

Keep snail bait around seedlings to protect them from slugs and snails and, if birds are a problem, try stringing thin wire or string across the beds with silver milk bottle tops threaded along it.

For more serious bird problems cover the bed with a chicken-wire-covered frame that can be lifted off. A new and effective solution is to tether a cut-out of a hovering hawk above the bed on a wire. They are available commercially or you could make your own.

CHECKLIST

April should be a pleasant month in the garden. The autumn season is in full swing with leaves on deciduous trees beginning to turn red, orange and gold and autumn flowers at their best.

Flowering now

The delicate pink waxy blooms of Crowea, an Australian native flowering now.

Trees and shrubs:
Azalea (spot flowering),
Camellia sasanqua,
Ceratostigma (Skybush),
Erica canaliculata,
Gordonia,
Hebe,
Hibiscus,
Holmskoldia,
Justicia,
Lantana hybrids and
L. montevidensis,
Luculia,
Malvaviscus,
Melastoma (pink Lasiandra),
Montanoa,
Plectranthus,
Tibouchina granulosa.

Berries on Arbutus,
Berberis,
Cotoneaster,
Crataegus (Hawthorn),
Holly,
Pittosporum rhombifolium,
Pyracantha (Firethorn),
some Roses.

Bulbs:
Dahlia,
Day Lily (autumn-flowering),
Nerine.

Annuals and Perennials:
Anemone hupehensis (Japanese Windflower),
Chrysanthemum,
Easter Daisy *(Aster ericoides),*
Goldenrod (Solidago),
Michaelmas Daisy (perennial Aster),
early Pansy,
Primula,
Poppy,
Viola.

Climbers:
Allamanda,
Ampelopsis (Chinese Ornamental Grape) in berry,
Antigonon,
Holmskoldia (Chinese Hat Plant),
Manettia,
Maurandya,
Polygonum (Bokhara Vine),
Tecomaria,
Vitis coignetiae (Crimson Glory Vine) in autumn foliage.

Natives:
Acacia terminalis (Sunshine Wattle),
Banksia ericifolia,
Crowea,
Epacris,
Lagunaria (Norfolk Is. Hibiscus),
Stenocarpus (Queensland Firewheel Tree).

APRIL

Plant

Trees, Shrubs and Climbers:
All container-grown shrubs including:
Conifers,
Citrus,
natives,
Azaleas,
Daphne.

Annuals:
Ageratum,
Alyssum,
Bellis perennis,
Calendula,
Candytuft,
Canterbury Bell,
Carnation,
Cineraria,
Cornflower,
Dianthus,
Lobelia,
Lupin,
Marigold,
Nemesia,
Pansy,
Penstemon,
Polyanthus,
Poppy,
Primula,
Schizanthus,
Snapdragon,
Sweet Pea,
Verbena,
Viola,
Wallflower.
(See also p. 69.)

Bulbs:
Anemones,
Babiana,
Bluebells,
Daffodils,
Dutch Iris,
Freesias,
Grape Hyacinths,
Hyacinths,
Ifafa Lily,
Ixia,
Ipheion,
Jonquils,
Lachenalias,
Ranunculus,
Sparaxis,
Triteleia,
Tritonia.
(See also p. 74.)

Vegetables:
Broccoli,
Brussels sprouts,
cabbage,
cauliflower,
celery,
lettuce,
onion,
silver beet,
red beet,
parsley,
peas,
broad beans,
spinach,
turnip,
strawberry runners.

Prune

This is not a pruning month and it is not a good idea to cut back shrubs now, particularly in cold, frosty districts where plants need the leaf cover to protect them from frost damage.

Spent perennials such as Phlox, Stoke's Aster, Michaelmas Daisy, Dahlias and others can be trimmed back and spent heads should be removed from annuals.

Chrysanthemums flowering now.

Pests and Diseases

Snails and slugs are out in force now. Protect seedlings and bulbs with snail bait. Check shrubs for snails too and spray with something containing copper oxychloride.

Aphids attack young growth on seedlings such as Pansies, Violas and others. Check Chrysanthemums for black aphids. Spray with a pyrethrum-based spray or Malathion or sprinkle Disyston and water in if you don't like to spray.

Leaf miner attacks Cineraria foliage, Nasturtium and Daisy leaves — pick off worst foliage and spray with Rogor or sprinkle Disyston.

Caterpillars are still busy so vegetables such as cabbages should be kept dusted with Derris.

Rust may attack Snapdragons, Hollyhocks, Calendula, etc., particularly in wet weather. Spray with Zineb or other fungicide.

Mildew may be a problem on Roses, Hydrangeas and vegetables as a result of damp weather or too much shade. Spray with fungicide. Black spot is still apparent on Roses and can also be sprayed with fungicide or a complete Rose spray.

All mummified stone fruit should be removed and burnt to eliminate sources of brown-rot fungus.

In wet weather watch for petal blight on early-flowering Azaleas and spray with fungicide.

Black aphids cluster round stems of recently developing citrus fruit — spray now.

Garden Care

Keep gardens weeded. Hand weed round newly planted annuals and bulbs. Cultivate lightly between vegetable rows to keep down annual weeds. Don't mow grass too short now as growth will slow down and weeds will encroach in bare spots.

If planting climbing peas or sweet peas, provide a sturdy trellis.

Keep plants moving with weak, fortnightly watering with Aquasol, Thrive, Zest, etc.

Divide clumps of perennials like Perennial Phlox and Shasta Daisies. (See also p. 63.)

THE APRIL GARDEN

I know it's really autumn when I see the fallen leaves swirling and scurrying along in front of me, like a flock of demented birds excited by the first chilly breezes.

The leaves drop quietly away from some trees without any sign of changing colour and you only notice that they've fallen when they start flying round your ankles. This is disappointing if you've planted a deciduous tree hoping to enjoy its autumn foliage. You can make sure of getting good autumn colour by buying deciduous trees while they are actually in autumn leaf at your local nursery.

Though autumn colour is fickle and dependent on the whim of wind and weather, it is still worth planting for. It adds drama and variety to our streets and gardens and the aromatic smell of autumn leaves lends something to the city atmosphere.

The planting position is important for deciduous trees. For dramatic impact the slanting rays of morning or afternoon sun are needed to light up the tree. Study the pattern of autumn sunlight in your garden so that you make sure you pick a good position.

The leaves of the English Oak (*Quercus robur*) are particularly disappointing as far as autumn colour goes. The leaves on this tree brown off rather than change colour, though they do take on a rusty yellow tint in cool climates. The Oaks that give the best display — particularly in hills districts — are the Pin Oak (*Q. palustris*) and the Scarlet Oak (*Q. coccinea*). These trees are large and suitable for street planting or large country gardens.

Leaves of two brightly coloured trees — Rhus which is scarlet and apricot and allergenic (don't touch); Liquidamber which has purple, red, orange and yellow leaves.

GARDENKEEPING

Autumn Planting

Easter usually brings a long-awaited change in the weather and takes us into autumn with the promise of some crisp, sunny days — good gardening weather. Anything planted out now stands a good chance of settling down well — the soil is warm but the fungus-inducing humidity has gone.

If you have been hesitating to plant bulbs and seedlings because of wet conditions, get busy now. Everyone has losses of seedlings (even nurserymen) during a wet, humid summer but replacements should get away quickly now and form good root systems before the cold weather starts.

Seeds of Virginian Stock, Mignonette and Nemophila can be sown among bulbs and will form an attractive ground-cover round bulb plantings. Nemophila is a charming annual with sky-blue flowers — popularly called Baby Blue-eyes — which provide a good contrast for Daffodils. I saw this flower growing wild in the Arizona desert, where it was providing ground-cover for cactus.

April days are meant to be spent out in the garden. The uncomfortable heat has gone from the sun but the earth is warm and ready to grow everything that's planted in it.

Plant out container-grown shrubs now and get them established before the cold weather starts. Nurseries and chain stores are full of sturdy seedlings and bulbs for spring flowers and with Mother's Day around the corner they are gay with potted Chrysanthemums in bloom.

While you're having your big April plant-out don't just plant the same old things. Look through your nursery for some of the new varieties.

Spring gardens can become very stereotyped when everyone grows the same plants — and nurserymen only raise the most popular plants for the seedling trade. Unusual things are just not profitable for big firms to handle. So browse among the seed packets and try some of the off-beat flowers to add personality to the garden.

Some plants, like Snapdragons, have changed out of recognition. Try the new Tetraploids — they are gorgeous though you might not feel they really are Snapdragons. Freesias have changed too and for once hybridists have managed to produce bigger, brighter flowers without losing the perfume.

Try to plant bulbs in clumps. Lachenalias or Soldier-boys — more than anything else — seem to tempt people to plant them in serried ranks. In all but cold areas Tulip bulbs lifted last season won't reflower unless they are put in the refrigerator for six weeks prior to planting.

Roses are enjoying their autumn flush and if you are planning to plant new roses later on take time off to look at roses while they are at their best. Rose nurseries are open for inspection right through autumn and neighbourhood gardens give the clue to which varieties do best in your locality.

Keeping Dahlias in Bloom

Dahlias ornament summer gardens with their fresh handsomeness — looking stately and self-satisfied. In autumn they undergo a character change. The foliage dries out and looks a little shaggy. The flowers glow in the sunlight like cheeky urchins.

Gardens should be at their most brilliant now and Dahlias are good company for the bright berries and coloured leaves of an autumn garden. When planning for autumn it is well worth regarding Dahlias as autumn flowers and maintaining them so that they will be at their best now. Snipping off dead heads will keep them blooming and looking good. They also need regular applications of snail bait. If the leaves show symptoms of mildew spray them with a fungicide.

Dividing Perennials

In warm areas perennials like Perennial Phlox, Michaelmas Daisies, Shasta Daisies and Stokesia which have formed big clumps can be divided up. Use the vigorous new plants from the outside of the clump and discard the old plant in the centre.

You will have lots of spare plants for give-aways to friends, or you could save them for a plant stall.

There will be plenty of fêtes later in the year and now is the time to pot any spare plants. Plastic ice-cream containers make useful and colourful plant pots.

Repotting

April weather is usually good planting weather — for both gardener and plants. Potted plants may need repotting, either into a larger pot or with fresh soil. Plants growing in large tubs too heavy to move can have the soil rejuvenated by replacing some soil with fresh soil, preferably from the compost heap.

Using Leaves

I've noticed people everywhere busily raking up fallen leaves in their gardens and burning them. If you grow Camellias, Azaleas or other acid-loving plants such as natives in your garden, don't burn the leaves. Use them to mulch round these plants — leaf litter is very important to their growth.

At this time of the year mulch will protect shallow root systems from the cold weather ahead, as well as maintaining the essential soil acidity. Keep the mulch away from the main stem, where it will cause collar rot. Don't forget to mulch potted Azaleas and Camellias too.

Surplus leaves can be added to the compost heap, raked into a corner and covered with a little soil or a bag to prevent them from blowing about or stored in big plastic bags. This will provide a convenient supply for regular mulching throughout the year.

Weeding and Feeding Annuals

Spring annual beds need constant attention to weeding. Weeds not only spoil the appearance of the garden, they compete for light and nutrients and are often hosts to pests and diseases which will spread to garden plants.

Applications of Aquasol will speed along annuals but avoid putting it on Camellias and Azaleas just now because it will stimulate new leaf growth at the expense of buds. In cold areas this new growth will be burned by frost.

Pests with Four Legs

First it was mildew, then black spot, then aphids. Now its **possums** at my roses. The way things are going, the only autumn flush in my garden will be on my face. However, I'm fighting back. We've used Zineb on the mildew and black spot and Clensel on the aphids. For the possums we are trying Quassia chips plus bread and honey. If the possums aren't discouraged by the repellent, perhaps they will be too full of honey sandwiches to bother about rose snacks.

If you're having similar problems, I recommend a Quassia chip repellent. Quassia chips are available from chemists but you will probably have to order them and they cost around $2.50 for 450 g. There are two recipes. For the first, simply soak 225 g (8 oz) of chips in 5 L (1 gal) of water for fifteen minutes. Strain and spray.

The second recipe requires: 100 g (4 oz) Quassia chips, 100 g (4 oz) soft soap, 20 L (5 gal) water. Boil chips for thirty minutes, strain and add the soap. Stir until dissolved and then spray. If you can't buy the soft soap commercially use pure soap such as Sunlight or Lux flakes (not detergent).

The chips can be dried and re-used, so they are not as expensive as they appear. You will probably need to spray several times to convince the possums that roses aren't for eating and, in wet weather, more frequent spraying will be necessary.

A rose nurseryman told me that spraying with Zineb is a very effective deterrent for possums. Neither remedy will harm possums or plants. Another anti-possum ploy is to crush a block of camphor, mix it with vaseline and smear the mixture along possum paths on fences and branches. A new commercial possum deterrent is D-ter which is effective and harmless.

In outer suburbs rabbits are a considerable pest. Some people shoot them, but a good rabbit-chasing dog is a help. The CSIRO will give a rabbit colony a dose of myxomatosis if all else fails.

Uninvited animals can certainly be a worry. But if you think you have problems, spare a thought for the man we once visited in Malaysia. We were obliged to go to the back entrance because the entire front drive was occupied by an elephant browsing contentedly on the herbaceous border!

TREES AND SHRUBS

Trees for Autumn Colour

If you are thinking of planting a tree for autumn foliage this is the time to visit the nurseries to see the trees while they are in autumn leaf. Some colour better than others and if you pick your tree now you will know that it does colour well.

If you have room for a fairly large tree you could plant a Liquidamber — a tall, shapely tree which colours well with shades of yellow, red and wine. The Claret Ash and the Golden Ash (*Fraxinus raywoodii* and *F. aurea*) look well together, one turning a rich claret colour and the other pale gold. The Golden Ash is also attractive while it is bare because the branches become yellow with black buds. In autumn the Silver Birch (*Betula pendula*) has golden leaves which contrast with the silvery-white bark.

For smaller gardens consider smaller trees such as the Flowering Cherries — which colour beautifully (cool climates only) — the Chinese Tallow (*Sapium sebiferum*) or the Japanese Maple (*Acer palmatum*) a graceful, small tree which does best in a slightly protected position with some shade from the hottest afternoon sun and hot winds in summer. These trees grow and colour very well in temperate areas but their appearance is often spoiled by hot windy summer days which scorch the leaf edges.

Japanese Maple — leaves colour best in temperate areas.

The showiest of all autumn foliage trees is undoubtedly the Rhus, but I would not recommend this tree for the home garden because of its dangerous allergenic properties. Not everyone is allergic to the Rhus but the slightest contact is enough to produce a violent skin eruption in many people. It is a tree to be avoided.

Instead plant a Pistachio (*Pistacia chinensis*) which has similar foliage, colours well and has attractive red berries. In cooler areas the Pin Oak (*Quercus palustris*) will turn rich red and scarlet. This is a more attractive tree than the English Oak, being a pyramidal shape and having deeply lobed leaves, pale green in summer and splendid in autumn. It is a good street tree for cool areas but do not plant it under power lines — it grows to 15 m (50 ft).

Poplars everywhere are leafless as a result of the fungus golden rust (*Melampsora medusa*) and Lombardy Poplars — which normally would be a pillar of gold — are bare. However, White Poplars (*Populus alba*) growing in some areas are a pale golden cloud, apparently unaffected by the rust.

Poplars have always been planted for their autumn colour, but if you are keen to plant one make sure it is immune to golden rust. The White Poplar may not be damaged by the rust, but it has a very bad habit of suckering which makes it a risk to plant — you plant one tree and end up with a forest. Admire from afar but do not plant it.

For a display of red berries to go with your leaf colours the two Cotoneasters *C. pannosus* and *C. parneyi* are well worth growing. They are loaded with berries now and will look good for weeks. The masses of orange berries you are seeing belong to *Pyracantha angustifolia.*

Many people have difficulty distinguishing these shrubs. The easiest way to tell Cotoneasters from Pyracanthas is to remember that Cotoneasters have no thorns. Both last well if cut for decoration. Trim away the surplus Cotoneaster leaves so that the berries show up well. Please, do not prune them until the berries have finished.

Water Nymph and Witch Repellent Trees

Nyssa sylvatica is an interesting tree. Nyssa is named for a water nymph and in its native North America it is found in damp places along streams or lakes. If you are looking for a tree which will grow well in heavy clay *Nyssa sylvatica* could be the answer. It also grows well under normal garden conditions and is a good street tree because it will grow under far from favourable conditions.

The horizontal branches which are a feature of the Nyssa give it a shape particularly satisfactory against modern architecture. Because it is bare for six months of the year it can be considered almost as an architectural feature of a house.

Nyssa sylvatica grows to around 9 m (30 ft) so it is not too big for the average garden. Its leaves are vivid yellow and scarlet in autumn and the female trees bear blue berries. The long leafless period means that the sun can stream through it all winter, making it suitable for underplanting with bulbs or spring annuals.

Readers in cold climates could grow a Rowan tree (Sorbus), a very graceful, pretty tree which features in lots of fairylore (a Rowan branch will keep you safe from witches). It has bright scarlet berries and the leaves colour rich red in autumn.

Unfortunately Rowans are not happy on the coast, but lots of other lovely autumn colourers are. *Pistacia chinensis* — which is related to the pistachio nut — grows well on the coast and is a good garden size at around 9 m (30 ft). It has a rounded head, good autumn colours — red, yellow and purple — and bunches of small berries which colour red and purple and stay on the tree for quite a while.

Some of the most striking autumn trees — like Poplars — are not suited to home gardens. They are generally far too big, have greedy root systems, and some species have bad suckering habits which can make them a menace.

Sasanqua Camellias

I spent a morning among the Camellias and Azaleas at a local nursery, admiring the espaliered Camellia Sasanquas. Sasanquas — whether espaliered, grown as a hedge or simply as a specimen plant — are charming and the daintiest of Camellias. The flowers are fragile and fall quickly (they are no good for picking) but they flower so freely that this does not matter. Actually the brief blooming is almost an advantage because there is no need to worry about the flowers burning or fading in the sun.

A few early Sasanqua varieties have flowers in February. Although their main flowering period is March to May, they actually bloom from February to June, when the Japonicas take over. Though not as glamorous as the Japonica Camellias, the Sasanquas are much less temperamental. They even seem to survive almost total neglect with equanimity (not that I am advocating neglect).

They come in many shades of pink, with white and reds at either end of the colour range. The flowers are dainty, single, semi-double or double and often strongly perfumed. Some varieties left to themselves will grow to almost tree-like proportions quite rapidly.

The obliging Sasanqua can be fitted into a small area if necessary. It can be espaliered on a wall or trimmed to hedge-like proportions. Most varieties will thrive in semi-shade, and a few are suitable for full sun. A visit to a Camellia nursery during the next few months will give you the chance to see them in bloom.

Like all Camellias, Sasanquas need acid soil and should not be planted near newly concreted or limed areas. Owners of new houses should bear this in mind, and avoid planting Camellias close to house walls.

Mysterious deaths of Camellias and other acid-loving plants can sometimes be traced to the aftermath of building — cement having been mixed or discarded or a bag dropped just where the new home-owner happened to plant a shrub.

In inland areas where soil and water are often alkaline, grow Camellias in tubs filled with acid soil or sprinkle a handful of sulphur round plants every three to four months.

Camellia sasanqua — *delicate blooms that add welcome colour to the garden at this time of year.*

Dwarf Shrubs

I know an unhappy gardener who planted a rockery with "dwarf" shrubs and now has a medium-sized jungle instead of the spreading carpet of plants he visualised.

The word "dwarf" probably causes a great deal of confusion among gardeners because it does not indicate that a plant is small, only that it is smaller than others of its species. *Grevillea robusta*, the Silky Oak, can reach a height of 25 m (80 ft) but *G. punicea*, the Red Spider Flower, reaches only 1.5 m (5 ft) and could justifiably be called a "dwarf" Grevillea.

To avoid being trapped into an unsuitable purchase by the "dwarf" description make sure you read the plant label, which usually gives the maximum height.

For gardeners who might be looking for plants which are around the 30 cm (1 ft) mark, here are a few suggestions: Nepeta, *Gardenia radicans*, Felicia, Thrift, Heuchera, Columbine, Pinks and miniature Roses.

These plants are small and dainty, free-flowering and all have attractive foliage, so that they earn their keep all year round. They can all be planted out now; even the miniature Roses which are sold in pots don't have to wait for the official Rose season.

Shrubs for Patio Planting

A friend of mine has moved into a house with a very large patio that gets afternoon sun, a view of bushland and parrots and, sometimes, a stiff breeze. We spent some time choosing plants to go in tubs on the patio. They had to be evergreen (buying a deciduous plant for a tub at this time of year would be pointless), decorative, and able to withstand windy days.

A tall, well-grown Holly (Ilex) was chosen to give height and substance to the display. Caution is needed in placing spiky-leaved plants on balconies, particularly if space is restricted or there are small children to consider. In this case neither had to be considered and the Holly had been grown in a standard form with a sturdy, bare trunk and the bulk of the leaves high enough not to be any problem. A slender, upright conifer such as Swane's Golden Cypress (*Cupressus sempervirens* "Swane's Golden") could be substituted instead.

Next we chose two bushy shrubs, both New Zealand natives — Coprosma and Metrosideros, the latter better known as Pohutukawa. Both make good tub plantings. They have dense growth and attractive leaves, Coprosma being very glossy and the other very dark. These shrubs also have variegated forms (the variegated Metrosideros, also called New Zealand Christmas Bush, is particularly showy) and we bought the variegated forms for extra colour.

Coprosma and Metrosideros will withstand salt breezes and are ideal for planting near the beach, either on balconies or in the garden. The Pohutukawa will grow into a tree if planted out, and has fluffy red flowers at Christmas.

The next choice was for colour. A bright scarlet long-blooming Bouvardia (Pentas makes a good alternative in warm climates); a dwarf Pomegranate with orange flowers and fruit; and the autumn-leaf plant, dwarf Nandina. These were joined by a silvery Lavender for fragrance and contrast. All these would be suitable for planting on sunny patios and balconies.

Variegated plants are not satisfactory in shady positions, because the leaves quickly revert to green, to supply enough chlorophyl for the plant's needs. Choose the green-leafed varieties if your patio is partly shaded.

While looking at the plants I discovered a variegated Buddleia still blooming. It is not as vigorous as the green *B. davidii* and has a rather horizontal growth under tub conditions which makes it an attractive choice for a pot in a sunny spot. The flowers are lilac and scented.

Where tub plantings are needed for coolness or privacy try a clump of one of the true bamboos. Bamboo will grow about 2 m (6 ft) high in a tub and the tall canes are decorative as well as providing shade.

Other suggestions for a similar situation are Sacred Bamboo *(Nandina domestica)*, Jade plant (Portulacaria) and a variegated Coprosma "Picturata". These three are hardy and attractive and will do well together in a sunny aspect. The taller stems and delicate foliage of the Nandina will provide a contrast with the shiny, stiff leaves of the others.

There are also lots of gay little pots of ornamental Chilis in the nurseries — just the thing for some bright colour. But keep them out of the reach of toddlers. The bright colours make them irresistible, but as a taste sensation they are not recommended. They will burn lips and tongues.

Some lovely containers are available if you are prepared to spend a little money. Most large nurseries carry a good range of pots in terracotta, concrete, fibro and plastic. They will also have some more expensive ones, like the glazed ceramic bonsai pots from Japan which can be used for Azaleas, dwarf Conifers and bonsai subjects. You may also find reconstituted sandstone pots and large salt-glazed containers.

If you are looking for something unusual you may like the imported Italian terracotta containers which come in a variety of ornamental shapes. The larger, more ornamental urns are decidedly expensive.

If you became carried away with these beautiful containers, you could easily find yourself putting a $5 plant into a $50 pot. There is no need to go to this extreme (it would not be difficult to find a $50 plant) but if your garden is restricted to a few plants on the balcony, beautiful containers will greatly increase the decorative effect of your plants.

PERENNIALS AND ANNUALS

Perennial Mainstays

The old-fashioned herbaceous border is not really a feature of modern gardens. Some perennials plants don't survive the wet humid periods of an Australian summer, but there are many easily grown and free-flowering perennials that will provide a succession of flowers throughout the year.

In my own neighbourhood I often pass a garden which is well planted with a succession of interesting perennials. The garden is old and well established and the house that it surrounds is of mellow brick with wide verandahs and plenty of white-painted gingerbread trimming. There are always flowers in this garden which has been cared for single-handed by one elderly woman who obviously loves to work in the garden but would not have been able to cope with much hard work.

This house changed hands recently and I have been dreading that I would pass it one day and find that the old-fashioned curving paths with their mossy basket-patterned bricks and the beds of old bulbs and perennials had all been swept away and replaced with one of those soulless, easy-care, low-maintenance, non-gardens consisting of mounds of cemented bush rock, Aloes and Golden Cypress. Mercifully this has not happened and the garden continues to look after itself undisturbed — the perfect low-maintenance garden.

This shows that it is possible to have plenty of flowers without a lot of work if you include some hardy perennials and bulbs that do not have to be lifted every year.

Look around at the perennials you see flowering during autumn and make a note of things you would like to have next season.

You will find perennials on sale — in flower if this is their season — at the perennial section of your local nursery and from specialist nurserymen. Later in the year there will be a selection of perennial plants on sale in their dormant state — crowns, bulbs, or tubers in peat moss and plastic bags.

Michaelmas Daisies put up a brave show for weeks and deserve to be grown more than they are. Michaelmas Daisies (Perennial Aster) were rather tall-growing plants, which may have accounted for their decline in popularity in suburban gardens where every centimetre counts. But there are now some dwarf hybrids which are very attractive and have a lovely colour range of lilacs, pinks, reds, blues and white. I particularly like "Winston Churchill", a rich cyclamen, and "Eventide", soft lavender and massed with flowers.

If your local nurseryman doesn't stock Michaelmas Daisies keep a look-out for them in gardening advertisements. Sending for things from catalogues or ads is rather fun and rewarding in

Michaelmas Daisies (Perennial Aster) which provide masses of autumn flowers of mauve, blue, violet and rose.

Japanese Windflower (Anemone hupehensis) — *a perennial for the autumn garden. Flowers are mauve-pink or white.*

Plectranthus ecklonii — *the lavender flower spikes add colour to autumn gardens.*

The smiling Penstemon — brilliant coloured blooms last for almost nine months of the year.

the way of new varieties. Otherwise, make friends with someone who already has them growing — they multiply readily and can be sub-divided in late winter.

Another mainstay of the autumn garden is Mock Erica (Physostegia), a vigorous plant — and one plant this year will mean dozens next year, but their lavender, heath-like spikes are welcome in the garden where they grow in sun or part shade. They are also good for cutting. They can be shifted even when they are flowering and if you get too many plants they are very easily pulled out and discarded.

Another autumn-flowering plant that never seems to be sold in nurseries is the delightful Easter Daisy (*Aster ericoides*) which sends up tall, dainty flowering branches covered in masses of tiny white daisies at this time of the year. Every year people ask me where they can buy it but unless you have a friend who can give you a few plants of this easily grown perennial, it seems you must do without.

One of my favourite flowers blooms in autumn — *Anemone hupehensis,* the Japanese Windflower. This graceful autumn-flowering Anemone is a perennial which forms an attractive clump of leaves in the garden for most of the year and sends up tall stems of single or double pink or white flowers. It grows best in filtered sunlight or part shade and needs almost no care and attention to surprise you each March with its dainty blooms.

In my garden at present, Plectranthus is providing a display of delicate flowers. One is a small shrub (*Plectranthus ecklonii*) now covered in spikes of purple-blue, and the other is a prostrate ground-cover which is often mistaken for Coleus, *P. oertendahlii*. I use this a lot as ground-cover for semi-shade. The soft, furry leaves are purplish underneath and look attractive all year, covering themselves in delicate spikes of pale, lilac-tinged flowers in early autumn. Try it as a ground-cover for shade-houses — the soft foliage will give a very attractive effect.

Penstemons are delightful perennial plants which are not grown nearly enough. You will find them among the seedlings at nurseries now — a punnet is well worth trying. You may be disappointed the first year, as perennials usually flower better in their second year.

They are related to Snapdragons, don't seem to suffer from any diseases and come in speckled pinks, reds and purples. Try them — they really do look happy in the garden. When mine smile, I smile back.

Chrysanthemums

The only flowers that can match Dahlias for glowing autumn colour are Chrysanthemums. Unfortunately, Chrysanthemums have developed into "florists flowers" produced for Mother's Day rather than real garden flowers.

However, their decline in popularity in shrinking gardens has coincided with the development of Chrysanthemums as pot plants. The potted plants on sale are more compact than the old garden varieties, making them ideal for flats or units. The flowers last well and buds continue to open for several weeks. They can be brought inside and used as table decoration. The plastic pot can be concealed inside a decorative pot for table use.

Don't wait for Mother's Day — think of "mums" now.

The Chrysanthemums in my garden are starting to flower and, as usual, I haven't staked them. One of the reasons for the popularity of compact dwarf varieties of taller growing plants like Chrysanthemums and Dahlias is that gardeners are not keen on having a garden full of stakes, partly because they are a lot of extra work and partly because they look like a cannibals' picnic.

If you don't like to stake Chrysanthemums trying growing the button varieties. They are small, compact and free-flowering. The pink ones seem to be the hardiest but they come in white and yellow as well. If they are pruned after flowering they will produce another flush of flowers and can be kept flowering almost all year round.

Chrysanthemums can be grown easily from seed and some pretty, mainly single, flowers will result. If you would like to try experimenting, save some seed from your flowers for spring sowing.

Chrysanthemums are often attacked by black aphids which cluster round the buds and will spoil the flower display if not controlled. Spray with Malathion or a pyrethrum spray.

Schizanthus and Sweet William

Seedlings of two favourite spring-flowering annuals are available this month. Schizanthus (known as Poor Man's Orchid or Angel Wings) is an easily grown and dainty annual suitable for a sheltered sunny position; it will tolerate partial shade providing it gets some hours of full sunlight.

Schizanthus is good in pots and baskets and can also be grown as a shade-house plant. Flowers are in soft pastel tonings like pink, mauve and white.

Sweet William (Wee Willie) is a good border plant because it is compact and only 15 cm (6 in) high. Flowers are single in mixed tones of red and pink. It flowers very early — in fact the plants often have flowers when you buy them. Wee Willie is another annual which is good in a container on a balcony.

Poor Man's Orchid (Schizanthus) — a dainty spring-flowering annual with Orchid-like flowers in jewel colours and ferny foliage.

ROSES

Autumn Splendour

This is a good time to go out to look at Roses, which are always at their best in autumn. This is also a good time to visit Rose nurseries to choose the plants you like while they are in bloom.

Looking at the lovely new season's offerings I was struck by the fact that, as well as being gorgeous, they all have plenty of perfume. So much for the fear that modern Roses were losing their scent.

The hedge of Rugosa Roses at a nearby nursery is carrying numbers of very large scarlet hips as well as a few mauve flowers. This old-fashioned Rose is somewhat too vigorous for the average suburban garden, but would make a good privacy hedge for either a large garden or a country garden where, when they run out of space, they move the fences.

One of the Roses I saw was a showy Australian-raised hybrid, "Olive McKenzie". Its flowers are a suffusion of apricot, salmon, red and yellow and beautifully fragrant.

If you do visit a Rose nursery this autumn you will notice the trend to vivid colour in the new Roses, the mixtures of colour — like "Olive McKenzie" — and the variegated colour like "Oriana" which has a red inner face and a white reverse.

Another thing to notice is the long, straight stems on many of the Roses — an indication of the popularity of long-stemmed Roses as cut flowers.

One of the new Meilland Roses will be of interest to those who have read *For the Love of a Rose,* the story by Antonia Ridge of the Meilland family and their Roses. Meillands have released a Rose named after her — the "Antonia Ridge", which is a rich red double.

"The Fairy" — a long-flowering dwarf garden Rose with large clusters of pink flowers.

BULBS

The Jersey Lily

The Jersey Lily, a Nerine — easy to grow bulbs with flowers ranging in colours from white through shades of pink to dazzling scarlet.

Lily Langtree was known as the Jersey Lily and the Jersey or Guernsey Lily, which attracted attention after the television series *Lillie*, is a Nerine (*N. sarniensis*) which grows wild in the Channel Islands. The name Nerine is from the sea-nymph who was a daughter of Nereus and *sarniensis* is from the old name for the Channel Islands.

This flower is not actually native to the islands but is said to have been washed ashore from the wreck of a Dutch or English ship coming from Japan with bulbs of the plant on board. The bulbs were buried in the sand and remained there for several years before suddenly bursting into bloom to the amazement of the local inhabitants. This romantic event took place in the mid-seventeenth century and the flowers quickly became popular with the cut-flower growers on Guernsey. For many years this Nerine was thought to have been a native of Japan and it was not until the end of the eighteenth century that it was discovered growing wild on Table Mountain in South Africa, and its true origin recognised.

Nerines grow quite well in mild to cool climates provided they are given very well-drained soil and full sun. If you have Nerines growing, don't disturb them any more often than necessary because they don't like to be moved and sometimes fail to flower for a year or so after being transplanted. They should be kept watered and fertilised with a half-strength mixture of Aquasol or a similar fertiliser until the foliage begins to yellow in spring.

Pot Now for Spring

If you garden on a sunny or partly sunny balcony, patio or window-sill, you will be able to enjoy spring-flowering bulbs in containers. Tulips make particularly handsome container plants and should be planted in late April, when the weather has become cooler. I prefer to grow Tulips in containers because they will not reflower in the Sydney climate unless they are chilled in the refrigerator for about six to eight weeks immediately before planting each year. If they are in containers it is easy to keep track of them for lifting and storing when the foliage has died down after blooming.

Other bulbs that can be grown this way for indoor use are Daffodils, Jonquils, Dutch Iris, Freesias and Bluebells. They should be planted with the top of the bulb just below the soil surface, then placed in a sheltered spot in the garden or on the balcony until they shoot.

They can then be moved into a sunny spot and fed with a plant pill and watered when necessary. Pots can be taken indoors when buds are close to opening.

Chinese pot planted with Triteleia (syn. Iphieon) the Star Flower. Plant now for spring in sun or partial shade.

Typifying all the mellow colours of autumn, the Liquidambar.

Delicate white highlights in the autumn garden from Anemone hupehensis, *Cyclamen, Zephyranthes and Ginger Lily.*

NATIVES

Autumn-flowering Plants

Like most plants Australian wildflowers reach their flowering peak in spring. However, they don't all wait for spring — many begin flowering as early as July and some seem to spot flower all the time.

Native Fuchsia (*Epacris longiflora*) has naturalised itself among the grey sandstone outcrops that pass for my front garden and there are always a few slender red and white bells to be found. At present it is like pink smoke among the rocks. The effect is more subtle than showy and is not even visible from the house. I have to stand down on the road and look up to admire it. This is because the house is high above the garden and the Epacris flowers hang down, concealing their colour from anyone looking down. This is very poor landscaping but as both flowers and rocks had possession of this land long before I did, I am not about to change things.

The Sunshine Wattle (*Acacia terminalis*) is more successful for looking down on (it is also native to the area) and I have planted several other wattles which can be appreciated from above. A lot of natives have flowers that droop down and it is quite difficult to find the plants that are colourful to look at from above. However, tree ferns, Umbrella trees (Brassaia), Bird's Nest ferns (Asplenium) and Coral fern (Gleichenia) form patterns when they are looked down on and are seen from their most effective angle.

Native Fuchsia (Epacris longiflora), *Queensland Wattle* (Acacia botrycephela) *and Waxflower (Crowea) — natives flowering in autumn.*

Native plants are improving all the time and many make good garden plants as long as you let them get on with it and don't fiddle with them too much. Callistemons adjust well to garden life and have attractive papery bark plus really bright, showy flowers. There are quite a lot of hybrids around which are well worth growing including: "Western Glory" (3 m upright; mauve-crimson), "Burgundy" (burgundy), "Reeve's Pink" (pink fading paler), "Candy Pink" (pink aging red), "Mauve Mist" (mauve/gold anthers), "Clearview Father Christmas" (white/red anthers), "Austraflora Candle Glow" (low, spreading growth; lemon brushes), "Little John" (1 m; red and amber), "Captain Cook" (1 m; red).

Other autumn-flowering natives worth a place in the garden include the Correas and Croweas. These plants form good, compact, small shrubs which are in flower for long periods of the year. The Correas (Native Fuchsia) have bell-shaped flowers which are colourful with red, orange, pink or green colours and they are very attractive to birds.

Croweas belong to the Boronia family and have masses of showy, pink, star-shaped flowers for months and are in full bloom now. You can distinguish between Boronias and Croweas by counting the petals. Boronias have four and Crowea has five. I feel that Croweas have been greatly overlooked — perhaps people are put off by the name, which is not appealing. There is a lot of prejudice against the poor old crow (which is more properly a raven) and there may be some association of ideas, in spite of Shakespeare's theory that a "rose by any other name would smell as sweet . . ." Anyway, *Crowea saligna* has the common name of Bright Pink Waxflower, which is pretty, though a mouthful, and there are a few improved hybrid forms of Crowea available as well as the species *C. exalta* and, occasionally, white-flowered forms may be found.

Grevilleas make great garden shrubs and some seem to flower all year round. One that is flowering now is *G. triloba*, a strong-growing and rather spreading shrub with masses of strongly scented creamy white flowers which are great for bees. If you plant it, make sure that it has room to grow without encroaching on paths because it has sharp spines. In spite of this slight drawback *G. triloba* is good for adding perfume to the autumn garden and a must if you have your own beehive. It also responds well to pruning.

Spider Net Grevillea (*G. thelemanniana*) — with scarlet flowers and grey foliage — is also flowering now. This is a prostrate grower which is suitable for a sunny position and tolerates coastal soils and frost.

Another bright orange-red native flowering now is the Robin Red Breast Bush (*Melaleuca lateritia*), an upright shrub growing less than 3 m (10 ft) which bears its colourful brushes for about six months of the year.

This is a good time for planting natives as well as exotics and a visit to a native plant nursery is always rewarding. The natives I have mentioned all need a well-drained, fairly sunny position though filtered sunlight is also satisfactory in most cases because this is the way many of them are found growing naturally. All should be available from nurseries that carry a range of native plants as well as from specialist native plant nurseries.

Though native plants can survive without a lot of water, remember to give them normal garden care including regular watering until they are established. Avoid digging around the roots, use mulch to suppress weeds and use organic fertilisers only and in small quantities, always watering before and after application. Use an organic fertiliser formulated specially for natives. Most of the foliar fertilisers are also safe to use on natives but too liberal a dose will encourage a lot of soft growth that is not as hardy.

Native plant authority Alec Blombery believes there are two ways of growing natives: You can feed them and grow them fast and lush and speed up their life cycle so that they have a shorter life; or grow them hard so that they are tougher and less luxuriant, a bit straggly in fact, and longer lived. This is a legitimate choice so if you like natives in the garden, but want them to conform to your idea of good garden plants, you can get them to respond to a regular programme of feeding, watering and spraying to get rid of the resultant insect attack. You must be prepared to replace them after three or four years to maintain the effect, however.

Purists will probably shudder at this suggestion but if natives are to keep their attraction as garden plants they should be grown where possible to blend in with the exotics in the garden.

The Queensland Firewheel Tree

The Queensland Firewheel Tree (*Stenocarpus sinuatus*) is a beautiful native tree in bloom round Sydney in April and is popular with parrots in our area.

Stenocarpus is tall — up to 12 m (40 ft) — with upright growth and dense, dark, glossy green leaves. The curiously shaped flowers are bright red and give the tree its common name of Firewheel. Each flower does indeed resemble a fiery wheel with many spokes and it is a more appropriate title than the botanical name (*stenos*, narrow; *carpos*, fruit) which refers to the leathery fruit follicle. The specific name, *sinuatus*, refers to the wavy margins of the leaves.

The Firewheel Tree is native to coastal Queensland and the north coast of New South Wales and enjoys a warm, frost-free position. It grows well in a wide climate range though it is best planted in spring when it will be free of the likelihood of frost damaging it before it has become established.

It is a member of the Proteaceae family and one of Australia's showiest native trees — well worth knowing and growing where there is space for it. The flowering time is long, from January to autumn. Give it a sunny position in good light loam with plenty of summer watering.

Queensland Firewheel Tree (Stenocarpus sinuatus) *— a handsome native tree suitable for the large garden or street plantings.*

EDIBLES

Strawberries and Vegetables

April is strawberry planting time and a bed of strawberries is one of the most satisfying things to grow.

Strawberries are called "straw berries" because they have traditionally been mulched with straw to keep the fruit out of the dirt. If the berries lie on the ground they not only become soiled, they are likely to rot and are more vulnerable to insects.

Cabbage, beetroot and silver beet are vegetables the home gardener finds satisfying to grow. There is a cabbage called Superette which matures very quickly, forming a hard head within seven weeks of transplanting. It can be eaten then or grown until it is 30 cm (12 in) across.

If you are planting lettuce remember that there are varieties for every season. Winterlake is suitable for planting out now and until June.

Slugs and snails are the worst pest of plants, particularly seedlings and newly shot bulbs. There are a lot of young snails about too and these are sometimes hard to see because they are so small. They will do a lot of damage if you don't find them, so check your plants carefully and keep some snail bait round them.

CHECKLIST

May brings in crisp, cool days and brilliant autumn foliage on deciduous trees and shrubs. The weather is great for working in the garden and planting out many trees and shrubs.

Flowering Now

Trees and Shrubs:
Arbutus (Strawberry Tree — flowers and berries),
Azalea (early and spot flowering),
Camellia sasanqua and early flowering *japonica* varieties,
Cassia,
Ceratostigma (Skybush),
Daphne,
Dombeya,
Euphorbia (Poinsettia),
Gordonia,
Holmskoldia,
Luculia,
Reinwardtia.

Berries on Cotoneaster,
Crataegus,
Pyracantha.

Perennials and Annuals:
Chrysanthemum,
Marigold,
Michaelmas Daisy,
Strelitzia,
Violets.

Bulbs:
Cyclamen (potted),
Iris stylosa,
Jonquil,
Narcissus,
Nerine.

Climbers:
Antigonon,
Clerodendron speciosissium.

Autumn colour on Ornamental Grape and Virginia Creeper.

Natives:
Callistemon citrinus (Crimson Bottlebrush),
Correa,
Crowea (Waxflower),
Epacris (native Fuchsia),
Grevillea triloba,
G. thelemanniana,
Melaleuca lateritia (some species),
Thryptomene (native Heath).

The evergreen Gordonia — flowering now.

MAY

Plant

Trees, Shrubs and Climbers:
Azaleas,
Camellias,
Citrus (Cumquat, Lemon, Orange, Grapefruit, Mandarin — see p. 103),
Conifers and all deciduous trees, shrubs and Roses. (See p. 87.)

Perennials and Annuals:
Last planting of bedding plants.

Bulbs:
Liliums,
Lily-of-the-valley,
Tulips.

Vegetables:
Broad beans,
cabbage,
lettuce (winter varieties),
onion,
peas (warm coastal areas only),
radish,
shallot.

Warm coastal areas:
Beetroot,
carrot,
parsnip,
tomato.

Bags of compost and mushroom spore ready to grow are available from many nurseries; also strawberry plants. Buy virus-free stock only.

Prune

Cut back spent summer/autumn perennials such as perennial Phlox, Dahlias, etc. Dahlias can be lifted with the soil intact round the tubers if the garden space they occupy is needed. Place soil-covered clumps in a partly shaded spot out of the way to harden off.(See also p. 82.)

Cotoneaster — long lasting red berries make an interesting addition to the autumn-winter garden.

Pests and Diseases

Apricots, cherries, plums and almonds should be sprayed for brown rot (symptoms: mummified fruit), for shot hole disease (symptoms: gumming of fruit buds) using Bordeaux when most leaves have fallen. (See also p. 82.)

Spray Chrysanthemums for leaf nematode or eelworm (symptoms: leaves become wilted, blacken and shrivel from the ground up the stem). Spray with Metasystox or Rogor. Burn fallen leaves.

Keep up snail and slug baits round bulbs, annuals and clump plants such as Clivea. Watch for aphids on young growth (Pansies are often attacked). Spray with pyrethrum sprays.

Mummified fruit and leaf showing shot hole of Prunus.

Garden Care

If you have deciduous trees and shrubs in the garden don't waste the leaves. When they fall, rake them up for mulch around the shrubs or add them to the compost heap. (See also p. 83.)

May is the beginning of the Rose planting season and new Roses can be ordered from nurseries. This is also a good month for planting Liliums which are available from specialist nurseries. (See also p. 91.)

THE MAY GARDEN

A lot of people — myself included — have a sudden outbreak of two-legged pests in the garden at this time of year. But although these pests do some damage to lawns, gardens and trees they respond very well to feeding and they will all go back to school soon. In the meantime, you might like to take them on bush walks — Wattles, Banksias and other natives are flowering and the trees are full of parrots. If there is no readily accessible bushland in your area, take them for walks round your own suburb or to the botanical gardens to look for autumn colour.

Apart from the more obvious colour on large trees — like the Liquidamber, Ash and Pistacia — there is a lot of more subtle colour to be found. Barberry (Berberis) colours well in temperate areas. This small, spiny shrub will provide good colour for a small garden. *Berberis thunbergii atropurpurea* (the purple Japanese Barberry) has colourful, bronzy leaves in summer which turn vivid autumn colours. It should be pruned in winter to keep its shape and encourage new growth.

The dwarf Flowering Almond (*Prunus glandulosa sinensis*) which is mainly grown for its stems of pink, double flowers in spring, develops red autumn colour. A larger Prunus (*P. serrulata* or Flowering Cherry) grows into a small tree with red and yellow autumn colours, and both these are suitable for small gardens.

Ceratostigma willmottianum is another small shrub which looks particularly attractive in autumn when the leaves have turned and the intense blue flower heads are still carried on the bush. Ceratostigma flowers from January and forms a low, spreading bush a metre high. It is a useful plant for a rock garden and combines well with the Berberis mentioned earlier.

Some of the deciduous Viburnums have a good autumn colour. *Viburnum opulus* (the Guelder Rose) has a good autumn colour, with berries in cold climates.

Virginia Creeper (Parthenocissus) has a brilliant red autumn colour that will provide an "antique" finish to the ugliest brick walls. If all the brash new brick high schools were planted with Virginia Creeper they would turn into traditional-looking hallowed halls of ivy in no time.

All the plants mentioned should be planted in full sun to get the best results. Autumn colour needs the sun and some cold nights to make it flame.

Quite a number of Roses, particularly the old-fashioned ones and species like *Rosa rugosa* set bright red hips in autumn which are an added attraction to their beauty.

Twining around amongst an old climber Rose in my garden I have a Chinese Ornamental Grape (Ampelopsis) which also contributes to the autumn berry display with its clusters of multi-coloured berries which change from pale lilac to turquoise, to deep violet.

Red shiny rosehips (top) and turquoise ornamental grape (Amelopsis) provide autumn interest and colour.

GARDENKEEPING

Diseases of Prunus

Now that the leaves are falling from Prunus species it is easy to see the mummified fruit hanging on these trees. If you grow Apricot, Cherry, Peach, Nectarine or Plum trees, either for fruit or flowers, don't neglect this sign of the brown rot fungus disease.

Mummified fruit both on the tree and lying on the ground should be removed and burnt. Trees should be sprayed with Bordeaux at late bud-swell to early blossom. If peach leaf curl is a problem, it will be controlled as well by spraying with copper oxychloride plus white oil at early bud-swell. This should be followed up by a spray with Captan at late full bloom to petal-fall.

Many of the ornamental fruit trees such as purple leaf Prunus are suffering from the shot hole of Prunus disease, which causes a peppering of holes to appear in leaves and, if infection is heavy, early defoliation of the tree. These same sprays will control this disease which weakens trees if left untreated.

Autumn Planting

May is the month for Thryptomene, the native Heath Myrtles. A hybrid form (*T. saxicola*) is a good garden plant as long as you have fairly acid soil (no lime) and do not disturb the roots. It has a long flowering period and a slightly spicy fragrance.

A look round your local nursery (or one specialising in Camellias and Azaleas) will produce such autumn bloomers as *Azalea* "Mauve Schryderi", a good single flowering now. In our own garden we have clumps of Paper Whites (Narcissus) and golden Jonquils adding a touch of spring. We seem to have the best of both worlds with both autumn colour and those buds of May.

This is also a good time for planting citrus trees. They can be bought in containers or bare-rooted and a lemon tree is a treasure in any garden. Cumquats are very decorative in pots, particularly the variegated one. They need plenty of sun and should not be exposed to draughts. And there is nothing better than Cumquat marmalade for breakfast.

If you live in an inner city suburb submerged in smog, plant deciduous trees in your garden or on the footpath. They stand up to the pollution much better than evergreens because they shed their leaves in autumn, stay bare for a few months and then start off in spring with a whole new overcoat.

Trimming and Lifting Dahlias

Dahlias are past their prime now and can be cut back to 30 cm (12 in) above the ground. The tubers can be left in the ground if the soil is well drained and you can spare the garden space. Otherwise lift them with plenty of soil attached and put them out of the way until the foliage shrivels and then store them for winter. Label Dahlias before actually lifting them if you want to keep the colours separate. Try fastening a plastic clothes peg the colour of the flower to each clump — a fairly rough method of identification, but quick and easy.

Composting Leaves

Many of the autumn leaves that had just turned bright gold, orange or red are now lying in heaps under trees waiting for eager gardeners to rake them up and burn them. If you are one of the leaf-burners, why not try composting them this year instead? You will help to reduce the suburban smog that hangs over our autumn-winter weekends and gain some rich mulch or compost.

Autumn leaves can be left where they are under the tree or shrub that bore them to return the nourishment to the soil, as nature intended. Or, more tidily, they can be raked straight on to shrub borders as mulch or put into the compost heap. Autumn leaves from deciduous trees compost down very rapidly. So even if you think you have huge, unmanageable piles of leaves, you will find that they will break down to about one-third of the volume in a few weeks with the right treatment.

If you have too many leaves for the normal compost heap or composter, just rake them into a heap, sprinkle with lime or dolomite, some blood and bone or all-purpose fertiliser, add a spadeful or two of soil, damp down if necessary and cover with a sheet of black polythene. Heat is important in the composting process and any compost heap should be in a position where it gets some direct sunlight to warm it up. The black polythene will absorb heat and retain the heat generated by the composting process.

A friend of mine in Brisbane with a large garden full of huge trees, many deciduous, is an enthusiastic composter of leaves. He has several large, open-ended basket-type containers in the garden which steam away like chimneys. He has had the leaves analysed to discover their mineral content. Having satisfied himself that they do indeed contain plenty of valuable plant food and that the larger the leaf, the bigger the return, he has planted even more trees, concentrating on deciduous, large-leaved species. Our friend has now started growing vegetables for his family using some of the rich compost with great success and very little trouble with pests and diseases. And all because, as a non-gardener, he was looking for a quick solution to the problem of surplus leaves without polluting the environment.

Sizzling Poison

A word of warning: most people are aware that all parts of the garden shrub Oleander (*Nerium oleander*) are poisonous. There are many tales about people who used the sticks to cook their sausages with fatal consequences. Recently I was asked if the Oleander wood could be used for the barbecue. The answer is definitely not. Even the smoke from this wood is poisonous.

I know that many people will be pruning their Oleanders now in frost-free coastal areas, even though they are better left until spring, so a reminder might be timely. Even if you put them in the incinerator, don't breathe the smoke and don't let it blow over your neighbours and poison them either.

Nerium oleander splendens variegata — *beautiful with its variegated foliage and rose-pink flowers, but like all Oleanders, deadly poisonous.*

TREES AND SHRUBS

Poinsettia (Euphorbia) — a magnificent shrub for warm, eastern gardens.

Poinsettias

Poinsettias are adding their red flames to winter gardens just now — and I don't mean the dwarf ones that are grown as potted plants.

Coming from Brisbane — where it flourishes mightily, to the extent that it is the State's floral emblem — I cannot understand why the Poinsettia is not grown more in Sydney gardens where it grows well, flowers for a long period in winter when bright colour is needed, is not troubled by pests or disease and does not take up too much room in the garden if it is pruned back hard after flowering.

Certainly, Poinsettia does not blend easily with the pastel colours of Luculia, Daphne, Camellia and Azalea, but it looks marvellous planted against a background of trees in autumn leaf. A clump planting of three colours — a pink, a cream and a red Poinsettia — near something grown for its autumn colour will keep the spot colourful long after the autumn leaves have been raked into the compost heap.

The Poinsettias are indispensable planted in a border of summer-flowering shrubs like Hibiscus and Oleander to provide some winter colour. If they are grown among other shrubs the rather unattractive lower limbs of the shrub are hidden. Poinsettia grows readily from cuttings taken in September to October, when the shrub is being pruned. If you are buying a plant look for the double varieties, which are more showy than the single forms of *Euphorbia pulcherrima*, the usual Poinsettia grown.

The addition of Reinwardtia (better known as Linum) as an under-shrub to a group planting like this will make it even more colourful. Reinwardtia is a small shrubby perennial growing a little over a metre (3 ft). It tolerates shaded conditions well but needs some sun to light up its bright, golden winter flowers. This makes it ideal for planting under deciduous trees. Prune it back hard after flowering.

The bareness of deciduous trees in winter worries some gardeners but some of the trees look beautiful bare when the sculptural lines of branches and trunks can be seen, particularly if they are outlined against the low winter sun. The ground is rather bare under these trees and this is noticeable when the tree is leafless. As well as the Reinwardtia mentioned, bulbs can be naturalised under deciduous trees to break up the bareness.

Another member of the Euphorbia family which is useful as a rockery garden plant is the Crown of Thorns (*E. splendens*). This is a low shrub with sharp prickles and showy red flowers almost all the time.

The Strawberry Tree (Arbutus unedo) *— an attractive small tree to enhance the autumn/winter garden.*

The Strawberry Tree

The Strawberry Tree (*Arbutus unedo*) is at its best in autumn and winter. This ornamental small tree is covered with both flowers and fruits at this time. The flowers are small, white and waxy, the size and shape of Lily-of-the-valley and are carried in arching sprays above the clusters of strawberry-like fruit which vary in colour from yellow and orange to bright red. Foliage is dark green and the attractive bark is reddish and flaking.

Arbutus is an evergreen, round-headed tree growing from 7-10 m (25-30 ft), is a member of the Ericaceae family and needs well-drained, lime-free soil. It does well in temperate areas and there are many good specimens in cooler mountain areas.

The fruit of the Strawberry Tree is edible or, perhaps more correctly, not inedible. The Latin name, *unedo*, comes from the words "one" and "to eat" and it has been suggested by people who have tried eating the fruit that this means you only want to eat one — that's enough. So I'm not recommending them, just mentioning that they are edible so that you won't panic if you find your children trying them.

Gordonia — a handsome winter-flowering small tree. The white, open flowers have golden stamens.

Gordonia

Gordonia has come into its own in recent years. This plant was once thought of as a shrub but has developed into a handsome tree in street plantings and gardens in many suburbs. This glossy evergreen is covered in large white Camellia-like flowers all through the autumn and winter months and is at its peak now.

Gordonias are easy to grow and trouble-free and are members of the same family as the Camellia (Theaceae). They are slow growing and though their height is generally given as about 4.4 m (15 ft) Gordonias can eventually grow to tree-like proportions.

Rhododendrons

Some interesting Rhododendrons are being grown experimentally in Australia. The late Mr Don Stanton of Wollongong devoted a lot of his time to Rhododendrons and had autumn-flowering Rhododendrons collected from places like Papua New Guinea, Indonesia, Borneo and Malaysia. The showiest was one called *R. zoelleri*, from Papua New Guinea. This species has huge trusses of yellow to orange flowers, each 14 cm (5½ in) across. It is not an easy plant to grow but is being used in hybridising and should produce some good garden hybrids in time.

All the Stanton's Rhododendrons had tubular or bell-shaped, single flowers. Several, including *R. jasminiflorum*, from Malaysia, were sweetly-scented. None of these interesting Rhododendrons are available commercially yet but they are being propagated slowly and will eventually find their way into our gardens. When this happens it will be possible to have Rhododendrons in flower for most of the year. Mr Stanton found that many of the tropical species are not affected by petal blight, which is good news for the future of the Rhododendron family (Azaleas being Rhododendrons too).

Rhododendron jasminiflorum — *an unusual scented Rhododendron from Malaya.*

R. jasminiflorum has slender, white tubular flowers in large clusters, reminiscent of Jasmine, which gives it the specific name. The leaves are leathery and dark green. It is not a recent discovery, but was found early this century. Mr Stanton has several named hybrids, most of which are strongly pink. This characteristic, surprisingly enough, has been inherited from a recessive pink gene of the white parent. Traces of pink can be seen on the stems and stamens of *R. jasminiflorum* and it occurs occasionally in a very pale pink form.

Daphne and Luculia

The first sprigs of Daphne are out in the garden, filling the air with piercing sweetness. It is notoriously temperamental, but well worth trying in your garden for its sweet scent.

Daphne needs much the same conditions as Azaleas and Camellias — a very well-drained, rather acid soil, plenty of surface mulch and a partly shaded position protected from the westerly and northern sun. Before you plant, dig in plenty of humus. This will make the soil more friable and also build up the level of the bed to aid drainage.

Take care not to plant the Daphne any deeper than it was in the pot. One reason for loss is collar-rot caused by planting too deeply. Mulch must never be put against the stem of the plant (this applies to all plants) because this will also induce collar-rot. My own Daphne is raised several centimetres above the bed round it. To avoid washing away the soil when watering, I have used a mulch of fairly small, flat stones. Small bulbs planted among the stones add colour.

Luculia gratissima — *the sweetly fragrant blooms of this winter-flowering shrub are rose-pink.*

One of the most beautiful winter flowering shrubs in temperate gardens is Luculia. Like Daphne, it has pink, perfumed flowers though the Luculia is far more showy with flower heads often 20 cm (8 in) across. Like Daphne, it can die suddenly and many gardeners buy this beautiful plant only to lose it. Luculia requires very special conditions. It likes lime and a deep, rich, well-drained soil, with plenty of watering in summer. Luculia also needs a very sheltered situation, protected from hot or cold winds and western sun.

Though I look longingly at Luculia in other people's gardens, I have never tried to grow it in my present garden, which is totally unsuitable. I have noticed that the best Luculia seem to grow in gardens below road level where they have good protection from wind. If you have the right sheltered garden with good, deep soil, by all means try a Luculia but otherwise spend your money on something tougher.

ROSES

Born and Bred in the Briar Patch

I cut my teeth on Roses. I was virtually raised on the family Rose nursery in Queensland. When I was very small I would go out in the paddocks with my uncles, the hired man and my own little "budding stool" to help bud the hectares of briar stock.

The scent of the sun-warmed earth was as heady as wine, I must have inhaled it clear into my bloodstream because I've been hooked on Roses (and gardening) ever since. There are many beautiful Roses introduced every year. Some stay in the catalogues and others fade out because they are not successful over the wide range of Australian conditions.

Some of the Roses I remember recommending confidently to customers over the phone (did they realise they were talking to a child?) are still in nurserymen's lists. They are tried and true Roses, well worthy of a place in the garden. There was "Etoile de Hollande", sultry perfume and rich dark red; "Red Radiance", double and also fragrant; "Editor McFarland", a good rose-pink with prolific flowers; "Pink Radiance", a fragrant, silvery-pink double with carmine reverse; "President Herbert Hoover" in shades of yellow, orange and crimson; and, of course, good old "Lorraine Lee". These old friends are not what are sometimes described as "old-fashioned Roses". They are something else again.

If you have just moved into a very old house with a garden full of strange and hoary old veterans, don't hack them out indiscriminately. Let them flower and then strike cuttings from the best of them. You could have something very rewarding and the beginning of a new hobby — collecting "old-fashioned Roses".

Among the newer Roses are the Meilland offerings and these are always worth considering. When "Peace" ("Madame A. Meilland") was first introduced we were all so enthusiastic about it that every time a customer arrived our dog "Rusty" would go out and stand beside the marker where it was planted. No matter that we had sold out and were trying to keep it a secret — Rusty never failed to give the game away.

"Madame A. Meilland" has been joined by stayers like "Michelle Meilland" (pink and lilac), "Papa Meilland" (a fragrant and beautiful red) and many more.

"Oriental Dawn" — one of a new fashion for "painted" Roses with cream to yellow petals brushed with pinky-red.

Planting Roses

Whatever Roses you decide to order, make sure you spend some time preparing the soil. Roses are long-lived and it is worth giving them the best possible start in life by ensuring that the soil is free of perennial weeds like onion grass and oxalis, and that it is well-drained and enriched with humus in the form of home-made compost, spent mushroom compost or rotted cow manure.

When we plant Roses we expect them to remain in the garden for several years, so it pays to prepare the ground well before planting. Roses need full sun to be really successful so plant them in a sunny spot, well away from trees and shrubs. They like good, well-drained soil and thrive in a fairly heavy loam. Too-heavy soil can be lightened by digging in sand, peat moss and well-rotted cow manure. Light sandy soil will be improved by liberal additions of compost.

If you have any doubts about drainage, raise your rose bed several centimetres above ground level by adding extra soil. If you are replacing old Rose plants or those which have died, replace the soil also. Roses like a slightly alkaline soil so dig a little dolomite into acid soil.

Don't add fertiliser to the soil before planting because it is liable to burn the roots. Bare-rooted Roses can be planted from

June to the end of August, while the plants are dormant. They should be planted as soon as possible after taking delivery of them. Keep the roots covered with a wet bag or stand them in a bucket of water right up to the moment of planting so that they don't dry out.

It is important that Roses are planted in full sun or where they will get at least six hours of full sun each day. Established Roses in the garden sometimes become shaded by other plants and if this is the case in your garden they can be moved to a sunnier position while they are dormant during the next two months. Prune before moving and re-plant and water immediately.

When you unpack your Roses, inspect them for damage. Broken roots can be cut away with sharp secateurs. Stems should be firm and unshrivelled. If a newly bought plant is wrinkled like a prune it has dried out. Return it and get a replacement.

There is more to digging a hole than meets the eye, so here are a few specifications for a hole suitable for any bare-rooted plants:

They should be about 1 m (3 ft) apart for bush Roses, but can be closer for floribundas. Make a hole wide enough to accommodate the roots without bending them, and deep enough for the bud union to be 5 m (2 in) above ground after planting. Make a mound of soil in the base of the hole and sit the Rose on it so that there is no air space under the plant. Cover the roots until the hole is half filled. Water with about half a bucket of water. Allow the water to soak away. Finish filling the hole, firm the soil with your hands and check the bud union to make sure it is clear of the soil. Use the rest of your bucket of water to water the Rose.

Rose purists plant nothing but Roses in a Rose bed, but in a small garden this is very restricting. It may mean you cannot enjoy other flowering shrubs in the garden and — let's face it — even Roses don't look beautiful all the time.

If you are planting a new shrub border you can mix Roses with other shrubs quite successfully, provided everything is planted about the same time so that the roots all have a fair go at the soil and nourishment.

Strong-growing bush Roses can hold their own under these conditions, but if you try to plant them in among established shrubs shading by the already established shrubs and competition from their root systems will make the new plants weak and sickly.

Once your plants are in, do not forget them. Inspect the soil around them daily and water when it is becoming dry. Westerly winds can damage newly planted Roses and dry the soil even in winter. Do not overdo the watering or you will kill them with kindness.

And remember, do not fertilise newly planted Roses and do not prune established plants until the end of July.

Tried and True Varieties

If your main interest is to have flowers for the house you would do better to disregard newcomers and choose familiar varieties from the nurserymen's lists.

These tried-and-true Roses have proved their worth in our gardens:

White — "Blanche Mallerin", "Iceberg", "Pascali", "Virgo";

Yellow — "Buccaneer", "Grandmere Jenny", "Lemon Elegance";

Pink — Michelle Meilland", "Tiffany", "Helen Traubel";

Red — "Avon", "Chrysler Imperial", "Papa Meilland", "Red Devil";

Autumn — "Montezuma", "Vienna Charm".

"Mister Lincoln" is a good deep red suitable for cutting. "Peter Frankenfeld" is a good deep pink and long lasting in the vase. "Blue Moon" is a must for flower arrangers. Its curious bluey-mauve colour looks elegant in an "arrangement".

If there isn't space in the garden for many Roses, standards will grow above low plants and look like bouquets on sticks. Remember you can have two or three budded on to the one stem.

If you are just beginning to grow Roses it is a good idea to try to choose established varieties which have proved themselves in local conditions. Some suggestions for reliable roses are: "Peter Frankenfeld" (rich, deep pink, fragrant, good for cutting); "Avon" (rich red, perfumed and reliable); "Red Devil" (dark red with silver reverse, named for the World War II parachutists who wore red berets and were known as Red Devils); "Helen Schoen" (tall-growing red); "Carla" (coral pink and free-flowering); "Iceberg" (large clusters semi-double white, fragrant flowers always in bloom); "Super Star" (soft vermilion, fragrant, free-flowering); "Friesa" (deep yellow, fragrant, free-flowering and resistant to black spot); "Vol de Nuit" (night flight), fragrant, deep mauve, nearly thornless); and "Diamond Jubilee" (deep buff yellow, sometimes tinged pink, fragrant).

"Double Delight", a hybrid tea-type Rose, is one of the best of recent releases – fragrant, double with creamy flowers edged with rich strawberry-red. The plants are sturdy and upright and very free-flowering.

One of the new trends in Roses in the tea-type floribunda. Classified as a floribunda, it has single Roses in the hybrid tea style rather than the cluster of small Roses which is, or was, the hallmark of the floribunda.

Some of these are very good and two new ones worth noting are "Patricia" (a soft salmon-pink colour which intensifies as the flowers develop) and "Marina" (a soft salmon-orange with yellowish undertones). A feature of this plant is its shiny foliage carried on a bushy, many-stemmed plant.

A couple of interesting things about new releases: "Olive Baden Powell" has been released throughout Australia under the auspices of the Girl Guides' Association to whom all proceeds will be donated. This Rose is fragrant and a brilliant scarlet colour. "Bendigold" is named for the gold of Bendigo and is a floribunda with mini-sized "button-hole" buds and flowers in an orange colour. The latest addition to the list of "blue" Roses is "Shocking Blue", described as blue to magenta. It is richly perfumed and has good growth and keeping qualities — a good addition to the flower arranger's garden.

The white Banksia Rose — an old-fashioned climbing Rose suitable for modern gardens being scented, easily trained and thornless.

Climbers

Climbers can give big returns for a small amount of ground space. Start building a good strong support for them in readiness for June planting. You'll find a lot of your favourites in climbing form: "Black Boy", a velvety red; "Lorraine Lee" (rose pink); "Chrysler Imperial" (red); "Queen Elizabeth" (shell pink); and others.

Don't overlook the yellow "Banksia" which gives a good quick cover on fences or trellises and is a mass of yellow clusters.

Some other climbers are: "Handel" (free-flowering deep cream, edged and flushed with deep pink); "Climbing Pinkie" (which flowers on and on, with clusters of small pink flowers carried all the way up the plant almost from the ground — not flamboyant, but pretty and reliable); "Climbing Peace" (the popular "Peace" in climbing form, with the same large yellow flushed pink flowers and vigorous habit).

One of my favourite climbers is "Mermaid", with its lovely single yellow flowers and prominent stamens. It has glossy foliage, flowers well and is large and vigorous.

Pillar Roses are suitable for arches and "Titian" is a good one, with carmine pink double flowers. "Golden Showers" is also a repeat flowering pillar Rose, with golden flowers and glossy foliage.

Choosing the Right Position

Choosing the right Rose for the right position is half the secret of successful Rose growing. The choice of colour is important, too — red Roses don't show up on red brick walls, for instance.

Roses look most effective in mass plantings of one colour. In our restricted suburban gardens we tend to plant as many colours as possible — one pink, one white, one yellow, one red. But if you have room for a bed of Roses all one colour you will find the effect very striking. I recently admired a bed of the deep mauve floribunda "Angel Face", surrounded by a border of the mini-rose "Lavender Lace".

Standard Roses look lovely in a bed with floribunda or miniature Roses under them as a ground-cover in blending or contrasting colours. Roses can be used in various situations as ground-cover. The white double, "Sea Spray" — a trailing Rose which flowers constantly — makes an excellent ground-cover.

Another charming way to grow Roses is to twine them on chains or tarred rope. Hung between posts, these will form a fence, or the rope can be looped on an existing fence and Roses trained along it in a design. This is a good way to decorate a fence or balcony rail without actually having the Roses clambering on the fence itself. People in units sometimes have difficulty with growing climbing plants on their balconies — this idea might solve the problem.

Some climbing miniatures are now available and could be just right for a balcony. They grow about 1.2 m (4 ft) tall. "Magic

Showy leaves and berries on Pistachia, a non-poisonous alternative to Rhus.

Sasanqua camellia—*a delicate and fast-growing beauty.*

Helianthus—sunny blooms for the autumn garden.

Lireodendron, the Tulip Tree, with beautifully shaped and coloured autumn foliage.

Dragon" (deep red), "Hi Ho" (deep pink) and "Candy Cane" (red and white candy stripes) are three beauties.

All miniature Roses are suitable for a sunny balcony or patio. The standard miniatures, which branch out from a 30 cm (12 in) stem, make very elegant pot-plants where space is restricted to a small area. Like all Roses they need plenty of sun to grow well and flower freely.

Not all minis have perfume but some — like "Baby Darling" and "Little Scotch" — are sweetly scented. Others are so pretty and have such masses of tiny flowers that they can be forgiven for having no perfume. I have "Robin", which has no scent but is smothered in tiny, double red flowers.

Some of the new miniatures are very attractive. "Fiesta Gold" is yellow with a pinky gold flush — very pretty — and "Mary Marshall" is a good double in deep coral with a yellow base.

Some nurseries specialise in old-fashioned Roses and you will find them advertised in gardening books during the season. If your garden is large enough to have space for a rosary, old-fashioned Roses will add to the charm.

R. rugosa scabrosa is an interesting old-fashioned Rose. The leaves are most attractive, crinkly and light green. The flowers are a striking rosy magenta with petals like crushed silk, followed by very large orange to red hips. One of the hybrid rugosas — "Schneezwerg", or "Snow Dwarf" — has semi-double white flowers with rich yellow stamens, and flowers freely.

R. rugosa has been called the Hedgehog Rose — I'll leave you to guess why. For this reason it is best planted where it can be left to its own devices; because the true rugosa is very hardy and disease-resistant, this is no problem.

Some Rose hybridists are turning back to the old Roses in an effort to breed better blooms so there may be some interesting and different Roses on the market. Among the new old-fashioned is the lovely "cabbage" Rose "Constance Spry".

One last word on the subject of Roses. Please don't prune them yet!

BULBS

Time to Plant Lilies

If you admired Liliums in other people's gardens last summer this is the time to do something about having some in your own garden next summer. Lilium bulbs can be ordered from specialist bulb nurseries now for planting during May and June. You will also find them at your local plant nursery, but wherever you buy them the important thing is to get them into the ground as soon as possible.

Unlike other popular garden bulbs, Liliums do not have a real resting period but grow throughout the year. Even when the

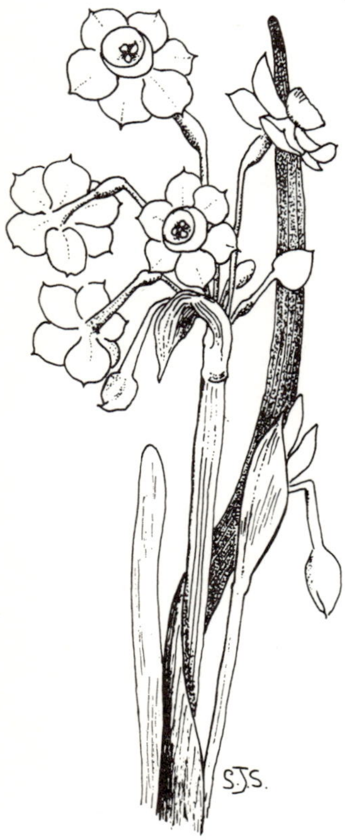

Golden Jonquils light up autumn gardens.

foliage has died back the root system continues to grow. Lilium bulbs left out of the ground for any length of time will deteriorate. A Lilium bulb should be firm and usually will have some live roots if it is in good condition. The base should be firm and show no signs of rot. Medium-sized bulbs are a better buy than large ones.

Liliums should be planted in well-drained, friable soil — they will rot away in heavy, wet soil. If your soil is heavy add plenty of well-rotted compost or leaf mould and a quantity of coke ash. Prepare the soil well, digging in plenty of old manure or an all-purpose fertiliser containing trace elements. Lilium bulbs must not come into contact with fertiliser at planting time so the bed must be prepared at least a week in advance. The planting depth varies but it is safe to work on the rule that the depth should be equal to twice the diameter of the bulb.

Plant your Liliums where they will be in filtered sunlight or partial shade. They grow well among Rhododendrons, Azaleas and Camellias and enjoy the same conditions.

There are a bewildering number of Liliums but the ones that grow best in humid coastal conditions are the Tiger Lily (*L. tigrinum)* and the November Lily (*L. longiflorum*). *Speciosum* and *auratum* hybrids grow well in tubs and can be grown on sheltered balconies or in the garden where they are protected by other shrubs. The Golden Ray Lily of Japan (*L. auratum)* is a spectacular tub plant. The Lilies are heavily perfumed and grow on tall stems which need the support of a stake.

Tulips

Tulips can be planted this month and late plantings of all spring-flowering bulbs can be made though they won't develop as much leaf as bulbs planted earlier.

EDIBLES

Strawberries

Strawberries are a popular treat. Because they are usually fairly expensive to buy, the only way to have them on the menu regularly is to grow your own. This is quite easy to do because strawberries do not need a lot of space for the amount of fruit they will provide and they bear for several months. It is well worth using whatever space you can to grow your own — a garden bed, a hanging basket, pots or a barrel.

Strawberries are available now from most nurseries and it is best to get them planted as soon as possible. Late-planted strawberries tend to develop runners rather than fruit. You will need a well-drained bed, preferably one that is raised above normal ground level. It is almost essential to use mulch between the plants or plant the strawberries through a sheet of black polythene. This is the only way to keep weeds down.

Because strawberries are perennials and because the plants

will remain in position for three years it is well worthwhile preparing the bed thoroughly with plenty of rotted manure or compost and some complete fertiliser which should be dug in and watered. There is no need to add lime to the bed because strawberries prefer slightly acid soil. Sandy soils will need lots of humus.

It is important to plant strawberries in good, straight rows spaced about 50 cm (20 in) apart. The plants should be abut 30 cm (12 in) apart with their roots spread evenly and the crowns clear of the soil. Mulch immediately and keep watered. Any runners that appear should be cut off or the plants will devote their energy to producing runners rather than fruit. Plant your strawberries in a good sunny position with a north or north-east aspect for the full morning sun.

If you don't have a suitable spot in the garden, strawberries can be grown successfully in a large barrel. Wooden barrels are not so easy to come by these days but plastic barrels can be used. To grow strawberries in a barrel it is necessary to remove the top and make holes at intervals round the sides. Drainage holes must be made in the base. Next you will need a piece of PVC agricultural piping which goes down the centre of the barrel, and the soil — rich with humus and compost, not ordinary garden soil — is filled in round it. As you come to a hole put your plants in from the inside out through the hole so that the roots can be spread properly and covered firmly with soil.

To prevent soil slipping into the holes, prop a piece of flyscreen gauze cut to size against the top of each hole after each plant is in position and wedge the bottom edge firmly into the soil. This helps to support the soil without interfering with the distribution of water and fertiliser. Fill to the top and then firm down and water lightly to allow the soil to settle.

Add more soil if necessary so that the barrel is filled to within 2 or 3 cm (1 in) of the top, with the top of the pipe showing. Plant the top and then do all watering and fertilising through the pipe. The water and fertiliser will seep out through the holes in the pipe and reach all the strawberry roots.

The ideal strawberry to grow in containers is the Swiss variety without runners. Strawberry varieties suitable for garden beds include "Torrey", "Red Gauntlet" and "Naratoga". Whatever variety you plant, make sure that it is certified virus free. Strawberries in existing beds should be trimmed back to remove any diseased leaves, and fertilised.

Strawberries are a good crop for the home gardener but insect pests can sometimes be a problem, especially in rainy conditions. Slugs, snails and slaters find the juicy berries irresistible and these pests are difficult to get rid of completely, particularly the slaters.

However, you can beat them all by picking the fruit when it is well coloured but not quite at that juicy ripeness which is so attractive to pests and people alike. Snail bait is useful. Baysol is particularly effective against slaters.

Sugar or Snow Peas

Sugar peas, also known as snow peas, are gaining popularity. These tender peas are cooked and eaten pods and all, saving the trouble of shelling peas and also the wastage involved in throwing the shells away (into the compost).

There are several varieties available, the newest being the Sugar Snap Pea in the Yates' packet seed range. This variety is crisp and crunchy and can be eaten raw or cooked because both pod and peas are tender and sweet.

These peas are quick and easy to grow in the home garden and crop heavily over a long period. They need sun, well-drained soil and some shelter from strong winds. Because they are vigorous growers — up to 2 m (6 ft) tall — they should also be given the support of wire or plastic netting.

Peas are sown directly into the soil, which should be prepared before planting with the addition of some lime if the soil is acid. A complete fertiliser can be added alongside the furrows where the seed is to be sown.

Peas are sown 3 cm to 6 cm (1½ to 2½ in) apart and can be planted now in temperate climates, though planting should be delayed until late winter in cold districts. Peas are damaged if frosts occur while they are in flower, so it is important to time planting to avoid frosts at flowering time.

Cut and Come Again

Unfortunately not many home gardens are big enough for a really worthwhile vegetable garden. However, there are some things which will give a good return in a small space. These are the cut-and-come-again plants like spinach and rhubarb. Several plants grown in a clump in a sunny spot will provide one or two people with meals for months.

Just pull a few leaves when needed and let the plants go on growing. Rhubarb crowns are available now. I have seen spinach growing well in a half cask along with parsley and chives as well as a tomato which had been supplying two people with lunches for months.

Mustard and cress can be grown in a seedbox and kept near the kitchen, snipped off with scissors and added to sandwiches and salads.

INDOORS

Winter Care

Indoor plants that have been growing luxuriantly through the warm months often develop problems during the cooler weather. These problems are usually caused by the shorter days which mean that plants may be getting less natural light than they were in summer, lower temperatures that slow down the plant growth and the drying effect of heaters.

Plants may need to be moved about once we are well into autumn — particularly those in rooms that face south or south-east where there has been plenty of light in summer but which become much darker when the sun shifts. These aspects also tend to be cold so if plants are not doing well move them to a warmer, lighter spot. Move plants away from fires or heaters and, if rooms are constantly kept heated, place pots on shallow trays filled with water and pebbles. The pots should be resting on the pebbles just above the water. This will ensure a level of humidity in the atmosphere. Otherwise spray the foliage with a fine spray of water regularly to keep the humidity up.

Once the weather cools down check your plants before watering them and don't water if the soil is still moist to the touch. Where you may have needed to water daily in the hot weather you may find that plants will only need watering once a week during cold spells. When watering plants in cold weather always use water that is at blood heat rather than cold water straight from the tap. Warming the water slightly will save the plants from being set back by the shock of cold water. African violets particularly will benefit from slightly warm water rather than cold in winter. Bear in mind that the water is only warmed to blood heat — it is not hot, just barely warm when you test it with your hand. Smaller amounts of fertiliser should be given too because roots that are in cold, damp soil become inactive and fertiliser salts build up in the soil because the plant is not able to use them.

During autumn insect pests often attack indoor plants. The false looper caterpillar damages foliage and if disturbed stays motionless and projecting out from the stem like a leaf stalk so that they are hard to detect. Pick them off or spray with a non-toxic, pyrethrum-based insecticide.

Scale insects are often found infesting indoor plants now and these can be wiped off with a cotton bud dipped in soapy water. Scale insects may be black, brown or pink colours and are found along stems, on the back and sometimes the front of leaves, often clustered along the veins. They will be found on plants from palms to ferns. Examine the stems and foliage of plants carefully for scale because this pest is very debilitating to indoor plants.

The effects of red spider attack also become more obvious at this time of the year although often the damage has been done earlier in the season and the insects have moved on. Indoor plants that have been attacked by red spider should be moved to a well-lighted position or moved outdoors into a sheltered spot to recover. If necessary spray with Kelthane, making sure that spray reaches the undersides of the leaves. Do this outside — not indoors.

Glossy-leaved Philodendron, Prayer Plant and Cissus are easily grown for indoor culture.

CHECKLIST

Growth slows down this month as soil temperatures drop. In frost areas frost-tender plants will need protection. All garden watering should be done in the morning now to give soils a chance to warm up again before night.

If you think winter is a time of no flowers, read the list of some of the winter-flowering subjects and look around the nurseries for some if you are short of colour in your garden now.

White Narcissus and golden Jonquils brighten the garden at this time of year.

Flowering Now

Trees and Shrubs:
Azaleas (early flowering),
Buddleia salvifolia,
Camellia (*sasanqua* and *japonica* varieties),
Chimonanthus praecox (Winter Sweet),
Daphne,
Erica,
Erythrina (Coral Tree),
Euphorbia (Poinsettia),
Garrya,
Gordonia,
Hamamelis mollis (Witch Hazel),
Hebe,
Heterocentron,
Hibiscus mutabilis (Rose of Sharon),
Iboza,
Lavendula dentata (French Lavender),
Luculia,
Montanoa,
Osmanthus fragrans,
Prunus mume,
Reinwardtia,
Salvia leucantha,
Senecio,
Tetrapanax (Chinese Rice Paper plant),
Tibouchina.

Berries and fruit on:
Arbutus,
Ardisia,
Aronia,
Aucuba,
Berberis,
Callicarpa,
Cotoneaster,
Crataegus,
Elaeagnus,
Elaeocarpus,
Eugenia (Lillypilly),
Euonymus,
Ilex (Holly),
Nandina,
Pistacia,
Pyracantha (Firethorn),
Ruscus (Butcher's Broom),
Symphoricarpos (Snow Berry).

Perennials and Annuals:
Begonia elatior,
Bergenia,
Euryops,
Helleborus,
Iceland Poppy,
Kalanchoe,
Primula,
Ruellia,
Schlumbergera (Christmas Cactus),
Strelitzia,
Tagetes (French Marigold),
Zygocactus.

JUNE

Bulbs:
Cyclamen,
Iris stylosa,
I. germanica,
Jonquil,
Narcissus.

Climbers:
Gelsemium,
Pyrostegia.

Natives:
Acacia podalyriifolia (Queensland Wattle),
Banksia ericifolia,
Chamaelaucium (Geraldton Wax),
Correa,
Crowea,
Epacris (native Fuchsia),
Grevillea (some species),
Leptospermum scoparium "Ruby Glow" (Teatree),
Swainsonia,
Thryptomene.

Berries on:
Pittosporum rhombifolium.

Plant

Trees, Shrubs and Climbers:
Deciduous trees and vines including fruit, nuts, ornamental and flowering trees, Roses, citrus (see p. 104), natives and container plants. Avoid planting out during severe cold spells.

Perennials and Annuals:
Alyssum,
Cineraria,
Hollyhocks,
Primula.

Herbaceous perennials such as:
Perennial Aster,
Canna,
Delphinium,
Filipendula,
Gerbera,
Liatris,
Michaelmas Daisy,
Russell Lupin,
Tuberose. (See also p. 108.)

Bulbs:
Calla,
Dutch Iris,
Gladioli,
Hippeastrum,
Ifafa Lily,
Japanese Iris,
Lilium,
Lily-of-the-valley,
Scilla (Bluebell),
Sparaxis,
Tigridia,
Triteleia,
Tuberous Begonias
Waterlily.

Vegetables:
Plant out or sow seed of:
Beetroot (warm areas),
broad beans,
cabbage,
onions (mid season),
peas,
radish,
silver beet,
spinach,
white turnip.
Rhubarb crowns and, in warm areas early potatoes may also be planted.
Strawberry plants (virus-free varieties) and in cool-temperate areas, raspberry and other berry plants can be planted now.

Prune

Abelias, Abutilon, Beloperone (Drejella), *Berberis thunbergii atropurpurea*, Ceratostigma (Blue Sky Flower), grapes (ornamental and fruiting), Plumbago, summer-flowering Tamarisk. Do not prune spring-flowering trees which are now in dormant bud.

Cut back Chrysanthemums, Cannas, Ginger Lily.

Take hardwood cuttings of Roses, Oleanders, Hydrangeas, deciduous trees and shrubs and vines (grapes, Wistaria). Dip in hormone rooting powder before planting.

Pests and Diseases

Watch for Aphids on new growth on annuals (particularly Pansies and Stocks) and spray with Malathion or pyrethrum-based spray. Slugs and snails are also about — use snail pellets round bulbs and seedlings.

Caterpillars on cabbage seedlings, etc., will need to be sprayed or dusted.

Watch for leaf miners in Cinerarias, Nasturtiums, Chrysanthemums, weeds, etc., and spray with systemic spray such as Rogor. Pick off and burn worst infected leaves.

Winter spray citrus for bronze orange bug using soft soap or Carbaryl.

Pick off and destroy mummified fruits on apricots, peach, plum, cherry.

Watch for canker on Cherry trees (gumming and die-back of limbs) — cut out and paint with Bordeaux, but there is no real cure.

Spray rust on Calendulas with fungicide.

Spray winter grass in lawns with Endothal.

Garden Care

Many herbaceous perennials can be lifted and divided. This includes summer-flowering Perennial Aster, Phlox, Canna, Helenium, Rudbeckia, etc., if they have been growing in the one position for about three years. Discard the old mother plant in the centre and replant small vigorous new plants from the edge of the clump. Replant immediately in some humus-enriched soil.

Lift Dahlias and store until spring. Remove spent flower heads from bulbs; remove and burn early Azalea blooms that show signs of petal blight; keep weeds down round growing bulbs and annuals.

Feed annuals and vegetables with liquid foliar fertiliser such as Aquasol to keep moving.

Compost or mulch autumn leaves.

THE JUNE GARDEN

Outdoor lights sparkled on wet leaves and shone on the flagged path and steps leading up to the house we visited one damp, dark, winter night. A huge Camellia reared beside the steps and fallen flowers — huge double, palest pink blooms — gleamed like nocturnal Waterlilies afloat on the wet flagging. A second glance showed that nature had been improved on by our hostess, to add a welcoming touch to the damp night — a charming idea and easy to adapt to your own garden.

Camellias have a maddening habit of falling while they are still perfect. So turn them right side up and float them on a pool or path. Or leave them where they are — but you will need some light on the scene. Hawaiian flares can be pushed in anywhere you want some light.

In Japan the spoil (fallen flowers) is admired more than the flowers on the tree. Australian gardeners often seem more intent on sweeping them all up than admiring the artistic effect.

The succession of damp, dark days that usher in winter really make us appreciate colour in the garden. It is conventional to think of winter as being a time when flowers are scarce — but this is not necessarily true. Camellias, Luculia and Daphne provide a wealth of pastel blooms through the cool months. But the plants which glow with colour really warm the cockles of a gardener's heart in winter.

Autumn leaves are still making a brave show round our way, and by far the brightest is the Rhus. There seem to be hundreds of Rhus trees springing up. They grow freely from seed, and if you find one uninvited in your garden it looks so magnificent in its blazing autumn colours that you come to regard it as a great treasure. However Rhus, for all its autumn glory, can be a menace. In some people it causes severe allergic reactions which can remain painful for months. (I have even heard gruesome stories of people needing hospital treatment after merely walking past it.) So if you have one of these uninvited guests growing, treat it with caution. In fact, I would recommend getting rid of it. Plant a Pistacia instead — it looks similar, and though its autumn colour is not quite so hectic it is far more subtle.

To help identify Rhus, each leaf is composed of a varying number of leaflets arranged in pairs along a red stem, with one leaflet at the tip. In summer the leaflets are bright green and in autumn fiery yellow to orange to vivid red. The tree can grow to 6 m (20 ft) in height and has an open umbrella shape. Branches and leaves tend to droop. Some carry drooping bunches of small berries.

Some people confuse Rhus with the Pistacia, but the Pistacia's branches are much more upright. It is a round-headed tree, with the berries arranged round the stem.

In our garden at present we have a splash of purple Salvia *(S. leucantha)* the Mexican Bush Sage. This has long spikes of flowers like purple velvet and long narrow, aromatic, felty leaves. Salvias really work for their living in the garden, from the sage we use in the kitchen to the decorative red of the summer Bonfire Salvia and the blue of *S. farenacea.*

Another unusual winter flower is Montanoa, the Tree Daisy. This is quite a showy plant which grows to about 3 m (10 ft) and flowers in June. It is most attractive to bees, and grows readily from cuttings. People are often puzzled about this tree full of Daisy flowers — it seems unreal. Worth growing for winter flowers if you have room.

Berry bushes are one of winter's joys and I have seen two which were a little uncommon and interesting. Aronia is a small deciduous shrub, growing from 2 to 2.5 m (6 to 8 ft) tall. The autumn colour is most attractive, combined with clusters of dark red berries. Callicarpa, the Bead Bush, is similar in size but carries tiny violet-blue berries in opposite clusters up the stem — for all the world like little beads. Both would be suitable for a mixed shrub border. Aronia has a suckering tendency but should not cause any problem. Callicarpa grows readily from cuttings and the berries hold well. The name means "beautiful fruit" which, though appropriate, makes me think of something large and showy rather than the tiny beads.

Quite a number of Azaleas also flower through the winter months and these can be used as cut flowers. "Agnes Neale", "Schryderii", and "Rosa Belton" are three good suggestions for winter flowers. "Rosa Belton", a striking white with a mauve border and lime throat, needs part shade. Winter flowering Azaleas — particularly the singles — are more tolerant of sun than those which flower later when the sun is hotter and more likely to burn and fade blooms.

Salvia leucantha — *purple plush flowers and pungent foliage which is green above, silvery below for autumn/winter colour.*

GARDENKEEPING

Winter Projects

After a long dry spell many gutters and drains will have become blocked with leaves, twigs and other debris. They should be cleared to avoid blockages in the first heavy fall of rain which may cause flooding and washaways in the garden. Any fallen leaves that may cause a blockage should be raked up and used for mulch round shrubs or put into the compost heap.

The ground is now dry and cold, and dry winds quickly dry out any remaining moisture. A good, deep watering plus a 5 to 8 cm (2 to 3 in) layer of leaf litter round shrubs will keep them from suffering too much.

Don't waste the cool, dry, sunny days we often get at this time of the year. This is the time to get busy digging drains and putting in paths and garden steps.

Before you start, have a look at some of the new materials available. For underground drains PVC contour pipe is much lighter to handle than terracotta agricultural pipes. And if you are mixing concrete, you might like to use expanded shale instead of the much heavier blue metal. Expanded shale (Litecrete) can also be used as a pebble mulch. In the mulch line, some bags of decorative pebbles have marked on them the area a bag will cover.

If you want to put up a trellis, remember that expanding trellis can be a godsend to the home gardener. Use it to cover old paling fences, as a windbreak or for privacy on a patio, round car ports, as light cover to filter sun instead of a roof over pergolas, or indoors for climbing indoor plants. It can even be put across windows to deter burglars. And, of course, it's great for climbing plants.

There is a line of instant trellis available at hardware and department stores and nurseries. Made of plastic in green or white, it is in a roll 3 × 1 m (10 × 3 ft). It is light, easy to handle and just the thing to support a small climber on a paling fence or whatever.

Don't Vegetate

Many home gardeners lose their enthusiasm for vegetable growing during the winter. Often the ground allotted to vegetables becomes shaded during this time, making it unsuitable for raising vegetables.

You can turn indifference into a virtue by using this time to let the beds lie fallow. Clear them of any stragglers from your summer/autumn crops, and dig over the beds thoroughly. Humus or animal manure can then be added and dug in evenly. Humus can be added in the form of home compost, seaweed, leaf mulch or spent mushroom compost.

If one of these is not available, buy a bale of lucerne hay or straw from your nearest produce store, spread it, sprinkle with lime and fertiliser or manure, and fork a light cover of soil over it. Water to dampen thoroughly and leave for a week before turning to ensure an even compost.

Water if necessary to keep damp but not wet and turn again at intervals. The beds can then be left to lie fallow until spring.

Tree Management

This is the time when we become conscious of the growth trees have made during the summer. Branches are cutting off sunlight, have grown inconveniently across paths, or are reaching out to tap, tap maddeningly against walls. Those branches growing in a wrong direction should be cut off flush with the trunk or limb.

It may not always be necessary to resort to surgery when branches grow in the wrong position. Removal can ruin the shape and appearance of Conifers, and it is possible to train a branch into a better position by wiring it. Light branches can be wired with plastic-coated copper wire, but a larger branch will need strong wire threaded through a length of hose pipe where it touches the branches.

If the tree is deciduous it is easier to tackle this job while the tree is leafless, when there are no leaves to get in the way and add extra weight, and the tree structure is clearly visible. Do not attempt to remove a branch with one cut. If you cut it off in several sections there will be less likelihood of damaging the rest of the garden, the tree or yourself.

Always saw round the underside of the branch to cut through the bark before you begin to cut it off. Otherwise the falling branch will carry a long strip of bark with it, leaving an ugly scar and opening the way for insect and fungus attack. Do not leave the stump of the branch jutting out like a hat-peg. Trim it off flush with the trunk and smooth off any rough and torn edges with a pruning knife. Paint the cut surface with a sealing paint to seal it against damage.

If you are growing creepers like Wistaria on the house, see whether long summer growths have sneaked up under eaves or roof tiles. Long, straggly summer canes can be cut back to keep it under control. But do not cut into the flowering wood.

The Irish Juniper (*J. communis* "Stricta") is grown for its neat, column-like shape, but sometimes the normally vertical branches bend out and it is necessary to bind the tree into a frame which will train the branches into the right position. Pass the wire right round the tree, making sure it will not cut into the wood and damage it. If you look closely at a well-shaped Juniper in someone's garden, you may see the training wires still in position.

Cypresses are ideal for trimming and so make a good hedge or wind-break tree. But it is always best to start pruning Conifers while young. Cutting heavily into old wood will sometimes kill a tree or leave it with bald patches where the foliage has not regrown. If you have planted Cypress trees that could grow too big, trim them regularly to keep them under control and start trimming before they get too big. They will be thicker and bushier if trimmed regularly.

TREES AND SHRUBS

Planting Fruit Trees

We are heading for the shortest day of the year and after that it's downhill all the way to spring which means that for gardeners there is no time to be lost in planting dormant perennials, Roses, fruit and nut trees and, if you live in cool areas, berry fruits.

All these plants should be permanent or, at least, long-lived additions to your garden and it is worth while spending some time in preparing beds or planting positions beforehand. A healthy, well-grown fruiting or ornamental tree is usually fairly expensive but the outlay will be very small indeed if you get a return of, say, twenty years of fruit or flowers. The first step in ensuring this return is the choice and preparation of the planting site.

Most plants need good drainage and plenty of sunlight to grow well. Choose a north aspect where trees should get maximum sunlight through the day and check the drainage by digging a hole and filling it with water. If it drains away quickly, drainage is good; if it drains away after a few hours, it will be satisfactory if some extra humus is added to the soil; but if there is still some water remaining in the hole overnight, you will need to improve the drainage if the tree is not to drown.

If you have sticky clay soil a dressing of gypsum, available quite inexpensively from nurseries and hardware stores stocking gardening supplies, will improve the soil structure by making it more crumbly and better draining. Where drainage problems are caused by seepage from higher ground, agricultural piping will carry off surplus water. The addition of humus in the form of compost, spent mushroom compost, cool animal manure, sawdust or seaweed will build up the soil level so that it is several centimetres higher than the original level and this will improve drainage too.

Planting holes should be wide enough and deep enough to hold the roots without bending or twisting them. Some trees and shrubs that are planted now are usually sold bare-rooted — Roses and some fruit trees for instance — and these roots must not be allowed to dry out, so do your digging before buying if possible or keep the roots covered and damp while they are waiting to go in. Don't add fresh manure or fertiliser to the soil when planting bare-rooted plants because it will burn their roots.

Another important point to remember if you are planning to plant several fruit trees is that they need room to spread. Fruit trees need good air circulation and good sun penetration through the branches to do well and overcrowding will cause problems. Allow spacing of about 5 m (15 ft) between trees and about half this distance on either side.

Home gardeners often make the mistake of planting trees — fruiting or ornamental — too close to fences, forgetting that trees grow out as well as up. The result is usually trouble with the neighbours after a few years when the branches begin to overhang their property, lean against the communal fence, which can be damaging to the tree as well as the fence, and drop fruit on their washing or into their pool.

You should find a good selection of fruit trees available in nurseries now, including Peaches, Nectarines, Apricots, Plum (Japanese varieties are most suitable for coastal gardens), Mulberries, Figs and Persimmons. For cooler climates, there are also Pears, Apples, Cherries, Walnuts and European Plums. Citrus trees of all kinds can be planted in coastal areas now but in the colder areas it is better to wait until August.

Many fruit trees need a pollinator so in such instances you will need room for two different varieties of each tree. Check before buying to find out whether the tree is self-pollinating.

Though having a supply of fresh, home-grown fruit is delightful, I am not one hundred percent in favour of reckless planting of fruit trees. They do require a certain amount of care and maintenance including spraying for fruit fly and fungus diseases that will, if neglected, ruin not only your crops but also those around your neighbourhood.

One fruit tree that can be excluded from this is the good old Lemon — the most useful tree for the home garden. Lemon trees do not need much in the way of spraying and, given good drainage and a reasonably sunny situation, they will bear masses of valuable fruit which is both ornamental and useful for drinks, marmalade, desserts and adding savour to meat and fish dishes.

Eureka is the best lemon for coastal gardens. It is an attractive tree, almost thornless and bearing most of its fruit in winter. Lisbon is reliable and heavy fruiting but is thorny. A newer introduction — Prior Lisbon — withstands cold winter temperatures and is hardy and strong growing.

The Meyer is also good for severe areas and can be grown as a tub plant. There is also a variety called Patio Meyer, a bushy, ornamental plant grown from cuttings (not grafted) which is an excellent tub plant for a sunny patio or small garden where there is not room for a larger variety.

If you have a Mediterranean-style house, why not plant tubs of Citrus — Lemons, Oranges, or Cumquats on the patio or use them as ornamentals for the front garden — as they are grown in Mediterranean gardens. However, Cumquats are particularly sensitive to winds and draughts. The poor things suffer badly because they are so often used as ornamental tub plantings on exposed steps and patios, where they quickly drop their leaves. If your Cumquats are looking somewhat less than decorative, check the draught situation and remember, too, that they like plenty of sun. You might need to replace them with something tougher — perhaps Coprosma or Indian Hawthorn (Raphiolepis).

When you are buying any bare-rooted plants, avoid any that have shrivelled or withered roots or stems which show that they have been allowed to dry out. Citrus that are being sold bare-rooted should have firm, green foliage. Don't buy any with wilted or yellowed leaves.

Camellias

In June the gardener's fancy lightly turns to thoughts of Camellias, with throngs of would-be growers yearning over the exquisite blooms on display. An afternoon among the Camellias is enough to give anyone visions of himself (like some latter-day version of Dumas' *Dame aux Camellias*) surrounded by a garden full of blooms.

By the way, the lady of the Camellias was not just Greta Garbo in pale make-up, but a real person responsible for a tremendous craze for Camellias. She was a young dressmaker who became famous in Paris society through her friendship with the composer Liszt and the author Dumas. Her habit of wearing a white Camellia started a fashion which became a cult when her coffin was filled with the blooms (she died at 22) and her admirers wore the flower in their buttonholes and strewed them on her grave.

So popular were Camellias then that when the first red and white striped Camellia — "Queen Victoria" — was introduced cuttings were raffled for 200 francs a ticket.

Today's Camellias are infinitely superior to the flower made popular by the little Parisian dressmaker but, even with inflation, advanced plants can be bought for a few dollars. The increased demand by landscape gardeners has resulted in short supply at some nurseries. You may have to visit several to find the variety you want.

Camellia *"Tip Toe" with bright pink-tipped petals pale to white and deep golden stamens. A delicate beauty which stands sun.*

Camellias are ideal for a shaded garden where more sun-loving plants will not flourish. The shiny foliage enlivens shady areas by reflecting light rather than absorbing it, in the way that Rhododendrons do. In fact, any shiny-leaved shrub adds an extra dimension to a garden with gleams of light and a real sparkle in the sun.

When planting Camellias, make sure they are positioned to avoid direct morning sun in the winter. It can burn the wet or frost-touched buds and flowers, which will then not open. This applies particularly to doubles.

Camellias are suitable for planting near the house — a much better proposition than those Conifer and Rubber trees, so often popular candidates for the front wall. Camellia roots will not interfere with foundations or drains, and are not likely to grow taller than 6 m (20 ft) during the next fifty years. Remember they like acid soil and good drainage. If the soil or drainage are not right, grow them in tubs filled with a commercial potting mix or compost.

Because of their dense, spreading growth, Camellias make good hedge plants. *C. sasanqua* is particularly suitable for hedging in narrow areas — in that space beside the driveway and the next-door property, perhaps.

Many Sasanqua varieties have a naturally side-branching growth habit and if unwanted outward growing branches are cut off flush with the main trunk they will form a hedge in a bed as narrow as 30 cm (12 in).

Huge Camellias in old gardens are sometimes axed because they have encroached over paths or windows. These can be pruned by having lower branches cut so that the bush has a single smooth trunk, and can start a whole new life as a small, graceful tree.

Camellia *"Shishi Gashira" a dwarf type with pink flowers suitable for containers or rockeries.*

Camellias are long-lived plants, so if you have moved into an old house with overgrown Camellias please do not think they are "finished". Do your bit for ecology — recycle a Camellia.

To find a Camellia you really like it is best to visit a Camellia nursery or one of the Camellia shows. In the meantime, here are a few suggestions for easily grown garden varieties: "Laurie Bray" a pale pink semi-double, is one of the best Australian-raised hybrids for the home gardener, and good to start with if you are new to Camellia growing. "Moshio" and "Dixie Knight" are two bright reds covered with blooms at this time of year, and "R.L. Wheeler Variegated" is a deep pink splashed white. Very reliable, it has the advantage of blooming from an early age.

Three delicate pale pinks are "Nancy Bird", "Magnoliaeflora" and "Dr Tinsley". This last is known to Camellia growers as a "shy flowerer". This means that it does not flower very much for about five years but, once established, covers itself in delicate pink and white blooms which open from pink buds.

As Camellias live for well over a century, this is not unreasonable. But it does mean "Dr Tinsley" is for the gardener who can afford to wait.

I am very attracted to "Magnoliaeflora", a very pale delicate pink with two rows of petals set apart so that each individual petal is displayed. This is a beautiful garden plant which flowers well and has upright, bushy growth which makes it suitable for use as a tub specimen.

Some unusual Camellias recently introduced are "Black Lace", a large, deep crimson touched with black and a perfect rose shape; a collection of small Camellias such as "Bokuhan", a tiny crimson-petalled bloom with a heart of large white stamens; and "Little Bit", a little pink and white striped pompom. Another unusual Camellia is "Hertzilia de Freitas Magalhaes" with flowers opening pink and turning purple. As well as having a most unusual colour, these flowers have a double centre forming a ball of tight petals, making them very interesting (and its name is not exactly easy to remember, spell or pronounce either!)

In warmer districts grow early-flowering varieties like "Polar Bear" and Sasanquas which bloom during the cooler weather.

Camellias are good balcony, patio and courtyard plants particularly for semi-shaded areas. Some suitable varieties are: "Susan Stone", soft blush pink, formal double flowers well displayed on a compact bush; "The Czar", deep red semi-double, stocky growth; "Yuletide", red single with prominent yellow stamens and close, compact upright growth, and "Bonanza", deep red semi-double flowers and growth which lends itself to espaliering.

"Bonanza" can be grown in a tub and espaliered against a wall to fill a narrow space and with regular trimming could be grown this way for many years. It can also be trained on to a frame pushed into the tub itself. "Yuletide" is ideal for a large container because the growth is compact and upright. It blooms freely, the brightness of the flowers making it quite eye-catching.

Camellias sometimes worry their owners with erratic blooming behaviour — buds that fail to open for instance. One beautiful variety which regularly sends its owners into a panic is "Hawaii". The bloom of this bush is magnificent when it is fully open being very large with pink, fimbriated petals with paler pink margins. The petals look as if they had been cut out with pinking shears and the flower is very striking. In bud however it is rather strange looking being quite green and ugly. The buds could be described as being like Brussels sprouts gone wrong but this is the normal way that "Hawaii" buds develop and, in spite of their strange appearance, they do actually open into the gorgeous bloom of the above description.

Many people don't realise that Camellias can be pruned after flowering — particularly the fast-growing Sasanquas. Pruning and shaping will also help to develop a good hedge growth where Camellias have been planted as a screen. If this is done as soon as the bush has finished flowering, you will get some good, dense growth.

Browallia and Bergenia

Browallia to most people is the small shrub with orange flowers, *Browallia jamesonii* (actually Streptosolen). My mother has always grown a small blue Browallia (*B. elata*), an annual with masses of small very blue flowers with a tiny white eye.

Two Browallia: The smaller flower (right) is not so deeply incised.

It is a little-known plant, supposed to have been introduced into our garden by my late grandmother, an ardent plant collector, after an expedition to the Brisbane Botanic Gardens.

I recently came across another blue Browallia (*B. viscosa*) in a nursery. This is a larger plant with larger flowers slightly tinged with violet and should be useful for a rockery or border — a plant to remember for that touch of blue in the garden.

Browallia will grow in any ordinary garden soil and likes plenty of sun and water in dry weather. I have found that too much fertiliser produces a lot of leaves at the expense of flowers.

Streptosolen (the orange Browallia) is a small shrub which could be in every garden. It grows easily, is not prone to pests or diseases and flowers all year in warm to temperate climates.

For a more shaded place Bergenia, a large-leaved rosette carrying spikes of pink flowers, is invaluable. The flowers last for many weeks on the plant, and can also be picked. During the rest of the year the rosettes of leaves look neat and attractive. If you have a narrow, rather shaded strip along your house or on the footpath between fence and paving, Bergenia will fill it perfectly.

Dwarf Flowering Shrubs

An attractive and rather unusual shrubby plant flowering now is *Heterocentron rosea.* It looks very much like a miniature Tibouchina and is a herbaceous plant which sends up 1 m (3 ft) canes with bronzy, reddish-green

Two shrubs for year-long garden colour:
Bird of Paradise Flower (Strelitzia reginae), *which blooms throughout the year and is a glamorous relative of the banana.*

Turk's Cap (Malvaviscus) is an easily grown shrub with bright red flowers most of the year.

foliage, square stems and clusters of mauve-pink flowers with red stems and calyx. It is a useful plant for a mixed border of small flowering shrubs. A good combination would be *Heterocentron rosea*, Daphne, dwarf Diosma (now Coleonema) and the pink Spiraea "Anthony Waterer" for summer flowers.

These dwarf shrubs are all about 1 m (3 ft) tall and have pinky flowers. They can be underplanted with clumps of bulbs or perennials for additional colour and interest to give an easy-care border.

PERENNIALS AND ANNUALS

Perennials to Plant Now

Some perennial plants are available for planting now while they are dormant. Astilbes are attractive, woody-rooted perennials which suit a moist position — of great value for that damp spot where nothing else will grow. They have fern-like foliage and feathery plumes of flowers in late spring or early summer. Colours are white, pinks to red. Very similar is Filipendula, with feathery peach-pink flowers and ferny foliage. It also likes plenty of moisture and will grow in a shady spot.

Still another perennial with feathery heads is Liatris (commonly called Blazing Star), which has cylindrical heads of flowers in summer and autumn. This plant is quite easy to grow and belongs to the Daisy family.

Nurseries in the cooler areas are offering Peonies this month. This beautiful flower needs a cool climate and deep, rich soil. Try it if your climate is suitable.

Another cool-climate gem available now is Lily-of-the-valley (Convallaria). Pips bought now will flower this season, though most coastal areas are not cool enough to establish them in the garden. I have seen a bed of Lily-of-the-valley which has been growing for about thirty years and flowers profusely each year.

Russell Lupins are for cool areas only. They don't do well on the humid coastal region but are splendid garden plants in the mountains or inland.

Hybrid Cannas make good garden plants and are a far cry from the old, tall-growing plants that need a really damp spot. The newer Canna varieties will grow in ordinary garden conditions, though they should be watered regularly during summer. Flowers are large and in a range of really bright colours. Some have colourful bronze foliage with contrasting orange or red flowers which make striking clump plantings. Cannas are not the sort of plants one usually thinks of as pot subjects, but I have seen them grown very well in tubs in a sunny position. Dwarf varieties are necessary for this.

If you have a well-drained bed in full sun, try growing some Gerberas. These bright members of the Daisy family are free-flowering and will flower most of the year in a good position.

They also make good cut flowers. Perennial plants such as Gerberas are good planted among Roses because they can be left to themselves and do not grow tall enough to interfere with the Rose bushes.

If you still haven't got around to planting your Roses, there is still plenty of time to put them in. You will find good supplies of Roses at most nurseries now. Remember that Roses need full sun to grow well and often as a garden grows trees and shrubs grow up and shade plants that were once in the sun. Roses grow weak and spindly in shade and are prone to white scale and mildew.

Hollyhocks and Geraniums

Remember old-fashioned Hollyhocks? They haven't been grown much for years because of rust problems. But now rust can be controlled with Zineb, and there are some very pretty double varieties of annual Hollyhocks available which would produce flowers by late spring or early summer, when the first spring flush is past its prime.

Hollyhocks need to be planted in a sunny position where they will get protection from the wind. Even where sheltered they may need staking to maintain the full effect of their willowy beauty. Apart from wind and rust, Hollyhocks are also attacked by snails and slugs. So keep some snail bait under the rosettes of leaves and as the plants grow taller, scan the stems occasionally for those snails that sneak up the stalks.

Another plant particularly susceptible to rust in the coastal areas is the Zonal Geranium. A lot of gardeners — myself included — have almost given them up in despair. But help is at hand. A fungicide called Difolitan is available and has been tested successfully by the Department of Agriculture.

In the meantime, a Geranium called "Ann Tilling" is apparently rust-resistant. This is mainly grown for its attractive bronze leaf marking and has small pink, single flowers.

Coloured-leaf Geraniums give interest to winter gardens when most Geraniums are fairly dormant. The coloured leaves are at their best during the cool weather and make good potted plants. There are a great many coloured-leaf varieties. One which took my eye at a Geranium show was "Bird Dancer", with a pretty star-shaped leaf and bronze markings.

Other members of the Pelargonium family are not troubled by rust. I have just bought an Ivy-leafed Geranium in bloom to brighten the kitchen window-sill. It is "Galilee", a rose-pink double.

People often complain that they cannot keep the Geraniums they buy looking as good as when they came from the nursery, and believe the nurseryman treats them with secret ingredients to make the blooms bigger and better. The only secret ingredient is constant care and ideal growing conditions — which they are hardly likely to get when they have to take pot luck in the garden. But one sure way to get bushy plants with plenty of bloom is to tip-prune regularly. This forces growth of side shoots, each of which will bear flowers.

Regal Pelargoniums will be putting out new growth ready for spring blooming and careful tip-pruning will keep bushes compact and produce more flower heads.

Look out for aphids on new growth, not only on Pelargoniums but on annuals and new Rose shoots. Spray with an insecticide. If your Pansies don't seem to be opening properly, they may be full of aphids. Unroll the petals to find them; they are not always noticeable by just looking at the plant.

CLIMBERS AND CREEPERS

Ivy

If you have lawns which are looking moth-eaten (or moss-eaten) because of winter shade and damp, perhaps you should consider Ivy as an alternative ground-cover. Ivy is very tough, and not prone to disease or insect attack. It is evergreen and remains handsome summer and winter, requiring no care other than occasional clipping to keep it within bounds and to encourage a more dense mat of growth.

Ivy is tough enough to withstand being walked on but does not attract people to walk or sit on it in the same way as a smooth lawn. Stepping stones should always be provided in a traffic area.

The common English Ivy (*Hedera helix*) will produce a dense, dark green cover which thrives in sun or shade and grows in any soil, tolerating quite poor conditions. English Ivy is easy to obtain in quantity — almost everyone has some and will happily give away a bundle of cuttings. This is an important consideration if you want to plant a large area without going to a lot of expense.

There are a number of most attractive Ivy varieties, all suitable as ground-covers. Variegated ones generally grow more slowly than green varieties but make light and colourful covers. Ivy is a good soil holder, and a variegated type will look particularly handsome on a sloping bank. *Hedera canariensis* var. *variegata* is green with greyish shadings and cream edges. Some leaves are completely cream, making this Ivy particularly showy and the leaves are large (perhaps to compensate for being slow growing).

The variety *cristata* (Parsley Leaf Ivy) has crinkly light green leaves and is quick growing. It makes a good ground-cover, the curly leaves forming a ruffled surface.

Ivy has other uses in the garden — it can be used to cover an ugly fence or wall, though it is so strong that it might eventually pull the fence down. It makes a decorative hanging basket for a windy or shady spot where more delicate plants could not survive.

If you have an old, dead tree in the garden you could turn it into an Ivy tree provided it is sound. Ivy planted at the base will completely cover a tree trunk and hang down in trailing "branches". As it can cost around $100 to have a large tree removed, covering with a creeper like Ivy can be an attractive alternative.

BULBS

Gladioli

With spring bulbs growing well and early-flowering Narcissus blooming, don't overlook bulbs which can be planted now for late spring and summer flowering. Gladioli, although suffering from the twin curses of Dame Edna Everage and thrips, are still a valuable flowering bulb for the summer garden. As they usually flower about 120 days after planting in winter or spring, planned plantings can be made to make sure that there are flowers in the garden at a specific time.

Gladioli have changed their shape somewhat recently. There are new hybrids with ruffled petals and butterfly-shaped flowers which are most attractive.

These bulbs are easy to grow and, as long as they are sprayed for thrips, are very reliable. Modern hybrid forms of Gladioli are really lovely, with ruffled petals and interesting blotches and markings. The corms can be bought at nurseries and garden centres and if you want something really special there are specialist Gladiolus nurseries.

Gladiolus should be planted in a sunny position in well-drained soil. Clump plantings are most effective in the garden but, if you are growing them purely as cut flowers, try planting a row in the vegetable garden. Gladiolus are picked as soon as the two lowest flowers begin to open so they won't be particularly decorative in the garden. A row or two among the vegetables won't take up much room and they will be easier to spray for thrips if they are grown this way, rather than dotted about the garden.

It is most important to spray the plants regularly from the two-leaf stage with Malathion to protect them from thrips. Thrips are very tiny greyish insects (very hard to see unless they are in plague proportions) which attack the buds and suck the colour out of the petals. When the damaged flowers open they begin to wither and any that do not open are grey and shrivelled. Spraying for thrip should start as soon as there are two leaves showing and should be repeated at 14-day intervals until the first buds begin to open and you are ready to start picking.

Lilies

Sprekelia (Jacobean Lily) can also be planted now. They have showy rich red flowers with an unusual Orchid shape. The flowers appear in summer after the leaves, and they can be grown in pots as well as in the garden.

The Pineapple Lily (*Eucomis punctata*) is a fascinating plant which is shown to good advantage in a pot. The flowers are carried on long stems covered with cream to green and sometimes pink scented flowers. They last for quite a long time and can be used as cut flowers — if you have enough growing.

Glowing red Sprekelia Lily, flowering this month. This is often called Jacobean Lily or Maltese Cross because of its unusual shape.

These bulbous plants are just as desirable as the spring-flowering Daffodils, Bluebells, etc. and carry the bulb flowers over into summer.

Summer-flowering Liliums can be also planted this month and some of the later-flowering ones can be planted up to the end of July. Some are better suited to cooler climates but *Lilium formosanum* has naturalised all round Sydney along road verges and railway lines, where I have seen elegant spikes growing from rocky railway cuttings.

L. formosanum flowers from January to March, and the white trumpets have a greenish-brown flush on the outside. It flowers in twelve months from seed and is well worth growing this way, as an inexpensive way of increasing your stock.

Liliums like a fairly acid soil and grow well with Azaleas. They can be planted among Azaleas where they will have the roots shaded and their heads in the sun. Do not plant them in windy situations — they are easily damaged by wind. When you buy bulbs, plant them as soon as possible. Unlike others, Liliums are never completely dormant and should not be allowed to dry out.

If you haven't tried Ifafa Lilies (Cyrtanthus) put in a clump beside your spring-flowering bulbs — they will begin blooming when the early ones are finishing. Ifafa Lilies are not big, but the cream or salmon, tubular flowers are long lasting and attractive in a good clump. Left to themselves they will multiply enough to give a good display after a few years.

A Rose by any Other Name . . .

While I was looking around a nursery, I noticed a scent of Roses in the air though there wasn't a Rose in sight. I finally discovered that the perfume was from a gorgeous Orchid in bloom, *Zygopetalum macaii.* The flowers were a combination of green and brown striped petals and purple and white striped petals, and looked as exotic as they smelled.

NATIVES

Winter Colour

Every morning we bound out of bed like gazelles at the first carolling of the currawongs — or they beat us to the milk. One morning, because of a strike, there was no milk, only disappointed currawongs. However, my chilly dash across the garden was rewarded by seeing the first rays of the sun turn the She-oaks to burnished bronze.

The "instant antique" look is caused by masses of minute red-brown flowers which cover the branches. The individual flowers are inconspicuous, but the overall effect is dramatic. She-oaks, or Casuarinas, are useful trees for coastal gardens. They are quick growers and can be combined attractively with other native trees like Queensland Wattle (*Acacia podalyriifolia*) which is also a quick grower and is in full bloom just now. I like the idea of the name Casuarina, from Casuarius the Cassowary, because the drooping branches resemble Cassowary feathers.

Some good garden hybrid Leptospermums which flower in winter and spring are well worth growing, like the double red "Red Damask" and "Lambethii", which has large pink and red flowers. Given a sunny, very well-drained situation, they flower magnificently. But you must be prepared to spend a few minutes looking over them for the stem-girdling web borer. Webs must be pulled off and burned. Spraying is generally ineffective because the grub is so well protected inside its web though the new spray Supracide is good in this situation.

These Leptospermums are at their best during their first five years. You must be prepared to scrap them if they become shabby and replant with new, vigorous plants.

Lillypilly — covered with cream to purple fruit in autumn.

When we think of berries, we usually think of exotics like Holly, Cotoneaster and Pyracantha, which are all traditional berry bushes. However, we have some excellent berry-bearing natives which should be valued more for their showy, decorative fruits. One that is making a good display now is the Lillypilly, which is covered in masses of large clusters of berries coloured from cream to purple.

The Lillypilly was known as Eugenia, a pretty and easily remembered name which most people still probably know better than the names it bears now — Acmena and Syzygium.

One popularly grown Lillypilly is *Acmena smithii,* a bushy tree with glossy, dark green leaves and white fluffy flowers which are followed by the berries. New leaf growth on Lillypilly is red — an attractive feature — and some have new growth which has pink and cream colours as well. It is an attractive tree for frost-free coastal gardens, though it may be attacked by white scale — particularly if nearby there are neglected citrus, Gardenia, Persimmon or other ornamentals that are hosts to this scale.

EDIBLES

Kiwi Fruit

In recent years New Zealand has been exporting and vigorously promoting something called Kiwi Fruit. Kiwi Fruit are really Chinese Gooseberries (*Actinidia chinensis*) which have undergone a metamorphosis and emerged twice the usual size and with a new name.

Chinese Gooseberries are native to China but have been grown so successfully in New Zealand that it is the world's major exporter of the fruit. Most of the Chinese Gooseberries on sale around Sydney come from New Zealand which also sends them to Japan, the US and Europe as Kiwi Fruit.

The new Kiwi Fruit is a very much improved version of the old Chinese Gooseberry and is a variety called "Haywood". As well as being a larger fruit, it has improved flavour and keeping qualities — an important consideration when you are exporting fruit from a place as remote from world markets as New Zealand.

There are a number of different species of Actinidia and though *A. chinensis* is the one usually grown, several others have edible fruit and two (*A. polygama* and *A. kolomikta*) are very attractive to cats. (This fascinating bit of information comes from the *Royal Horticultural Society Dictionary of Gardening* and I'm passing it on because I am collecting a list of plants which are attractive to cats.)

If you have developed a taste for Kiwi Fruit you might like to try growing your own. Plants are available from some nurseries and as the plants are dioecious — that is either male or female — you will need either two plants or one that has been grafted and budded with both types. They can be grown from seed saved from ripe fruit but you will have to wait for four years before they commence to bear and you know whether you have male or female plants.

Apart from the delicious fruit, Actinidia is an asset in the garden because it is an attractive climber, vigorous and with large fleshy leaves, red hairs on the stems and scented flowers. It will grow well in a warm, fairly frost-free position sheltered from cold winds and with well-drained soil. Being deciduous, it provides shade in summer but lets the sun shine through in winter.

If you plant one be sure to provide a good strong support such as a high trellis, pergola or carport where it can grow in comfort. Among its other assets, Actinidia is winter-ripening, an unusual time to harvest a fruit crop.

INDOORS

Colourful Blooms

Brighten up your indoor plant collection with some winter-flowering plants. You will find a wide choice at your local nursery or garden centre now.

Several showy flowering plants for indoor use are available: Cyclamen with decorative foliage and masses of flowers and buds, making it a long-lasting investment; the lovely *Primula abconia;* Elatior Begonia, with cascades of pink or rose flowers; and Christmas Cactus (Zygocactus) with bright rose, cyclamen or red flowers on the ends of succulent stems.

Christmas or Crab Cactus (Zygocactus). Plants look well in a hanging basket or placed high so that foliage can be displayed. Flowers range in colour from white through pinks and reds to deep purple.

Zygocactus has become very popular and is much easier to buy than ever before. Most nurseries seem to be carrying stocks in bloom or about to flower. This plant gets its common name of Christmas Cactus from the northern hemisphere where it flowers at Christmas time. It makes a showy basket plant and can be used on a sheltered patio or balcony in filtered or morning sun. Indoors, it should be given a well-lighted spot near a window during its flowering period. After flowering, move it out to a shade-house or sheltered position and protect it from snails, which are very attracted to the succulent foliage.

Nurserymen also have good supplies of flowering Polyanthus Primroses which can be used as a flowering houseplant or put into a shady area in the garden to add colour. Polyanthus come in many pastel shades of mauve, blue, pink, red and yellow, and well-grown plants have many more buds developing to provide a long flowering period. African Violets are ideal for well-lighted window-sills indoors, where they do not get any direct sun.

Orchids in bloom are beginning to appear in nurseries and stores. They are a wonderful buy for use as a flowering indoor plant. The flower spikes can last for many weeks so that, though an Orchid in bloom can be expensive, you get a good return for your investment. After flowering, the pot can be put out on a balcony. Orchids are not suited to constant indoor life.

If you are an indoor-plant enthusiast, a Cyclamen is a must for winter blooms in a range of cyclamen, pinks or white. The foliage is large and handsome with marbled and veined heart-shaped leaves held on pink-tinged succulent stems. The flowers are suspended over the foliage like a flutter of butterflies. Cyclamen is undoubtedly the most floriferous of indoor plants, a single plant having twenty or more blooms.

If you buy a Cyclamen, make up your mind that it is probably only going to flower for one season. They do sometimes re-flower the following year but more often will produce nothing but leaves. After the flowers have finished, move your plant into a sheltered position outdoors or in a bush-house or sheltered balcony where it will get plenty of light and some filtered sun. Water and fertilise it until it begins to die down. During summer, when it is dormant, just give it enough water to prevent it from drying out completely. When it begins to put out new growth begin to water and feed it again — it may reward you with another season of blooms.

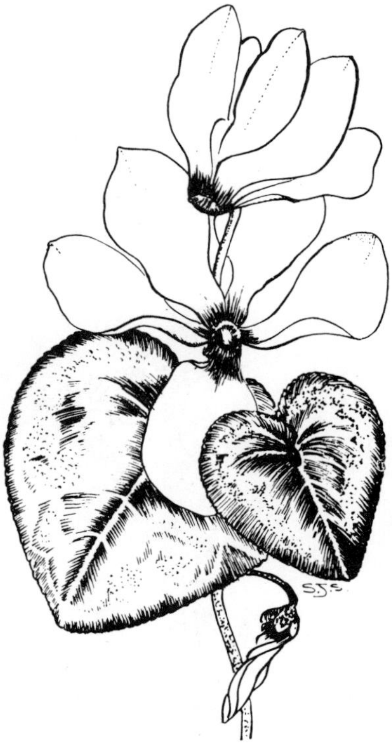

Potted Cyclamen flower prolifically throughout winter if placed in a well-lighted position.

CHECKLIST

July is a good month to concentrate on garden construction work — putting down new paths, garden steps, agricultural pipes — that can be undertaken by the home gardener-handyman as well as more ambitious projects, such as putting in a swimming pool or a deck for summer garden living.

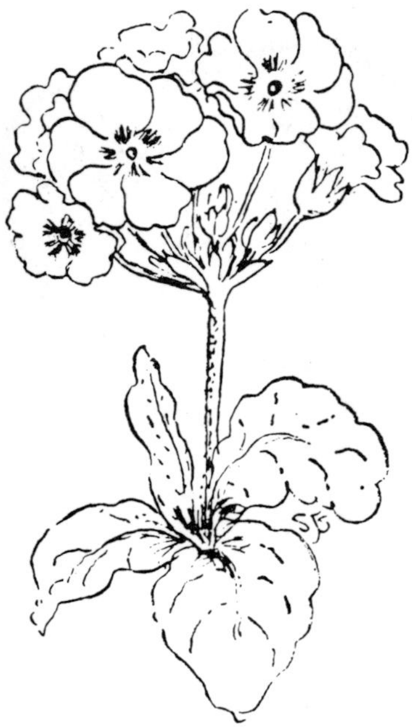

Flowering now: Polyanthus, a colourful addition to gardens, troughs or pots.

Flowering now

Trees and Shrubs:
Azalea,
Buddleia salvifolia,
Camellia,
Coleonema (Diosma),
Daphne,
Erythrina (Coral Tree),
Euphorbia (Poinsettia),
Gordonia,
Hebe,
Iboza (Moschosma),
Japonica,
Lavendula dentata (French Lavender),
Luculia,
Magnolia,
Podalyria sericea,
Polygala,
Prunus campanulata (Bell Cherry),
P. mume (Almond),
P. persica (Winter-flowering Peach),
Reinwardtia,
Viburnum tinus.

Berries on Ardisia,
Cotoneaster,
Euonymus,
Hawthorn,
Holly,
Melia,
Nandina,
Pistacia,
Pyracantha.

Perennials and annuals:
Bergenia,
Calendula,
Helleborus,
Iceland Poppy,
Kalanchoe,
Mignonette,
Pansy,
Primula,
Rochea,
Stock,
Violet,
Wallflower,
Zygocactus.

Bulbs:
Clivea,
Cyclamen (potted),
Daffodils,
Hyacinth,
Iris stylosa,
Jonquil,
Narcissus,
Snowflake.

Climbers:
Clerodendron splendens,
C. speciosissimum,
Gelsemium (Carolina Jasmine),
Pyrostegia venusta (syn. *ignea*).
(See also p. 127.)

Natives:
Acacia baileyana (Cootamundra Wattle),

JULY

Chamaelaucium (Geraldton Wax),
Grevillea (some species),
Leptospermum (hybrid varieties),
Thryptomene.

Berries on Elaeocarpus (Blueberry Ash),
Lillypilly,
Pittosporum rhombifolium.

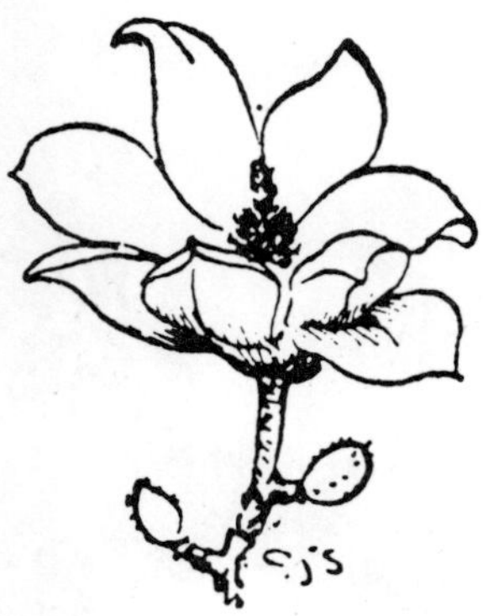

Magnolia denudata — *a beautiful winter-flowering tree.*

Plant

Trees, Shrubs and Climbers:
Deciduous flower and fruit trees,
nut and citrus,
grape vines,
Roses,
raspberry,
loganberry,
black currant,
gooseberry,
boisenberry (cool districts only) and strawberries.

Perennials and Annuals:
Astilbe,
Gloxinea,
Liatris,
Perennial Phlox,
Russell Lupin (cold areas only).

Advanced bedding plants of
Alyssum,
Arctotis (Aurora Daisy),
Calendula,
Candytuft,
Delphiniums,
Dianthus,
Gypsophila (seed),
Larkspur,
Linaria (seed),
Lupin,
Mignonette (seed),
Statice,
Violets,
Virginian Stock (seed).

Bulbs:
Agapanthus,
Bearded Iris,
Calla,
Eucomis,
Gladiolus,
Hippeastrum,
Hymenocallis
Ifafa Lily,
Ismene,
Liliums,
Lily-of-the-valley,
Tuberous Begonia,
Valotta (Scarborough Lily).

Vegetables:
Broad beans,
cabbage,
lettuce (winter varieties),
onion,
peas,
radish,
rhubarb crowns,
shallots,
silver beet,
spinach,
turnips.

Warm areas:
French beans,
beetroot,
carrots,
herbs,
parsnip,
tomatoes.

Prune

Quite a lot of pruning can be done towards the end of the month though in very cold districts this may be left until August.

Though a range of plants can be pruned this month, care should be taken not to prune spring-flowering deciduous shrubs and flowering fruit trees grown for ornamental blossom. Prune: Caryopteris, Ceratostigma, Cestrum, *Clerodendrum ugandense* (Butterfly Flower), Duranta (after fruit fall), Heliotrope, Holmskoldia, Hydrangea (if not pruned in summer), Hypericum, Lagerstroemia (Crepe Myrtle) if grown as a shrub, Lantana, Luculia (moderate as flowers finish), Oleander (in frost-free areas), Plumbago, Roses, Sambucus (Golden Elder), Tamarisk (*Tamarix pentandra*), Wistaria (shorten canes to plump flower spurs only), grape vines, and cut back spent Chrysanthemums.

Pests and Diseases

Spray citrus for tissue paper stage of bronze orange bug with Carbaryl, Malathion or soft soap if available. Deciduous vines with oblong scale insects should be sprayed with red oil as directed on pack. Spray winter-flowering Prunus for peach leaf curl at bud swell using Bordeaux or lime sulphur. (See also p.120.)

Spray all Rose bushes after pruning with lime sulphur (Harola), also soil under plants to clear up spores of fungus diseases. Spray with Dormant spraying oil after pruning for white scale infestation.

Cup moth infestations occur in Eucalyptus, Brushbox and Angophoras. Spray with Malathion or inject with Rogor. Larva has stinging spines at each end of body.

Spray Cinerarias for leaf miner using Malathion, Rogor or Metasystox. Keep all Azaleas sprayed once buds show colour to protect against Azalea petal blight, using fungicide such as Mancozeb.

Check deciduous trees for borer and treat with Malathion. (See also p.121.)

Spray winter-flowering Azaleas for petal blight. (See also p.167.)

Garden Care

Keep all spent heads off bulbs and annuals.

Scatter snail pellets round growing plants, also in clumps of Clivea where snails are a problem from now on as flowers develop.

Keep plants moving with water-soluble fertilisers such as Aquasol and if dry weather is prolonged, keep water up to Azaleas.

Dig up bulbous weeds like oxalis and onion weed now before new bulbs form in spring.

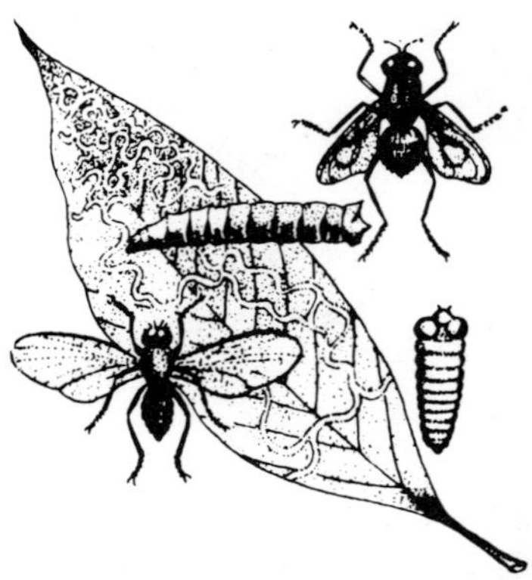

Leaf miner on Cinerarias should be sprayed this month.

THE JULY GARDEN

There seems to be a myth — no doubt carried to these shores by our European ancestors — that there is no colour in winter gardens. While this is fairly true of cold-climate countries that are snow-bound for several months through winter, it should not be applied to Australian gardens, other than those in areas of extreme climate.

There is plenty of colour to be found though you may have to look for it. In cold areas where there are many deciduous trees you will find a wealth of subtle colour in the bare branches and some trees display a sculptural beauty when their shape is revealed after the leaf cover has fallen.

Nyssa sylvatica is a stately tree with beautifully shaped, horizontal lateral branches and the Crepe Myrtle that fills gardens with flowers all through the warm months displays an elegant curved trunk (or trunks) with satiny silver branches when it is bare. Some of the Maples develop brilliant red stems while the Ash shows golden stems and black buds. And what could be lovelier than a clump of Silver Birch trees with their black and silver trunks and slender, weeping bare branches.

Flowers are plentiful in the warmer coastal gardens. Poppies, Pansies, Primulas and early flowering Narcissus, Jonquils and the earliest Daffodils are with us in winter. Poinsettia displays huge red, pink or cream heads in frost-free gardens, winter-flowering Wattles, such as the Queensland Wattle (*Acacia podalyriifolia*) finishes blooming as the Cootamundra Wattle (*A. baileyana*) begins to bloom. Winter-flowering Peaches, the flowering Almond (*Prunus mume*) and the first of the Cherries, the Bell Cherry (*P. campanulata*) are also coming in to bloom. These are just a few winter colourmakers that spring to mind. Look around, you will find that there is colour in gardens everywhere.

Perennial Wallflower, a shrubby plant flowering most of the year. Flowers change from yellow-pink to orange to mauve and are easily grown in a sunny spot.

GARDENKEEPING

The Depths of Winter

Once we get into July we really do seem to be in the depths of winter. It gets dark early, there are westerly winds, frosts and even snow in some areas to make life difficult for gardeners. If you live in a frosty spot remember to get out and hose plants before the sun gets on them after a frost. This will save them from a lot of damage. Young, frost-tender plants should be protected by having some sheets of newspaper wrapped round their trunks.

Some gardeners in cooler areas might be worried by leaves on young Papaw trees drooping and falling off. This is just the result of the cold weather. Papaws are warm-climate plants and do feel the winters. They can't stand frost or even cold and should be covered when there is any likelihood of freezing weather.

Frost-tender plants like Crotons should be moved indoors or given the protection of a roof overhang. These tropical foliage shrubs are popular potted plants but will not survive outdoors if they are hit by frost. Shrubs which have been blackened by frost should be left until spring before being pruned.

There's not much growth in the garden at this time. Deciduous plants are dormant and annuals seem to stand still. However, there are plenty of flowering plants at your nursery or garden centre if your garden needs brightening up.

Spray Peaches now at bud-swell stage with Bordeaux to prevent peach leaf curl.

Peach Leaf Curl

Another seasonal task — early-flowering Peaches are at the bud-swell stage and now is the time to spray for peach leaf curl. This is a parasitic fungus which shows up in spring, when the leaves appear. The affected leaves are thickened and distorted.

If your Peach trees had this disfiguring disease last year, you should spray with Bordeaux mixture or lime sulphur before the trees get beyond the bud-swell stage. Only one application is necessary, but extremities of all limbs and twigs must be well sprayed.

Pruning

There are many pruning jobs that should be done in July. This month is an ideal time to remove a lot of dead wood from the inside of some shrubs, an important aspect of pruning which is often neglected. The gardener tends to reduce shrubs by chopping away the outer growth, which is often new and vigorous, and leaving the inside of the shrub, which may be full of old or dead wood.

Have a good look at your shrubs — it is easy to spot dead wood on both deciduous and evergreen plants in July when they are not densely clothed in leaves. Even evergreen plants are generally sparser in winter. Try to work in the morning while the low winter sun shines through the branches. It makes the job a lot easier.

Abelias can be pruned by removing old canes carrying dead, twiggy wood. These must be cut out at ground level. If the natural arching shape of Abelia is taking up too much space in the garden, it can be trimmed to fit. I keep mine under control by picking long sprays during the flowering season. It looks attractive in a big flower arrangement.

If you grow Crepe Myrtle as a shrub, it can be cut back now to within several centimetres of last year's growth.

Some people prune their Crepe Myrtles back to the same point every year, so that they develop ugly, thickened calluses at each branch. As the shrubs are deciduous, they look most unattractive until they have put on enough summer growth to conceal the scars. This ugly appearance is easily avoided if you cut a little higher each year. If the plant begins to get too big after a few years, simply go back to the lowest cut and start again. All pruning cuts should be made on a slant so that water runs away, otherwise the cut ends can become waterlogged and will be attacked by fungus diseases.

Don't prune spring-flowering deciduous shrubs like Prunus, Weigela and climbing Roses or you will be cutting off the blooms.

Borers

Though July may seem a fairly quiet time in the garden there are many things that should be done now to ensure healthy plants and plenty of flowers when the weather warms up.

Take a good look at all your deciduous trees while there is no foliage to conceal the branches. Damage from borers of various kinds is clearly visible and easy to get out while the branches are bare. Look for signs of gumming or bleeding and patches of sawdust and webbing which conceal holes in the trunk.

Scrape away the debris and you will find the hole usually with the grub still in residence. You can often kill it by inserting a piece of wire into the hole and prodding around inside. Then squirt some methylated spirits or Malathion into the hole with an old eye-dropper or syringe and plug the hole with soap. Leaf eaters high up in trees can be controlled by injection. Drill three or four holes into the trunk of the tree at an angle of 45 degrees. Don't drill deeply, just into the sapwood. Fill the holes with Rogor or Metasystox diluted with water and with a few drops of detergent added. When the poison has been absorbed, plug the holes and paint over with a bitumen sealer. It will take several days to take effect. Though trees sometimes can withstand the damage done by borers and leaf-eating pests they do seriously weaken them and, if left unchecked, trees may eventually die.

Check your flowering Prunus, particularly flowering Cherries because they are susceptible to borer attack. Take a look at native trees and shrubs, too — particularly Gums and Wattles. Bleeding, gumming, lifting and cracking of the bark indicates attack from various insects such as Longicorn beetles. Longicorn beetles feed on the phloem-cambium tissue and the bark may conceal quite extensive damage. All damaged and loose bark should be lifted and cut away as soon as it is noticed. Check for insects and scrape the damaged area to remove all loose bark and damaged tissue.

If you think there may be insects still present spray with Malathion then paint or spray the area with a fungicide to prevent further damage from fungus attack. Holes should be plugged and the area painted with tree wound dressing. Small holes can be plugged with soft auto putty or ordinary wood putty. Fill only to the level of the sapwood so that the bark can grow over the scar.

Damage to tree trunks near ground level sometimes can be the result of mower attack. Treatment is the same with the additional recommendation of more care when mowing round trees. Help damaged trees to recover by fertilising round the root area to the outer edge of the foliage and watering.

TREES AND SHRUBS

Prunus

Like Candide, I sometimes think this is the best of all possible worlds. Here it is, the deepest, darkest depths of winter — and already the first of the spring-flowering trees is blooming.

This is *Prunus mume,* the flowering Apricot, which starts flowering in Sydney this month. If you live in cooler areas it is a joy still to come.

Prunus mume is a small tree about 3 m (10 ft) and the flowers are sweetly perfumed — literally a breath of spring. The double white variety is particularly pretty, but it also comes in red and pink. It is not particularly fussy about soil, but thrives best in a well-drained position, with plenty of sun and some shelter from winds.

Prunus mume is not the only source of winter flowers. With a little planning we can have our gardens blooming right through June and July. A number of Camellias are flowering now and these combine well with the flowering Apricot for a look of springtime.

The ground should now be in good condition for planting deciduous trees. Nurseries have received their stocks of flowering and deciduous types, but if you leave buying until late in the season the best will have gone and those left tend to get "shop-soiled". The spring-flowering trees are particularly suitable for small gardens, as they usually are within 6 m (20 ft) high.

Flowering Peaches (*Prunus persica*) come in two types — the winter-flowering, beginning to flower now, and the later spring bloomers. Buy in flower, so you can choose the colour you want. Prunus such as flowering Peach, Plum, Cherry Plum and Almond will do well in humid coastal areas, while the flowering Cherries and Crab-apples do better in cooler districts.

Nurseries in areas where flowering Cherries do not do well rarely carry stocks. So if your local nursery has no Cherries, settle for flowering Peach or Plum. Prunus "Elvins" is a favourite of mine. It has creamy blooms which turn pink with age. If you are looking for a spectacular flowering Peach, "Lillian Burrows" has huge pink double blooms and the most popular Cherry is pink-to-white "Alba Rosea" — not new but a well-tried favourite in temperate areas.

Purple-leaf Cherry Plum—a small-foliage tree for the garden. The single flowers are shell-pink.

Magnolia denudata—*dramatic blooms start appearing in July.*

Geraldton Wax—a native with prolific winter blossom.

Helleborus—a cool-climate perennial for winter-spring flowers.

Year-round colour from a collection of silver plants, including Artemesia and Lavender, set off by red gravel and a dark-green backdrop of conifers.

However, for the areas where Cherries do well, selection may be made from a number of beautiful varieties. *Prunus serrulata* varieties generally available are "Amanagawa", which has semi-double, light pink flowers; "James H. Veitch", with double rosy-pink flowers; "Mount Fuji", with double white, perfumed flowers; and the unusual, green-flowered Cherry "Ukon". If you like weeping plants look for the lovely *P. subhirtella pendula* (the weeping Rose-bud Cherry) with rose-pink flowers on pendulous growth weeping almost to the ground.

Prunus varieties grow in any good garden soil in a sunny position, and the blossoms will last longer if they are planted with some protection from the westerlies. They are sometimes attacked by borer, and it is worth keeping a lookout for signs of trunk attack — sawdust, webs and a gummy ooze are the usual symptoms. (See p. 121 for methods of eradication.)

Flowering Cherry (Prunus serrulata) *one of the most beautiful flowering trees for temperate and cool areas.*

Conifers

If I had five cents for every specimen of that popular gold-splashed Conifer *Chamaecyparis obtusa* "Crippsii" growing around Sydney I would be a rich lady.

The most unpretentious citizen, on becoming the owner of a front gate, can be seized by the overwhelming urge to plant a "Pine" tree on either side of it. But it is not always "Crippsii" — some people flank their gateways with *Pinus radiata* or *Cedrus deodara,* neither of which will stop short of 18 m (60 ft).

It is easy to get carried away with the neat elegance of Conifers. In the nursery they look so small and innocent that the gardener carries them home and plants them 15 cm (6 in) from the gate post — with not a thought of their ultimate height or spread. In a few years he will have to cut a tunnel through them to get in and out of the house. And while this may look very quaint, the Conifer's elegant shape is lost forever.

If you are already in this situation you have two choices. You can keep trimming the tree to keep it within bounds, and resign yourself to the curious shape the poor thing develops. Or you can tell yourself you paid a couple of dollars for it, you've had ten or fifteen years of pleasure from it, but now it has outgrown its situation and has to go. After all, you wouldn't expect a car to last as long, and cars cost a lot more than Conifers.

Once you have come round to this way of thinking, everything becomes simple. You buy the Conifer of your choice, enjoy it for ten or more years — then chop it down and start again.

But it really is better to plant Conifers which will not grow too big for your garden. Unless you have a really large garden it is best to avoid the big boys like Norfolk Island Pines which will rear up for 30 m (100 ft). There are plenty of Conifers suitable for small gardens.

A visit now to a Conifer nursery gives you the chance to see them in their winter coats. Many develop colours very much richer than their plain summer greens and blues. There you will find some short Conifers with long names like *Platycladus orientalis* "Minima Glauca". which grows only to 1 or 1.2 m (3 or 4 ft).

Cryptomeria japonica "Elegans", for instance, is bright green in summer but turns a rich russet colour in winter. "Elegans" grows to about 4 m (15 ft) with a spread of about 1 m (3 ft), making it a good size for the garden.

Junipers, tough and hardy, are useful and popular with many gardeners. Some have been reclassified Sabinas, which may be confusing when you buy them. The Meyer Juniper (now *Sabina squamata* "Meyeri") is a good garden size, about 2 × 1 m (6 × 3 ft). Junipers are useful for "privacy planting", but be cautious in using them to screen a swimming pool. Many Juniper leaves are very sharp, particularly the dead ones, and can be very painful to bare feet.

Some of the most charming Junipers are the prostrate varieties so useful to landscape gardeners. *Juniperus conferta* is a good ground-cover, spreading and quick growing, and useful for softening large areas of pebbles or cement. I have a much slower-growing juniper, *Juniperus scopulorum* "Repens", which is green in summer but at present has rich red stems with silvery purple foliage.

The subject of Conifers is so vast that I can't even begin to scratch the surface here but dwarf Conifers alone form an interesting facet, and a dwarf Conifer garden can be safely planted without fears for the power lines or danger of swamping a small garden. A little blood and bone for potted Conifers (not too much at a time or you'll encourage too much growth), and regular watering so that they don't dry out is all the care they need.

Many out-of-town gardeners have plenty of room for trees of nobler proportions than those mentioned above. Araucarias like the Norfolk Island Pine, the Bunya Pine and the Hoop Pine are splendid trees, reaching 30 m (100 ft) or more. They are adaptable to many soils and conditions and will give a handsome landmark — if you have the room. All three thrive on the coast and the Bunya also does well inland. It is well known for its large, pineapple-like cones — good to eat, but not too good to stand under when they are ripening.

Cedrus deodara (the Himalayan Cedar) is a handsome tree reaching about 18 m (60 ft) with a 6 m (20 ft) spread. The Atlas Cedar (*Cedrus atlantica*) likes deep soil and a cool climate. There are some lovely cultivars — "Aurea", gold tipped, and "Glauca pendula", a blue colour with drooping branches.

Pines are popular in the country as windbreaks — *Pinus radiata* is often used. *Pinus patula* is another very attractive Pine with distinctive drooping needles about 25 cm (10 in) long which hang like fringes all over it.

Callitris is a pretty and useful tree, even for fairly small gardens. *Callitris columellaris* (the Coast Cypress Pine) is denser than the Port Jackson Pine (*C. rhomboidea*) but both have a spread of only 3 m (10 ft). Callitris has the advantage of being only rarely attacked by borers, which makes it a good bet for a hedge. The Monterey Cypress, in contrast, is prone to borer in humid coastal areas.

One of the nicest things about Conifers is their smell. Have you ever noticed that the Golden Cypresses smell of lemons, and that *Chamaecyparis lawsoniana* smells like parsley when bruised? They don't all have a smell which appeals. I have heard the Savin Juniper (*Sabina vulgaris*) described as smelling of tom cats. But it is a very good hedging plant, and will grow near the beach.

If you long for one of these Conifers and don't have much room, they can be grown in tubs. Even the big ones will stay in a pot for years with care. They take on a rather gnarled and attractive "bonsai" look. An ideal Conifer for a tub is *Thuya occidentalis* "Reingold", a golden ball 1 m by 1 m (3 ft by 3 ft). And remember that all gold-tipped conifers need full sun to keep the golden look.

Japonica

Japonicas (Chaenomeles) are flowering well now and these thorny shrubs are one of the plants that should have old wood removed from the centre of the plant. People naturally avoid doing this because of the sharp thorns, but the plants will flower much better if they are kept open in the middle and not left cluttered with old and dead canes.

While the Japonicas are in full bloom is just the time to spot old non-flowering branches — mark them by tying a piece of coloured wool round them so they can be cut out when the plant has finished flowering. Use a pruning saw and gardening gloves or a pair of long-handled "high pruners" which will reach into a prickly shrub while you keep your distance.

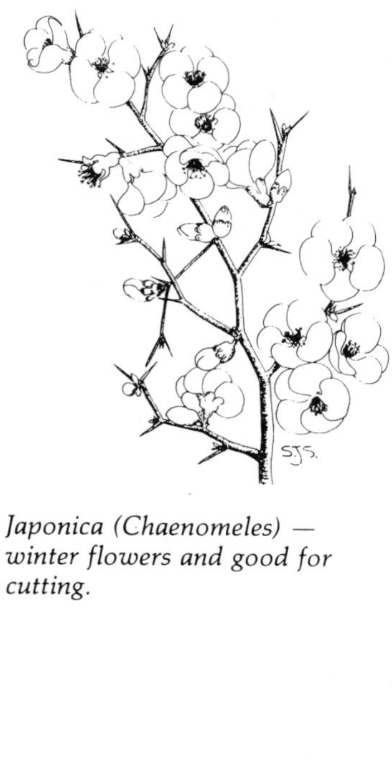

Japonica (Chaenomeles) — winter flowers and good for cutting.

Don't let the thorns put you off growing Japonicas — they are good sturdy shrubs that grow easily and provide brilliant winter flowers. Japonicas will tolerate poor soil, drought, frost and wind once they are established, although like everything else they need a little care when they are newly planted. Put them in full sun to get the best results and to get the effect of sunlight shining through the flowers on bare, brown stems.

Japonicas, or Flowering Quince, come in white, pink and white, rose pink and vivid reds. There is also a double pink variety. They have no perfume but, as well as adding colour to the garden, they make good, long-lasting flower arrangements if they are picked when the flowers begin to open. Bud-laden branches will continue to open for weeks in water.

Don't plant Japonicas near entrances or on paths where the thorns will be a problem to people passing or children playing. There is one position in the garden that is ideal. Japonicas make a good animal and people-proof hedge, though, being deciduous, they don't provide much privacy in winter. If you live on a busy street you will find a Japonica hedge across the front of your garden will deter people from putting their hands into your garden beds to steal plants.

Winter-flowering Azaleas

Winter-flowering Azaleas are a good source of colour for the July garden and there are a number blooming well now. I have been enjoying two plants of

Azalea *"Betty Cuthbert" — a winter-flowering Azalea with small semi-double, pale pink flowers.*

"Betty Cuthbert" blooming (in pots) among my Narcissus and Jonquils. This is a kurume type Azalea with small semi-double flowers, shell pink, with a cerise spotted throat. It is a charming flower, not spectacular but very appealing.

Other good winter-to-spring flowering Azaleas are "Agnes Neale", which has large, soft mauve, single blooms; "Autumn Beauty", a silvery-rose sport of "Searchlight"; "Early Splendour", also a sport of "Searchlight" which is new and has soft pink flowers edged with white; "Pink Champagne", pink semi-double; "Rose Queen", bright pink, semi-double; "Eclaireur", crimson with a dark blotch; "Orchidflora", orchid pink; "Pauline Mardner", double, bright pink; "Veronica", cerise, double; and "Deuche Perle", a white double. These are just a few suggestions.

Azaleas in bloom can be used for a week or two as indoor plants, but they need a well-lighted position. Azaleas are not very happy as house plants for very long. They start to drop their leaves which is a sure sign of stress. They make ideal patio or balcony plants in a sheltered, semi-shaded situation and can also be used in the garden to brighten up a special spot — beside a sitting-out area or near the entrance, for instance.

Azaleas make good container plants and can stay in fairly small pots for a number of years which makes them easy to move about for display purposes when they are in flower. Some make good basket plants for a sheltered position out of the wind. Choose smaller-growing doubles, perferably varieties which spot bloom over a long period before breaking into their spring flush. Here are some small-growing doubles: "Balsaminaeflora", rose pink; "Bouquet des Roses", red; "General Bridges", red; "Silver Jubilee", cerise with variegated foliage; and "Vervaeaena", pink, with a white border.

Although the winter-blooming Azaleas are not so prone to petal blight as those that flower in the more humid weather, petal blight is still around so pick off and burn infected flowers and spray with a fungicide as directed. If spraying is neglected now there will be a strong build-up of the disease in the garden ready and waiting to attack the spring flush.

Azaleas need well-drained, acid soil with plenty of humus, compost or peat moss dug in before planting. They prefer a situation where they get filtered sunlight, particularly during the flowering season. Some Azaleas — particularly the tall singles — will do quite well in a sunny position but the flowers fade quickly.

Keep Azaleas away from newly built brick walls as the lime in the soil from the concrete work will kill them. If the garden has heavy clay soil, grow your Azaleas in containers or build up a bed raised about 50 cm (20 in) above ground level, using compost, peat moss and sandy loam so that the Azaleas are growing well above the clay. Because they are shallow-rooted plants the root system will stay in the specially prepared soil and not find its way down into the clay.

If you have some Azaleas already established which you want to move, this is a good time to do the job. If the plants are not too big just cut right around them in line with the outer edge of the foliage, using a sharp spade. Push the spade down under the mass of roots which will be quite close to the surface and lift the plant with the root-ball intact. Replant immediately.

Larger bushes will need a slightly different technique. First make the cut around the plant and leave it for a few weeks to recover from the root loss, then begin lifting it, pushing a sheet of heavy plastic or bagging under it as you work so that by the time you have loosened the root-ball, you have the material right underneath it.

The plant can then be dragged to its new home or, if it is to go some distance, wrapped. To wrap, bring the sides of the material up around the stem of the plant and tie it firmly but not tightly. If not replanting straight away make sure the plant is kept watered. Azaleas die very quickly if allowed to dry out for even a short time.

When replanting make sure that the Azalea is not planted any deeper than it was before and keep it watered until it has recovered from the shock of moving.

Clerodendrum splendens — *scarlet clusters of winter flowers.*

CLIMBERS AND CREEPERS

Bright Winter Colour

In Brisbane in July the winter sun is so warm that it feels like spring. Two winter-flowering creepers make brilliant splashes of colour in gardens there — the orange *Pyrostegia ignea* (better known still by the old name of *Bignonia venusta*) and the scarlet *Clerodendrum splendens*. Both of these creepers can be grown quite well in humid coastal areas and it is surprising that they are not grown more out of the tropical zone.

Pyrostegia is a warm-climate plant but it stands up to frost quite well. Being a member of the Bignonia family, it is vigorous and fast-growing and looks spectacular covering a carport (roof and all), shed or wall. The clusters of drooping, tubular flowers hang like a curtain of brilliant colour through winter and into spring.

Clerodendrum has clusters of scarlet flowers with protruding stamens which are quite a feature of the flowers. The large, dark foliage is also attractive but is almost hidden by the shower of blossom. In temperature climates it seems to flower in late summer or autumn and continues into winter. A friend in Brisbane has a pergola covered in this climber right across the back of the house. Long flowering streamers trail through the beams and swing in the breeze, while the front of the pergola is a solid mass of red where the arching canes have twined together to make a living wall. (This is a great protection from the sun in summer.)

In temperate areas, Clerodendrum is best grown in a warm northerly aspect where it is protected from cold winds. It will grow in full sun but flowers that have some shelter from the hot afternoon sun will last longer and stay bright over many weeks. People in more tropical areas usually grow it where it is in part shade for some of the day. These two climbers are so showy that I would like to see more of them in home gardens.

Pyrostegia — a vigorous climber with pendulous orange winter flowers.

ROSES

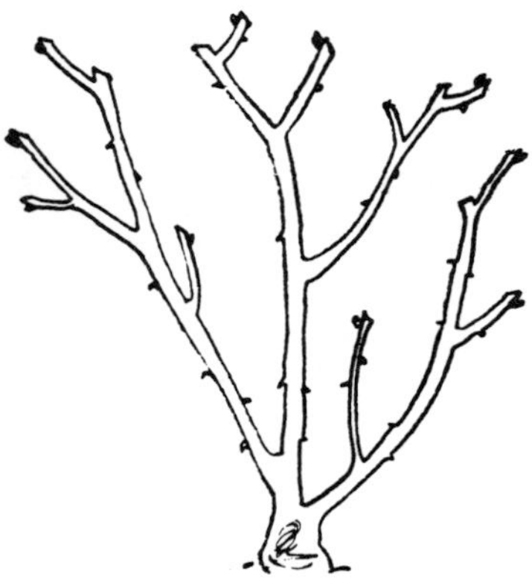

Prune Roses to healthy, outward-facing eye; make slanting cuts. Prune out dead wood.

Pruning Time is Here

Sharpen up your secateurs — it's Rose pruning time. Roses should be pruned now in all but frosty areas, where it is best to delay until August. To do a good pruning job on your Rose bed, you will need a pair of clean, sharp secateurs, a pruning saw — available from your nursery or hardware store and invaluable for cutting through wood that the secateurs can't handle — and a pair of gardening gloves. You should also have on hand some wound treatment paint such as Colgraft, and some lime sulphur (Harola) for use after pruning.

Roses flower best on young wood — particularly watershoots — and the main aim of pruning is to remove some of the older, unproductive wood to keep the plants young. All dead or diseased wood must be removed and spindly growth that is choking the centre of the plant can be taken out.

Roses should not be pruned too hard. Many gardeners make the mistake of chopping their Roses back to within a few inches of the base of the plant. This robs the plant of all the food stored in the branches. Some Roses never recover from this treatment and remain weak and sickly and die off after a few years.

Another bad habit home gardeners have is to prune all their roses off at the same height, regardless of the size of the plant, in the interests of neatness and uniformity. If you are growing a row of tall growers such as "Queen Elizabeth" or "Pink Parfait" as a hedge, you will naturally want to keep them an even height. But where a Rose bed has been planted with a mixture of small, medium and tall growers, each plant must be treated as an individual and pruned to suit its growth habits.

Don't prune spring-flowering climbing Roses — these must be pruned later when they have finished flowering. If you have a winter-bloomer — like "Lorraine Lee" — just remove the spent flowers with a few centimetres of stem to keep them blooming.

When you take out dead or diseased wood, remove it flush with the trunk. Don't leave a stump of dead wood to spread disease through the plant. Wipe your secateurs and pruning saw over with a cloth dipped in some antiseptic so that you don't carry disease on to healthy wood.

Shorten healthy stems back to a firm, plump eye. Choose an eye that faces outward and make the cut close to the eye and at the same angle.

If you have a lot of die-back in your Roses paint cut surfaces with Colgraft. Branches suffering from die-back should be cut several centimetres below the obviously damaged wood, as the infection travels downwards and the tissue inside the branch will be diseased, though the outside still looks healthy.

After pruning, spray plants with Harola to control fungus diseases like mildew and black spot. Rake up and burn prunings — they are difficult to compost and usually carry fungus spores. Although I don't usually advocate burning garden prunings, it is probably the safest course with Roses.

Roses should be fertilised after pruning, using animal manure or an all-purpose fertiliser. There are also special Rose fertilisers available. Roses prefer soil that is not too acid and an application of dolomite will improve Roses growing in acid conditions. Don't use too much fertiliser — it will encourage soft growth that will be more prone to disease. Always water well after applying fertiliser.

If you want to shift any of the Roses in your garden, this can be done after pruning. Dig the plants and replant in the new position immediately. Roses that have become too shaded or overcrowded will take on a new lease of life if moved to a better position, so don't hesitate to move Roses that are not thriving because of unsatisfactory conditions.

New Roses can still be planted and Roses put in now will get away quickly in the warming soil. Don't overlook the weeping Roses and climbers when you are choosing Roses because they add variety to the appearance of a Rose garden.

The Roses we buy are all grafted onto a rootstock, Japanese Brier (*Rosa multiflora*) is used in New South Wales because of its vigorous root system. In America it is generally used a lot in mass plantings 6 m (20 ft) high for crash barriers on highways — much more attractive than the white posts and steel railings of our highways.

Winter-flowering Peach, Snowflakes, Jonquils and early Daffodils bring a touch of spring.

BULBS

Armchair Gardening

Sometimes the weather in July is more suitable for armchair gardening than the actual outdoor type. Just the time to sit by the fire and look at catalogues and gardening books. Remember the time when nurseries put out those free catalogues in full colour? High printing costs have put an end to most of them but large nurseries still produce catalogues although they are no longer free. I have just received one from a Victorian nursery, with their winter list showing Gladioli, Dahlias, Liliums, Canna and Perennial Phlox, plus many others, suitable for planting between now and September.

Hippeastrums

Hippeastrums are gorgeous flowers, also easy to grow, and will last for many years once bulbs are established. Hippeastrums are sometimes called Amaryllis although this name is not correct — they are also called Hippies. Whatever common name you give them, they are well worth growing. The bulbs are very large and the Lily-like flowers are huge in shades of white, pink, cerise, scarlet and crimson. Some flowers are plain colours while others are striped or mottled. Like most bulbs they need well drained soil and should be planted so that the neck of the bulb is above the surface. They make good clump plantings but also make very handsome potted plants.

Hippeastrum — handsome striped or solid-colour Lilies flowering now make striking potted plants.

Hippeastrums are very popular in Europe where they are commonly grown on a sunny (or at least light) window-sill through the winter to flower as soon as the first warm spring days arrive. I have some in pots and bring them inside when they are about to flower. They are not prone to any pests or diseases but should be protected from snails with a little snail bait around them.

Hippeastrums make spectacular potted plants that can be raised on a window-sill if you do not have a garden, or brought indoors from the garden when the buds begin to open to serve as a showy houseplant. Because Hippeastrums do not have to be deeply planted they can be grown in quite a small pot with the neck of the bulb showing above the soil level. Add a couple of snail pellets to the pot to protect the young shoots.

Lilies

Liliums are also available from the perennial plant stands now. These gorgeous flowers are welcome additions to the summer garden and need well-drained, slightly acid soil with some shelter from the summer sun. If you grow Camellias and Azaleas, Liliums will make good companion plantings among them because both enjoy the same conditions of humus-rich soil and filtered sunlight.

Liliums can also be grown in a container on a balcony sheltered from strong winds or on a patio, the taller growing ones looking very handsome supported by a pillar or trained up a stake. Liliums never become completely dormant and should be planted as soon as possible after being lifted, so don't delay planting if you have bought bulbs or have lifted those already growing.

November Lilies (*L. longiflorum*) are probably the easiest to grow in the humid coastal areas and, unlike most Liliums, prefer some lime added to the soil. The November Lily grows on a sturdy stem up to 1 m (3 ft) high, each plant carrying several large, fragrant, pure white trumpet flowers. It is prone to mosaic virus infection and should be grown in a different part of the garden from other Liliums. However, because it needs the addition of lime while the others need acid soil, you would do this in any case. There are a number of named hybrid varieties of the November Lily, such as "Dutch Glory", which are very much improved versions of the old species.

A fairly recent development which is still going on is the dwarf Lilium. Only one has been released in Sydney and bulbs are still expensive (round $25 each). However, they multiply well and soon establish themselves in the garden.

Trumpet-flowered Liliums such as the "Aurelium", "Green Goddess", "Lotus" and "Superstar", can be planted now.

Asiatic hybrids introduce yellow, orange and red into your Lilium display, one of the most popular varieties being "Enchantment" which is nasturtium red with upward-facing flowers spotted black. Interesting Lilium hybrids which could be grown more are the American Bellinghams. These also have yellow, orange and red but have Turk's Head flowers with reflexed petals held on long stems. In humid coastal regions they grow about 1 m (3 ft) tall but reach twice this height in the mountains, where they do very well.

Unusual Bulbs to Pot

Many gardeners grow spring-flowering bulbs in pots but there are bulbs suitable for pot culture for other seasons too.

Apart from Hippeastrums, mentioned earlier, the Pineapple Lily (Eucomis) is another bulb that can be planted in a pot now for long-lasting spikes of flowers. *E. punctata* has very large spikes, cream with green tints and purple stamens and a sweet perfume. *E.* "Pink Sensation" is a beautiful variety with pink shaded flowers and lush bronze-green foliage.

Calla Lilies have elegant foliage, glossy green and spotted with white. The flowers resemble small Arum Lilies and these too make good pot-plants or can be planted in a fairly sunny part of the garden for plenty of flowers. Ismene, popularly called Peruvian Daffodil or Spider Lily, is another striking bulb for a pot. The flowers are borne four or five to a head on a long stem. They are unusually shaped, white with a green striped throat and perfumed.

Valotta, Scarborough Lily, is good in a pot or tub in semi-shade. Plant the bulbs with the neck showing above the soil and, if planting in the garden, make sure that drainage is very good. Flowers are intense scarlet in clusters.

NATIVES

Wattles

If you are thinking of growing more native greenery, you could start with a few Wattles. There are more than 400 species in Australia and their scent makes a big contribution to the mystical fragrance of the Australian bush.

Wattles (or Acacia) are valuable trees for the garden. They are quick growing and rather short-lived, as are many quick growers. But this should be no deterrent — simply plant another. They are good for the new garden because they will provide quick cover while more permanent trees are becoming established. Wattles are also suitable for small gardens because, apart from the Cedar Wattle (*A. elata*), they are all small trees or shrubs.

The fluffy golden flowers of the Queensland Wattle (*A. podalyriifolia*) brighten the chilly depths of June. Queensland Wattle is a pretty, small tree with silvery leaves and masses of scented, golden blossom. It grows quickly and does not have a troublesome root system.

It is followed this month by the Cootamundra Wattle (*A. baileyana*) and the two make a good companion planting. The silver-grey leaves (actually phyllodes) of the Queensland version contrast well with the soft, ferny, bipinnate leaves of the Cootamundra Wattle and as they flower in close succession, they provide a show of blossom through June, July and August. Purists will shudder, but I like the combination of the Queensland and

Cootamundra Wattle (Acacia baileyana), *one of the loveliest Wattles, blooms when it is most welcome — mid winter.*

Queensland Wattle (Acacia podalyriifolia). *It has golden flowers with grey felted foliage and provides bright colour in June.*

Acacia saligna *is a rapid-growing Wattle with big balls of bright golden blossom in spring.*

Cootamundra Wattles with Prunus varieties. If you think native plants should only be planted with other native plants try the compatible Purple Mint bush *(Prostanthera ovalifolia)*.

A. longifolia — the Sydney Golden Wattle — blossoms in August. It is good for coastal planting because it withstands salt winds and will grow in sand. Another Wattle I admire is *A. pycnantha*. It is a rapid grower, with green phyllodes and really big balls of bright golden blossom in spring. Grey Sally (*A. prominens*) — from the Central Coast of New South Wales — is a graceful tree growing to 6 m (20 ft) with yellow flowers in August and September.

A Wattle that grows freely in gardens and bushland is *A. saligna*. This native of Western Australia is fast-growing and graceful, forming a slender tree with long phyllodes (25 cm — 10 in) and very large deep gold balls of blossom. Black Wattle (*A. decurrens*) has bipinnate green leaves and creamy yellow flowers in August and September. It is a fast-growing tree which reaches 10 m (30 ft) so it is short-lived but attractive.

Summer-flowering species for garden use include *A. mollissima* (Green Wattle) which is from the central and southern tablelands of New South Wales and has creamy-yellow flowers and dark green bipinnate foliage. This tree grows to 10 m (30 ft) and flowers in November-December. The tall, stately Cedar Wattle (*A. elata*) is long-lived and grows to a height of 20 m (60 ft). Cedar Wattle has bronze new foliage turning green later and large cream balls in December-January.

There are many other good Wattle varieties, but those I have mentioned are available at general nurseries. Those specialising in natives would carry more unusual species, all well worth trying in a sunny, well-drained garden. They thrive in such conditions and once established they will survive dry conditions and total neglect.

They are prone to border attack, which often shortens their lives, but their fast growth balances this hazard and, like most fast-growing trees, Wattles are most beautiful while they are young. A succession of trees is an advantage and not expensive because they usually seed freely.

The best protection against fatal borer attacks is vigilance. Look for the tell-tale sawdust and holes — sometimes ring-barking a branch. Squirt methylated spirits into these holes with an eye dropper, and seal the hole with soap.

Wattles can also be subject to fungus gall infestation, a disease which causes large brown galls or swellings on the ends of branches. The galls grow quite large and cause the twigs to become deformed and develop a witch's broomstick effect. The galls are attacked by an insect but this is not the cause of the galls. Wattles attacked by this fungus should have the galls removed if the infestation is not too severe and the tree should be watered and fertilised with a complete fertiliser to improve the vigour of the tree and reduce the infestation.

EDIBLES

Herb Gardens

Mid-winter is not usually the time to think about herb gardens, but a mid-winter visit to Rosemary Hemphill's herb garden at Dural gave me food for new thought. While most herb beds have gone into temporary retirement during winter, Rosemary Hemphill's seem to have a charmed life — as befits the plants in a garden belonging to a writer on and grower of herbs.

Rosemary grows her herbs in a small, walled garden which provides them with a micro-climate. The westerlies are kept at bay and the walls also form a sun trap. The rough stone walls are double and filled with enough soil to support a hedge of Lavender on top.

Among the herbs flourishing inside the walls of stone and Lavender I found Watercress growing happily in damp, rich soil in full shade. This is true Watercress which normally grows by running water. Rosemary told me that so many people who bought seeds told her they were growing it this way that she decided to try it herself. The Watercress had been growing for about four months and was doing well. During dry weather she lets the hose drip on it for a while each day so that it does not dry out. True Watercress is delicious with salads or as a garnish and as the traditional English Watercress sandwich for afternoon tea.

1. Salad Burnett, 2. Chives, 3. Mugwort.

Two varieties of land Cress were also growing — Curled Cress and American Upland Cress. These grow in normal soil conditions and do not need to be kept constantly damp. As well as the Cress, Rosemary had Oregano, French Sorrel, Florence Fennel, Parsley, Garlic, Chives, Tansy and Salad Burnett growing.

The Fennel was from an autumn sowing which produces the thick, bulbous stems rather like celery at the base of the plant. This is white and crisp and can be sliced like celery or onion and added to a salad or used alone with a French dressing. It has a slight aniseed flavour which is very pleasant.

Spring is the time to plant most herb seeds but if you would like to grow them in a herb garden you will need to set about preparing it now. Rosemary's herb garden has paved paths around a sundial centrepiece. The garden beds are raised for better drainage, and the low stone walls provide a frame and protection for the herbs.

A herb garden should be put in a sunny spot and if you don't have room in your garden for a specially built section for herbs here are a couple of simple suggestions: The sunniest part of most back gardens is usually chosen to plant the rotary clothes line and the space under it is ideal for herb growing. Put down a couple of large paving stones where you stand to hang clothes and lay out the rest as a circular bed planted with the low growing herbs that form good ground-covers — Thyme, Parsley, Oregano, Salad Burnett and Chives. Don't plant Mint among it unless you put it in a large pot partly sunk into the bed so that you can control its spread.

Another way of growing herbs so as not to take up much room is to use hollow cement blocks as a garden edging with an open side facing up. Fill each with good soil and plant with the low-growers mentioned above. Herbs need good drainage and if your soil is on the heavy side planting them this way would help them grow better.

A window-box outside the kitchen window is another space and time saver — the closer the herbs are to the cook the better — and the effect looks as attractive as more conventional annuals. Include a plant of Tansy in your window-box. It is a good fly and moth repellent and will be appreciated particularly if you don't have fly-screens. Rosemary, who has a lot of Tansy growing said that she had had less trouble with flies in the garden since growing it. Bush flies can spoil gardening in summer so you might like to try some Tansy.

Vegetables are expensive and home-grown ones take up space. It is worth remembering that herbs are a rich source of vitamins and minerals, and do more than just add flavour to food. If you have not got room for a full-scale vegetable garden, create some space for a herb garden.

In the USA, indoor herb planters are obtainable with a built-in light so that they can be put on a shelf in the kitchen of a flat or unit without access to a sunny garden. This is a marvellous idea and one that could be used here. It would be no trouble for a handyman to build and Gro-lux lights are available in Australia.

It is no good growing herbs if you do not use them, and there are a number of books on the market devoted to herb growing and cooking. Rosemary Hemphill has written several books on herbs and spices and there are several other locally-written books on herbs.

Tomatoes for Christmas

If you want to raise some early tomatoes, try planting seeds in small pots (Jiffy pots or similar sized containers) and put them on a sunny window-sill. Plant two or three seeds in each pot and when they are well up cull the weaker ones so that you have one strong plant in each container. When the pot is full of roots, move the tomatoes into a slightly larger container.

When they get too big for the window-sill you can move them outside into a warm, sheltered position against a sunny, north-facing wall or fence. Cover your plants at night with a cloche made from a plastic flagon with the bottom cut out (this enables you to hang all your cloches up on a hook with a piece of string through the handles).

By the time the weather is warm enough to plant them out in the garden, your tomatoes will be super-advanced, giving you the chance to pick the crop before Christmas — the goal of all home tomato-growers.

INDOORS

Pots for Pleasure

I find that pots of flowering Primroses have a soothing effect and have a window-sill sporting a collection of them at present. I am more fond of the simple Primrose with its stems of single flowers rather than the larger Polyanthus Primrose with heads of flowers carried on a stout stem. Lately there seem to be quite a lot of the single Primroses in pale or deep blue, yellow, red and pink, rather than the odd single among the Polyanthus varieties. However, they are delightful flowers, whether single or multi-flowered, and definitely soothing to the spirit.

Single Primroses in pale or deep blue, yellow, red and pink — soothing to the spirit and ideal indoor colour at this time of year.

Not all flowers are soothing to live with. One popular flower which seems often to be infuriating rather than relaxing is the African Violet. Most people have succumbed to the charms of this plant at some time and carried it home covered in blooms, treated it tenderly and then watched it fade away or, perhaps worse, grow luxuriantly but never re-flower.

Some people have success with African Violets by accident. They happen to put the plant down in a spot that suits it perfectly. I met a woman once who had a large collection of African Violets which grew and flowered like magic. Apparently, while waiting for her husband to put up some shelves when they moved into a new house, she had put her African Violets on the dining-room table. The shelves somehow didn't get built and the African Violets grew so well on the table that after a while it was completely covered with pots and the family ate in the kitchen.

During this month you might be able to buy pots of bright golden Reinwardtia (Linum) in flower. It, fortunately, is easily grown and is a cheerful plant which carries its flowers right through winter.

There are also some pots of early golden Daffodils in flower now. A nice idea, if you can find it, is the combination of Daffodils and one golden Jonquil which adds perfume. Pots of Daffodils are intended for indoor use and, as long as they are given a well-lighted position, they will continue to flower indoors for some weeks. When the blooms fade the plants should be moved outdoors to a sunny spot and fed and watered until the leaves begin to yellow.

Also easy to grow indoors are dwarf Poinsettia. Their bright red flowers would warm up any indoor or balcony garden and they last and last.

Pots of Daffodils require a well-lighted position if taken indoors.

CHECKLIST

August is Magnolia month in many districts. These beautiful trees are flowering in many gardens with pure white or pink to mauve blossoms on bare branches. They make good specimen plantings in a lawn and need good drainage, acid soil and protection from hot or strong winds.

Flowering Now

Trees and Shrubs:
Azaleas,
Buddleia salvifolia,
Camellia (*japonica* and *reticulata* varieties),
Coleonema (Diosma),
Crassula,
Japonica,
Lantana montevidensis,
Magnolia,
Michelia,
Polygala,
Prunus cerasifera (Cherry Plum),
P. campanulata (Bell Cherry),
P. blireana,
P. persica,
Psoralea,
Virgilia.

Perennials and Annuals:
Daisy (Marguerite),
Helleborus,
Iceland Poppy,
Pansy,
Polyanthus Primrose,
Primula,
Ruella,
Viola,
Violet.

Bulbs:
Clivea,
Daffodil,
Freesia,
Hyacinth,
Lachenalia,
Narcissus,
Snowflake.

Climbers:
Clerodendron splendens,
Gelsemium (Carolina Jasmine),
Jasminum polyanthum,
Pyrostegia venusta,
Thunbergia grandiflora.

Natives:
Acacia,
Boronia,
Chamaelaucium (Geraldton Wax),
Clematis aristata,
Correa,
Crotalaria (Bird Flower),
Epacris,
Eriostemon,
Grevillea,
Hardenbergia,
Prostanthera (Mint Bush),
Thryptomene.

The chill winds of August are with us but so are the spring flowers — Violets, Roman Hyacinths and Snowflakes

AUGUST

Plant

Trees, Shrubs and Climbers:
This is the last month for planting out bare-rooted Roses. Deciduous fruit trees, nut and citrus trees can be planted, also deciduous flowering trees and vines. Many ornamental trees are offered in bloom through spring. Azaleas and Camellias are also available.

Perennials and Annuals:
Finish planting herbaceous perennials as soon as possible.

Seeds and seedlings where available of Ageratum,
Alyssum,
Antirrhinum (Snapdragon),
Candytuft,
Cleome,
Delphinium,
Dianthus,
Gloxinia,
Godetia,
Gypsophila,
Larkspur,
Linaria,
Lupin (annual),
Mignonette,
Statice,
Virginia Stock.

Warm districts only:
Balsam,
Marigolds,
Petunias,
Phlox.

Bulbs:
Agapanthus,
Bearded Iris,
Calla,
Canna,
Eucomis,
Gladiolus,
Hippeastrum,
Hemerocallis (Day Lily),
Ismene,
Tuberous Begonia,
Valotta (Scarborough Lily).

Vegetables:
Potatoes put in this month will grow well and seed potatoes are available from nurseries.

In all districts plant:
Artichoke (Jerusalem),
asparagus crowns,
carrot,
lettuce,
parsley,
parsnip,
radish,
silverbeet
sweet corn.

Coastal areas:
Aubergine (egg plant),
capsicums,
choko,
cucumber,
marrow,
pumpkin,
rhubarb crowns,
tomato,
squash.

Cool-temperate areas only:
Broad beans,
cabbage,
carrot,
peas.

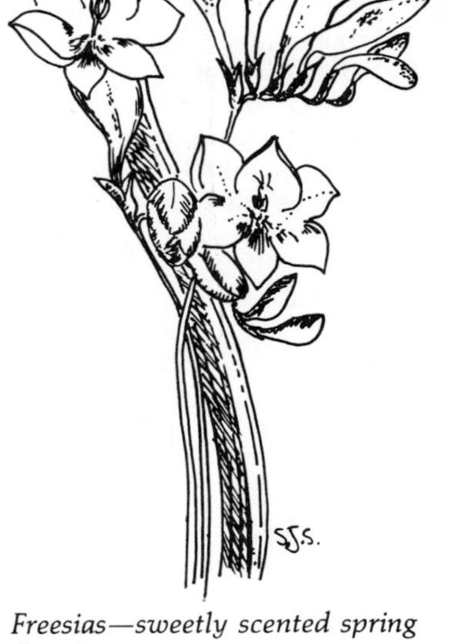

Freesias—sweetly scented spring flowers.

Fertilise

Help annuals along with water-soluble fertilisers such as Aquasol, Thrive and Zest or with side dressings of an all-purpose fertiliser.

Citrus should be fertilised with citrus food or sulphate of ammonia spread to outer line of foliage and watered in well.

Strawberries require side dressings of complete fertiliser.

Fertilise blue Hydrangeas and water well. If desired apply Hydrangea blueing compound as directed on container. Further applications are made in September and October.

Narcissus that have finished flowering, Agapanthus and other summer-flowering shrubs should also be fertilised with an all-purpose or foliar fertiliser.

Prune

Finish pruning Roses in cold districts (except spring-blooming types); Cotoneasters if not already cut back (or shaped if hedges); winter-flowering Peach as soon as flowers finish.

Camellias can be trimmed or pruned to shape if necessary after flowering.

Remove dead wood from lemons and shorten fruiting laterals as crop is picked.

Prune to shape Oleander (Nerium), Fuchsia, Hypericum, Heliotrope, Tibouchina (Lasiandra), Vitex (Chaste Tree) and Poinsettia when bracts have finished.

Pests and Diseases

Watch for aphids on new growth, buds and flowers. New Rose growth is often attacked by the Rose aphid. Spray with pyrethrum-based garden spray as directed on pack or use a garlic spray. (See p. 142.)

Slugs and snails are prevalent on vegetable and flower seedlings and bulbs, particularly Clivea — protect plants with snail pellets.

For cabbage moth caterpillars starting to attack cabbage, stocks and other members of the crucifer family, dust with Derris.

Leaf miner in Cinerarias and Marguerites should be sprayed with Rogor as directed on pack.

Bindii in lawns should be sprayed with Weedoben as directed on the pack.

Watch for cup moth larva on Eucalyptus, Brush Box, Angophoras and Pittosporums. Stinging spines at each end of the body cause a painful rash on contact. Spray Malathion as directed on pack or inject Rogor as directed on pack.

Mealy bug on Norfolk Island Pines is usually controlled by ladybirds.

Byrobia mite (light pink eggs on bark) on Almonds, Apples, Pears and Plums require spraying with red oil as directed on pack.

*Cheerful winter colour is provided by both the Cootamundra Wattle (*Acacia baileyana*) and* Jasminum mesneyi.

Both "The Czar", a Camellia, and Japonica bloom from July to September giving months of vivid colour and a foretaste of spring.

For citrus gall wasp (swellings on branches) remove and burn infected branches before the end of August when insects reach adult stage.

For shot hole of Prunus (small holes in foliage, die-back and gumming) spray with Bordeaux at pink bud stages.

Leaf curl of peaches (swollen distorted leaves with pink and yellow colouring on Peaches and Nectarines in particular) spray at bud swell with Bordeaux.

Mottle leaf on citrus (yellow, irregular mottle on leaves) should be sprayed with zinc sulphur spray.

Spray Azaleas for petal blight with Mancozeb.

Citrus gall wasp: cut and burn before the end of this month.

Garden Care

Spring annuals are coming on well and need attention to keep up the quantity and quality of blooms. Remove all spent heads. Iceland Poppies will reward you well for this and for regular applications of liquid fertiliser.

Nip the centre head of flowers out of Wallflowers to force side shoots and produce a sturdy bush with plenty of flowers.

Keep Azaleas regularly watered to extend blooming time. Don't wet flowers as this spreads petal blight.

THE AUGUST GARDEN

The wind now might be straight off the snow, but in the draughty canyons of the city the word is spring. Department stores are dazzling with Daffodils (real ones, praise be!) and baskets of Daffodils, Violets and fragrant brown Boronia are being hawked on street corners.

Once the Daffodils and Prunus start flowering I can't help feeling it's spring — even though the official date is next month. Every day there is something else in bloom, and it is like meeting old friends to go out and see your favourites in flower again.

Early flowering Peaches are at their best. My own are a little disappointing because they often come into leaf as well as bloom — but others I have seen flower while satisfactorily bare.

Prunus blireana also looks delightful now. It is a small tree and smothers itself in double, rose-pink flowers. When they appear, the leaves will be a light purple-green. The Prunus varieties are a bit confusing to some people because they cover the stone fruits — Peach, Cherry, Plum, Almond, Apricot, and Nectarine as well as crosses between them.

P. blireana, for instance, is a hybrid of *P. mume,* the flowering Apricot and *P. cerasifera atropurpurea,* the Cherry Plum. Perhaps the trickiest is *P. laurocerasus,* the English Laurel, an evergreen bush used as a hedge and responsible for so many houses in England being called "The Laurels". Though it does bear fragrant flowers, it is not in any sense a "blossom tree" like other Prunus grown for their beautiful flowers.

One of the nicest things about most spring-flowering trees like Prunus and Magnolias is that they are so suitable for small gardens. The largest will not grow taller than 6 to 8 m (20 to 25 ft) and, being deciduous, they will provide shade in warm weather but let the winter sun stream through.

A rustic planter — a hollowed out Birch log filled with Pansies, as seen in Germany. An idea for Australian gardeners.

GARDENKEEPING

Mossy Lawns

What can you do with moss in a damp part of the lawn? A good control is to use a solution of sulphate of iron at the rate of two tablespoons to half a bucket of water and repeat after a week. For long term results it is best to improve the drainage of the area of lawn that becomes mossy. Moss in lawns is usually more evident in winter when the lawn is more shaded and stays damp.

A quick and easy way to improve drainage in lawns is to lift the turf and spread several centimetres of clinker ash or coke ash over the soil before replacing the turf and pressing it down firmly. This will raise the level of the damp area slightly as well as helping moisture to drain away below the grass.

If large areas under trees or at the side of a house that is heavily shaded in winter are suffering badly with moss, it is better to get rid of the grass and plant a shade and damp-tolerant cover like Selaginella, Helxine (Baby's Tears) or Ivy. Or you can gravel the area with decorative pebbles about 6 cm (2½ in) deep.

Fuchsia Care

Fuchsias are growing vigorously now and should be gently tip pruned by nipping off the growing tips with the thumb. This will force side growth from lower on the stem, and give a bushier shrub with more flowers. I like to keep my Fuchsias low and bushy, but there are other ways of treating them.

At the Chelsea Flower Show I saw one which had been grown as a creeper and trained up a tall, curving pole so that the flowers cascaded the whole length in a most decorative way. To try this idea you would need a very sheltered position out of the wind.

Fuchsias respond well to feeding and can be given fortnightly watering with Aquasol, Zest, Thrive or similar foliar fertiliser.

Blue or Pink Hydrangeas

If you want to keep Hydrangeas blue, water on some Hydrangea blueing compound available from nurseries and hardware stores. I love all those half-pink Hydrangeas that are neither blue nor pink but subtle variations of mauve. But if you prefer them one or the other, blueing compound will make them decisively blue and lime will pink them up. Water the Hydrangeas before applying the blueing mixture to avoid any burning.

Oxalis

Another fairly prevalent problem is Oxalis. I have a query from a gardener whose vegetable garden is full of it and he is desperate because weeding only seems to encourage more growth.

This is a familiar feeling for anyone who has suffered from infestations of Oxalis which multiplies rapidly. Each bulb produces countless tiny bulbs beside the "mother" bulb. It is these tiny bulblets that do the damage when you are weeding. They drop away from the parent plant so that instead of one plant of Oxalis you have dozens.

Oxalis is difficult to poison but this can be done if you are as persistent as the plant. Water or spray the leaves with Zero weed killer and the poison is translocated to the bulb. The leaves turn yellow, or rather a whitish colour, and die off. Any re-growth has to be sprayed again.

This treatment is difficult when there are plants growing round the Oxalis because if the spray touches them they will be killed too. Zero (a Ciba Geigy product) leaves a shiny residue on any plant sprayed and it is easy to see if you have accidentally sprayed a valued plant. If the spray is washed off at once the plants will not be harmed.

In a vegetable garden, the most satisfactory method of getting rid of the pest would be to sieve the soil — a tedious but effective method. Do this by degrees, marking off the bed with a stringline which can be moved as each section is completed. Tip all bulbs and bulblets into a carton and burn or wrap up and put it in the garbage bin.

Some people claim that Oxalis is fire proof. This is because the small bulbs will drop unburned through the fire and when the ashes are scraped out and used on the garden they go back and grow again.

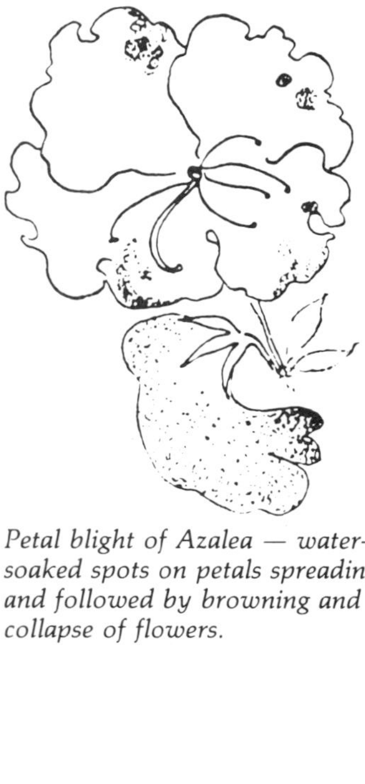

Petal blight of Azalea — water-soaked spots on petals spreading and followed by browning and collapse of flowers.

Azalea Care

Azaleas are coming into their spring flush. Regular watering round the bases of the plants will help extend the blooming to the longest possible time. Azaleas wilt quickly if allowed to dry out and though they respond dramatically to water, the flowers will fall quickly if they are treated this way.

Azaleas are particularly susceptible to petal blight as a result of wet weather which spreads its spores. All Azaleas that are either blooming or in bud should be sprayed with fungicide to prevent sudden losses of blossom. Petal blight is more familiar to gardeners now. One of the reasons for its rapid spread in past seasons has been the failure of gardeners to recognise the disease, so that it has spread unchecked. If your Azaleas collapsed quickly last spring, don't wait for symptoms to reappear but get in and spray.

Garlic Spray

Aphids are already attacking new Rose shoots. A mild winter means that pests are not killed off by the cold weather and insect and fungus pests come out in full force to attack new spring growth.

Several friends have asked for a non-toxic spray for aphids. The recipe for the one I recommend — garlic spray — is very effective for aphids and cabbage moth caterpillars and is sudden death to mosquitoes. Experiments are being carried out to see if it can be used for control of malaria in countries where the mosquitoes have become resistant to DDT. It is not the sort of thing you spray round the living-room, but can be used on stagnant water where mosquitoes breed.

Garlic Spray: Soak 90 g (3 oz) chopped garlic in 2 teaspoons of kerosene or white oil for forty-eight hours. Dissolve 8 g (¼ oz) of oil-based soap in a little hot water, add more water to make 500 ml (a pint) and add to the garlic mixture. Use 1 part garlic solution to 99 parts water.

The mixture should be strained and stored in a plastic container; it becomes stronger after being kept for a few weeks, but may be used immediately. Use the garlic spray as often as necessary and always repeat after rain.

Lemon Scab

Lemons, in coastal areas particularly, can be infected with the fungus disease lemon scab. Lemon scab attacks Lemons at the time of blossoming and petal fall, but the disease may not be noticed until the fruit develops warty growths accompanied by scabby areas on the fruit skin and on leaves and twigs.

The fruit is not damaged internally, but lemon scab can cause severe fruit-fall in the young crop. The treatment is to spray with Bordeaux mixture, with the addition of a little white oil as a spreader, applied before all the petals have fallen from the spring blossom.

A second spray should be given around the second week in February after about half the petals have fallen from the blossoms that appear in the early weeks of the new year.

Another pest to watch for is the citrus gall which shows up as swellings on branches of lemon trees. The affected branches must be pruned and burnt. It is actually illegal to have trees infected with galls and the Department of Agriculture might catch you if you don't cut them out.

Lemon scab — a fungus disease causing wart-like growths and scabby areas on fruit and leaves.

Frost Treatment

If you have had plants blackened by frost don't be tempted to prune them to make them look better. The upper canopy of foliage, even though damaged, is still protecting the lower parts of the plants. Wait until the frosts are over to tidy up. And in most cases the plants will send out fresh growth in spring.

Gardeners growing Hibiscus where there is any likelihood of frost could also take this to heart. No matter how tatty your Hibiscus is looking, don't prune it until the weather warms up. The outside of the bush acts rather like a blanket, keeping the air round the plant warm.

TREES AND SHRUBS

The Advantages of Deciduous Trees

Several people have said to me "I hate deciduous trees." I don't know why anyone should hate deciduous trees. All those fallen leaves in autumn worry some people, but they are a wonderful source of leaf mulch for the

Catalpa, a beautiful deciduous spring-flowering tree. The frilly bell-like blooms are pale pinky-white with splashes of purple and yellow.

garden and the leaves fall all at once rather than throughout the year as the evergreens do.

Since deciduous trees are at their most attractive in spring, it is an opportunity to remind you of their good points. Most trees and shrubs that lose their leaves flower before the new leaf appears, so that the blossom display has a much greater impact than it has on trees that have their flowers partly hidden in leaves. Even before the new flowers or leaves appear, deciduous trees look interesting. The downy new buds catch the sunlight and shimmer in any breeze. Flowering trees change colour from day to day as they go from bud to blossom and then to spring leaf.

A deciduous tree is suitable for a small garden where it will provide shade in summer, when it is appreciated, but let the sun shine through during autumn, winter and spring so that spring flowering bulbs and annuals can be grown successfully round it.

If you are prejudiced against deciduous trees, take another look at them this spring. Perhaps you'll decide they're not all that bad. There are plenty of deciduous trees available for planting from your local nursery now.

Magnolias

I did a double-take when a friend remarked that after such a windy day his Magnolia would be out when he got home. I looked at all the Magnolias I passed on the way home — and they were all coming out! The effect of the dry westerly wind on the buds is to dry the calyx so that it splits, allowing the bud to open. It is quite obvious but, I must admit, I had never thought of it before. Anyway, the Magnolias are all in full bloom now and looking exquisite.

Apart from the large evergreen *M. grandiflora,* Magnolias are ideal small trees for the home garden. *M. denudata* and the purplish-pink and white *M. soulangeana* are the best. *M. soulangeana* reaches about 4.5 m (15 ft). *M. denudata* has the common name of Yulan Tree and it is a native of central China. It is an upright tree with spreading branches growing about 9 m (30 ft) tall, though it is taller in its native environment. The large, pure-white flowers are an open bell shape and very sweetly scented and are well displayed on the bare branches. It is a beautiful sight in full bloom and makes an ideal specimen tree for a garden. Foliage is large, green above and downy below and dense in summer. *M. denudata* is not a common tree but Magnolias of many kinds are now more readily available from nurseries and there should be no difficulty in obtaining them.

For the very small garden there is the more shrub-like *M. stellata* which only grows to 3 m (10 ft) and covers itself with starry white flowers which are very pretty but lack the grace of the others. A dainty pink variety is also available.

The evergreen *M. grandiflora* is very different from the deciduous Magnolias. It is a warm-climate tree from the southern USA, growing to around 10 m (30 ft). It has glossy green leaves and in summer bears masses of scented white flowers up to 25 cm (10 in) across. In the Neutral Bay-Cremorne-Mosman area of

Sydney there are many splendid Magnolias in old gardens, framing the beauty of old cast-iron verandahs and gingerbread eaves, and thriving in the warm coastal atmosphere.

The Port Wine Magnolia is worth mentioning for its fruity fragrance though it is no longer classed as a Magnolia and is now named Michelia. The flowers are small, purple and insignificant but they fill the garden with perfume and the glossy foliage is dense and attractive. The name of Port Wine Magnolia is sometimes mistakenly applied to *M. soulangeana nigra* which has dark wine-coloured blooms, but since the real Port Wine Magnolia has lost its status, perhaps this does not matter.

I recently saw a member of the Magnolia family, *Michelia doltsopa*, which I have not seen before. It is a shrubby small tree, about 5 m (16 ft) tall in Australian gardens although it can grow to around 28 m (90 ft) in its native region of the Himalayas. *M. doltsopa* has large, white, semi-double flowers with a tinge of lime green at the base of the petals. The flowers are highly perfumed with a fragrance of mingled Gardenias and spice. I don't know whether this Michelia is sold by many nurseries, although the tree I saw came originally from a local nursery, but its perfume is every bit as fascinating as the better-known *Michelia figo* (Port Wine Magnolia) and the flowers are far superior to the insignificant little purplish-brown flowers of that shrub.

Another Michelia which is available from some nurseries is *Michelia champaca* — an evergreen which grows to 6 m (20 ft) with yellow, scented flowers. *M. champaca* is suitable for humid coastal climates but requires a sunny position sheltered from winds and frost.

Magnolias need a loamy garden soil with plenty of leaf mulch to retain moisture during summer. They like similar conditions to Camellias and Azaleas and should not be limed. If possible, plant them in a position where they will get some protection from hot or strong winds. They do not need pruning and should be allowed room to grow naturally.

In addition to their great beauty, Magnolias are generally free from pests and diseases, though some people have trouble with birds (usually Bulbuls) pecking holes in the base of buds to reach the nectar.

Magnolia stellata — *a spreading shrub with scented white flowers gracing gardens this month.*

An unusual member of the Magnolia family — Michelia doltsopa.

Psoralea

Psoralea is just beginning to flower. This is a very pretty, shrubby plant — a large shrub or a small tree, depending on how you look at it. It covers itself in a dense mass of sweetly-perfumed mauve-blue pea flowers and grows quickly and easily in any ordinary garden conditions. Like all quick growers it can be short-lived, but is well worth a place in a small garden.

Coleonema

A small, heath-like shrub which is covered in masses of pink flowers at this time of year is Diosma. The name of this plant has been changed to Coleonema, by the way. It is very easy to grow — so easy that many people believe it to be a native plant.

Coleonema enjoys full sun and will grow in any average garden soil. Its dense growth habit makes it particularly suited to clipping and it can be used as a low hedge. If it is clipped immediately after flowering and trimmed again to tidy up summer growth it will produce a mass of flowers in spring. Plants left untrimmed develop into rangy shrubs and lose the rounded shape that is part of their charm.

Helleborus — the Christmas Rose. A useful perennial for a shady position. Flowers are white, pinks and purples of varying shades.

PERENNIALS AND ANNUALS

Helleborus

I was given a gorgeous bouquet of spring flowers recently and among them an unusual flower — the Christmas Rose (Helleborus) — attracted attention. The flowers (actually sepals) are green-flushed and spotted with pinkish mauve. They also have tubular yellowish nectaries and fairly prominent stamens.

There are a number of Hellebores, usually called Christmas Rose or Lenten Rose, though *H. niger* is specifically the Christmas Rose. They are not related to the Rose family, but belong to the Ranunculaceae. It takes a vivid imagination to see any resemblance to a Rose.

Their rather curious charm lies in their greenish flowers and winter-flowering habit. They make an interesting addition to the perennial garden. Hellebores like moist, shaded conditions with rich, well-drained soil. Once established, the clumps should not be disturbed. They should not be allowed to dry out. Use a thick mulch to keep the soil moist in summer.

Hellebores are occasionally available from nurseries, but it would be easier to get them from a specialist perennial nursery. Sometimes Hellebores droop when you use them for cut flowers, but they will last in a float bowl.

Spider Lily (Hymenocallis) — delicate white summer blooms — which can be planted now.

Spider Flowers

If you suffer from arachnophobia, perhaps you should skip the next few paragraphs about Spider flowers.

Cleome, a shrubby annual with two-tone pink or lilac flowers, earns its Spider flower name from the masses of long, conspicuous stamens that curl out from each flower rather like a spider's legs. It is a quick-growing, sturdy annual with a long flowering period into late summer. It grows and flowers very quickly from seed sown where it is to grow.

My first experience of this flower was when, some years ago, I noticed some visitors arriving at the door. A quick glance at the sitting-room revealed a bunch of faded Cleome which I hastily dispatched out of the windows into the garden bed below. The following summer, and every summer after, a splendid clump of Cleome grew unbidden on the spot — a reminder of my emergency housekeeping and an example of how easy it is to grow from seed planted at this time.

Another Spider flower is the bulb Hymenocallis or Ismene (commonly called Spider Lily) belonging to the Amaryllidaceae family. The Spider Lily forms a large clump of green, strap-like leaves and has white flowers in summer. It is one of those things that will grow almost anywhere and can be grown in full sun or partial shade, in any well-drained garden soil.

Violets

A common cause of complaint with Violets is that they never flower (they're not called "shy" for nothing). The reason is generally a lack of sun. Violets will flower best where they get full sun through the winter months and some summer shade, preferably from lightly foliaged deciduous trees. Too much nitrogen is another reason for plenty of leaf growth and lack of flowers.

If you are having problems with your Violets move them into a more sunny position, and prepare the bed beforehand with well-rotted manure. Violets like the soil with a pH of 6.0 to 7.0, similar to Sweet Peas. Water regularly in spring and summer to deter red spider attacks (they like dry conditions) and use a fertiliser low in nitrogen.

A number of named varieties are available from nurseries. Most trade growers use "Princess of Wales". "King of the Doubles" is a most attractive deep violet blue with a white centre. Then there are the Parma Violets beloved of heroines in romantic novels. These are a little different from *Viola odorata* and more sweetly perfumed. "Duchess de Parme" has large double flowers, lavender blue on 15 cm (6 in) stems.

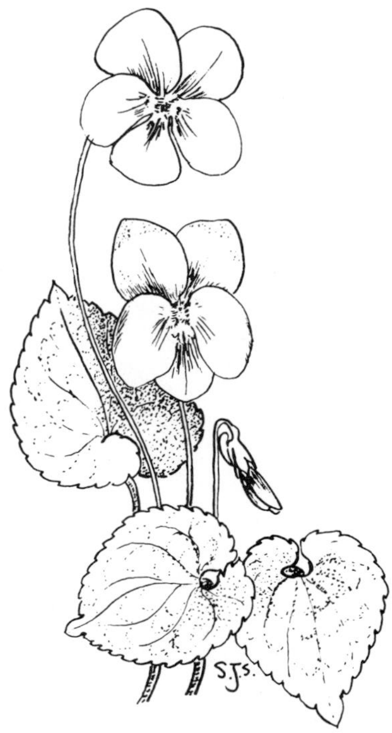

Violets are available in flower at present. This is "Purple Robe". The large, scented flowers are held well above the foliage.

Godetia

An easily grown summer annual is Godetia. This flower does not seem to be grown much these days but it is worth trying.

The seed can be sown directly into the garden where it is to grow. Godetia seed is fairly fine and you will find it easier to sprinkle any fine seed if you put it into an empty container with a shaker top (like talcum powder for instance) and add some dry sand. Give it a shake to mix well and then sprinkle over the planting area. Cover the seed with a thin layer of soil. Don't cover too deeply or the tiny shoots will never make it above ground. Keep the soil damp. Seed planted in this way will be more evenly spaced and there will be less wastage with thinning.

Keep spring annuals blooming with regular watering and an application of liquid fertiliser.

ROSES

Green Roses

Looking round a garden recently I saw a completely green Rose — not a victim of "greening" virus but a real, green Rose. It is *Rosa chinensis viridiflora* and is similar to the Cecil Brunner Rose in size and shape though not in colour. The petals are an unusual shape, narrow with irregular serrations at the ends. The colour is a clear green, with a brown tinge developing on the outer petals as the flower ages.

This Rose bush would be a must for the flower arranger, with the advantage of flowering throughout the year and of lasting well as a cut flower. I don't think it is sold at many nurseries but *R. chinensis viridiflora* can be grown from cuttings because it has a vigorous root stock.

Cool-climate Pruning

For gardeners in cold and frosty areas Rose-pruning time is here again. Roses flower best from young, vigorous wood, and pruning, which encourages plenty of new growth, is done for other reasons too. It enables a bush to be maintained at a suitable size and shape to fit its position in the garden, and is an opportunity to get rid of dead or diseased wood. Shorten stems back to a plump bud, taking care not to leave "hat-pegs", the result of cutting too far above the bud so that you end up with a peg of dead wood above the new shoot.

Water shoots — the lush red shoots which usually come from fairly low down on the bush — should not be cut off. They will produce plenty of flowers later.

Don't prune newly planted Roses or climbers, which are pruned after flowering. Remember, the smaller the Rose, the smaller the amount of pruning needed. Don't get carried away and hack into minis too much because you'll have nothing left to flower.

BULBS

Prepacked Bulbs

There are some bulbs, rhizomes and crowns in little nets or plastic bags on the bulb and perennial stands this month.

Japanese Iris (*Iris kaempferi*) which grow in water and flower in December, can be planted out now. They grow beautifully in pools but should be planted in a pot and gently submerged for the summer growing season. This Iris likes wet feet in summer and dry ones in winter, when it can be lifted from the water and set aside until the following spring.

Hippeastrum bulbs planted now should flower in late spring. This bulb is also a member of the Amaryllis family and should be planted with its neck above the soil. It makes a very handsome potted plant and can be grown on a patio or balcony and brought indoors when it comes into bloom.

You will also find Day Lilies (Hemerocallis) in several good colours. These make marvellous clump plants and are good soil holders. Sprekelia, or Aztec Lily, is another summer flowering bulb available now for spring planting. Being another member of the Amaryllis family, it has its neck at soil level. In summer it has dark red flowers which are an unusual shape, sometimes described as a Maltese cross. Leave them undisturbed to form good clumps and they will provide you with plenty of flowers.

Gladioli bulbs are there, too for immediate planting. I had some which had developed a white fungus on the base of the bulbs which turned out to be a harmless penicillin mould, which will not affect growth in any way.

The fungus is a symptom of the difficulties of packaging these plants in plastic bags. There is nothing basically wrong with the packaging system which allows the customer to see the bulbs or crowns inside, but they react to the conditions they are exposed to in the nurseries and stores. Sometimes they are kept in air-conditioned buildings, where they dry out quickly. Others are in hot, humid conditions which make the bags moist inside and can start the bulb rotting. However, these bulbs and perennial crowns are in good condition when they come into the shops and if you buy them quickly when they first appear on the stands you will be assured of a healthy bulb.

Day Lilies (Hemerocallis) easily grown members of the Lily family.

Daffodils and Hyacinths

Daffodils are making a brave show — they manage to look so important bobbing about in the breeze. We have a couple of delightful miniature Daffodils — one an Australian hybrid called "Little Gentleman", which is bright gold with a long, narrow trumpet and narrow petals, very attractive and well worth growing.

Some of the Daffodils we bought recently seem to be suffering from bulb eelworm or nematode disease. Fortunately the infected bulbs were all planted in pots, so we should be able to keep it from spreading. The symptoms of this disease at this stage will be noticed in the leaves which become slightly twisted and distorted and may be pale. There are lumps or thickenings along the leaf which can be felt if the leaf is drawn between the fingers. The flowers do not appear to be affected, but the bulbs will show brown decay.'

The cure is the hot water treatment. Wait until the bulbs have died down naturally after flowering and then lift them. Cut off the leaves and burn them, and leave the bulbs in a cool, airy place on a wire-netting frame for several weeks until dry and dormant. They should then be soaked in water kept at 43°C (110°F) for four hours. You will need a thermometer because it is important to keep the water at the right temperature. Faulty heat treatment will result in malformed blooms next season.

Any soft or rotted bulbs should be burned. Tools used should be dipped in boiling water and Daffodils should not be replanted in the infested soil for three years. Do not forget to nip the heads off spent flowers. If the plants are left to set seed, nourishment will be diverted from the bulb.

Another bulb blooming this month is the Roman Hyacinth. The flowers — a rich blue and smelling the same as the Dutch Hyacinth — are not so thickly clustered on the stem, rather like the English Bluebell.

Watch out for grubs and snails on flowering bulbs. A little snail bait scattered round will get the ones on the ground, but examine flower heads for lurking snails.

NATIVES

Boronias

One of the pleasures of spring is getting out in the garden and just breathing! Even stepping off the train at our station at dusk is a pleasure. The air is saturated with the perfume of Stocks in the prize-winning station garden.

Our own garden is a heady mixture of scents — brown Boronia, Freesias and Jasmine mingle with the Daphne which has been flowering all winter. If you like perfume in the garden find a corner for these plants. None takes up much room, but their perfume fills the whole garden.

Like most natives, Boronias prefer acid soil and need a well-drained situation. Plant them where their roots won't be disturbed — they don't like to be dug round at all. If they are growing among other plants they can be watered and fertilised along with the rest, but use organic fertilisers like blood and bone rather than artificial fertiliser. Tip pruning after flowering will encourage fresh new growth and denser flowers for the next season, and produce a less straggly plant than nature produces in the bush.

Thryptomene paynei — *a dainty, free flowering and very reliable native shrub for the garden.*

The scent of Boronia sends the blood surging through the veins of city dwellers (it's more potent than Gum-leaves in Earls Court) and inspires people with the desire to grow it. The brown Boronia (*B. megastima*) is a native of Western Australia and unfortunately tends to be short-lived under garden conditions. It is a small bush with little brown and lime flowers, which though dense are inconspicuous.

Sydney Boronia (*B. ledifolia*) with masses of rosy flowers, is blooming in our moist sandstone gullies. It does not have the perfume of the brown variety but makes a bright splash in a wildflower garden.

Boronias can be found at nurseries specialising in native plants and I have seen a few in chain stores occasionally. Seeds can be bought from seed specialists and sown now and on through September and October. You will need a deep sandy loam, perfect drainage and a cool aspect where the plants will not dry out in sun or wind.

Forestry Commission Nurseries

There are still areas where koalas survive, and you may be interested in planting food-trees to help in their support. It is a popular misconception that koalas eat only one species of Eucalypt. In fact, the Forestry Commission's tree nursery at Pennant Hills near Sydney grows thirty-one species suitable for koalas.

I recently visited the nursery to look at their native plants. Rather appropriately perhaps it is past the Koala Park Sanctuary at Pennant Hills. The nursery is approached by more than a kilometre of road winding through peaceful forest glowing with spring Wattle. The Pennant Hills nursery specialises in tall trees, though they do carry some shrubs, and the stock includes exotics as well as natives.

All plants are sold in tubes, the best way to buy natives. They can be slipped out of the bottomless tubes without injuring the root system so that the trees are able to grow quickly without any setback at planting. These small trees only cost 60¢ and will usually make better growth than expensive advanced trees grown in conventional pots and rootbound.

Visitors to the nursery should ask for the very good handbook on trees and shrubs which is inexpensive. Trees are listed by botanical and popular name, and the information includes those suitable for fodder, honey, koalas, tannin and oil, as well as soil, salt and wind tolerance. I was intrigued by *Erythrina vespertilio*, which is listed as useful for cow bails.

Sydney gardeners can visit the local nursery and New South Wales country readers will be able to call or write to nurseries at Narrandera, Muswellbrook, Forbes or Dubbo. There is an order form in the back of the catalogue, and plants will be sent by rail. All States have Forestry Commission nurseries stocked with both native and exotic plants suitable for their localities.

There are many interesting trees at the nursery. I bought an unusual *Acacia baileyana* called "Purpurea", which is similar to the usual Cootamundra, but has purplish foliage. This variety was developed in New Zealand, and only a small stock is kept in Sydney.

The Scribbly Gum (*Eucalyptus haemastoma*) is popular on poor sandstone soils and again a purplish variety is available. This is *E. haemastoma sclerophylla* which has a slightly broader leaf than the usual scribbly and does not grow as high. The new foliage is a purplish colour and the tree usually has enough new growth to maintain the purple cast.

There is a Eucalypt for almost every soil condition. Some will thrive in dry areas, some in wet and there are Eucalypts that will withstand salt. *Eucalyptus leucoxylon* var. *macrocarpa* "Pink" is a pretty pink-flowered gum which grows well in gypsous clay loam and will withstand wet feet and frost. An ornamental tree, it grows up to 10 m (30 ft). If you want a tree for a difficult situation, look for the right Eucalypt.

I was anxious to buy a Bastard Box because of its marvellous name, but it is stocked only at Dubbo and Forbes. The tree is a cross between an Ironbark and a Box. Botanically it is *E. affinis* "Pink". Instead of the Bastard Box I bought another interesting gum, *E. acaciiformis*, which has fine leaves like some wattles. A large, handsome tree with a dense dark-green crown, it grows to 20 m (60 ft) in clay soils.

Eucalypts are easy to grow, but not always so easy to keep looking handsome because of insect attack. Borers are one of the biggest worries, but it has now been found that trees adequately fed are able to resist by producing substances that overwhelm the borer larvae before they can do much damage.

Organic fertilisers are suitable for native plants, and new packaging on some lines lists plant suitability. Use any fertiliser labelled safe for natives.

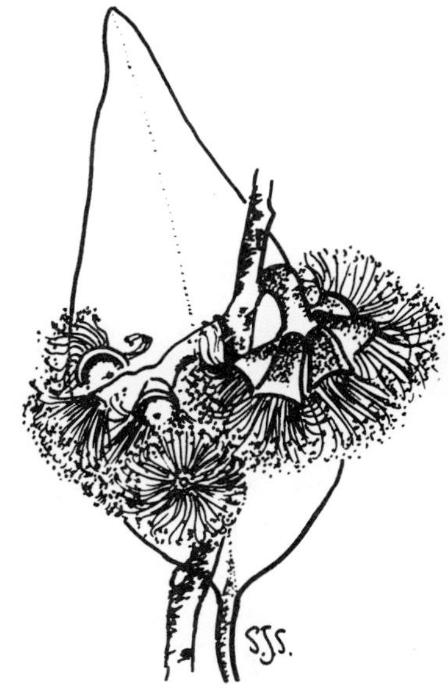

Two of the many varieties of Eucalypt — a decorative, small-flowering Mallee and E. ficifolia*, the exuberant, red-flowering gum.*

A complete fertiliser recommended by the Forestry Commission is Shirley's Poplar Special (no relation). Hortico has a blood and bone plus trace elements designed for use on native plants.

EDIBLES

Vegetables — Tame and Wild

Rising food costs are tempting people to grow their own vegetables and in the United States, where things are worse, some people have gone to the extent of planting their front yards with wheat.

Things may not get so bad here that all our carefully-tended lawns must be transformed into fields of waving wheat, but the luxury of lawns must be considered. If you grow vegetables with the idea of feeding the family, you might consider replacing the lawn with something edible.

Suburban gardens do not have the space for a full fruit and vegetable garden unless the lawns are rotary-hoed — so choose your favourite food and concentrate on it.

There is a great deal of satisfaction in growing something usually too expensive to be on a regular menu, such as strawberries or, with summer round the corner, sweet corn. Sweet corn can be planted from now on (except in frosty areas). It needs full sun, good drainage and rich, well-fertilised soil.

Dig the bed over and add a good dressing of complete fertiliser, watered in well, a week before planting. Corn makes a good wind-break and can be planted where it will protect other vegetables. Corn should be kept moving and watered regularly for tender luscious cobs. They should be picked and eaten or preserved by pickling or freezing as soon as they are ripe.

Grow tomatoes and lettuce in the shelter of the corn — you will find tomato and lettuce seedlings in the nurseries and garden departments.

A lemon tree is a must for the home garden — if you have a sunny spot, this is a good time to plant one. You will find them fruiting in nurseries now. Lemons are full of vitamins and can be used in drinks, desserts and salad dressing instead of vinegar.

Lemon trees in home gardens are often totally neglected, and now is the time to do something about it. Citrus trees may be fed now with sulphate of ammonia, which should be applied after a preliminary watering, and watered again after the fertiliser has been spread. Keep the fertiliser away from the trunk of the tree. Use fertiliser at the rate of 0.5 kg (1 lb) for each year of the tree's age. Alternatively, spread a mulch of fowl manure mixed with composted lawn clippings.

Lemon trees that show signs of powdery mildew can be sprayed now with the lime sulphur used on Roses. Citrus gall wasp will be apparent now, and any branches with swellings should be cut off and burnt. This must be done before the end of August, or the wasps will emerge and reinfect the same or neighbouring trees. The citrus gall wasp is a declared pest — so please examine your trees for the galls.

Lemons should be picked as soon as they begin turning yellow. They should be clipped off with a piece of stem intact, and stored in a cool place. The fruit will keep well, and gradually the skin becomes thinner and the juice content increases. The tree in the meantime is able to spend its energy on the still-maturing fruit.

If you are not a successful vegetable grower you can still save money by eating your weeds. This is not recommended unless you know what the weeds are — but many are edible.

Chicory grows wild in some areas and is eaten as a vegetable called witlof when young. The roots may be dried, roasted and ground to cook as caffeine-free coffee. Dandelion (*Taraxicum officinale*) roots can be used the same way for dandelion coffee, and young leaves can be picked for salads or tea and the flowers used for dandelion wine.

Pig-weed can be cooked as spinach, and nettles used for soup. Mustard grows wild (it looks like lettuce gone to seed) and can be picked — the whole plant, flowers and all — and used as a hot vegetable. Acorns may be used for coffee, and the fruit of Ginkgo trees is also edible. The seeds may be roasted and used like nuts. The low-growing plant called New Zealand spinach, which can be found growing wild round beach areas, makes a good hot vegetable.

Many weeds are full of vitamins, and seeds such as sunflower are rich in vitamin E. But do not eat weeds at random. Many are poisonous. Make absolutely sure you have the right weed before you eat it.

Dr Enari, senior biologist at the Arboretum in Arcadia, Los Angeles, has been giving lectures on edible weeds. This would be a good subject for one of our biologists or botanists. Anyway, whether you eat the weeds or not, if your lawn is full of dandelions at least you will know it is more nourishing than grass.

Rotation to Avoid Disease

Some people have difficulty growing disease-free lettuce. Random plants develop a yellow, leathery appearance on the outer leaves while the inner leaves seem to shrink and also turn yellow. If the plants are left they eventually rot, but do not infect surrounding plants.

This sounds like a virus disease called necrotic yellows of lettuce. Aphids spread this virus disease and the recommended control is to get rid of the aphids. The aphids responsible also infest the common milk thistle or sow thistle, so all thistles must be destroyed. Diseased lettuce should also be culled and burnt.

This sort of problem draws attention to the importance of crop rotation in successful gardening. Rotation can be difficult in small suburban gardens where there is often no alternative space for vegetables. However, constantly growing the same crop in the same bed allows a build-up of the pests and diseases which affect the crop.

Several virus diseases can live in the soil for years and each successive crop will be re-infected. However, if no host plant is grown in the soil, the disease will eventually die out.

If you are having repeated failures with a crop, I would suggest you stop growing it for a couple of seasons. At the same time avoid growing other plants of the same family nearby. Remember that many weeds belong to the same families as garden plants, and are infected by the same diseases and insect pests. Better still, rotate your crops before any disease problems arise.

INDOORS

Terrariums

Thousands of Australians live in flats or home units and do all their gardening on balconies, window-sills or planter-boxes, which need constant supplies of indoor plants. Space is usually so limited that avid gardeners soon feel frustrated by the lack of scope for their green thumbs. If you are bored by the possibilities of pots and baskets why not try terrariums?

Terrariums are usually called bottle gardens and almost any glass container can be planted as a terrarium as long as it is clean. The difficult part of planting a bottle is getting everything through the narrow neck — like the problems of building a boat in a bottle, it is tricky. However there are some bottles on the market today that have suitable swan-like necks but their secret is that the whole top section can be lifted off, making the planting process very easy and also making it possible to use quite large plants.

I have seen a number of these bottles planted with spectacular plants such as Bromiliads, flowering Authuriums and dwarf Palms with a base of more conventional bottle-garden plantings of Saxifrage, Selaginella, Fitonia, Maidenhair fern and African Violets. The combination of high-quality glass and good planting makes them the handsomest bottle gardens I have seen. They are also expensive — a large carboy costs around $60, though there are fairly small bottles for under $7.

If you would like to try your hand at making your own bottle garden look round for clean, preferably clear glass bottles of any size or shape or use glass storage jars, aquariums or brandy balloons. Start with a layer of pebbles and a few pieces of charcoal — the depth of the pebbles depends on the size of your container but use enough to provide good drainage — the pebbles should be visually attractive too. Then add a layer of potting mix fed in through the neck of the bottle with a funnel made from a twist of stiff paper — this keeps the soil from dirtying the glass.

Never use soil from your garden in terrariums — buy sterilised potting mix from your nurseryman because it will be weed, insect and disease free. Dust or spray plants with a fungicide before planting — never attempt to spray into a bottle after it has been planted because the spray will coat the bottle.

Start your venture into bottle gardening by using easily grown plants like ferns, Selaginella, Saxifrage, Kenilworth Ivy, Ivy and Helxine. Choose very small plants that can be slipped through the neck and plant them with the aid of a fork tied to a length of dowelling. Water by dripping in just enough to moisten everything, top with a layer of gravel and seal your bottle with a cork.

Your bottle garden should be placed somewhere where it will be out of direct sunlight which will scorch the plants, near a well-lighted window or beside a light. Terrariums can be used as the base for a standard lamp. The plants do very well with this built-in source of warmth and light.

A terrarium should not need to be watered very often because the moisture in the sealed container is constantly recycled. Droplets of moisture will form on the glass and drip back into the soil at the bottom. If the bottle becomes too fogged up, the cork can be taken off for a few hours. Should the plants look a little dry, water by dripping a small amount of water in, taking care not to make the soil soggy because this will cause rotting of the plants.

Terrarium plants don't need fertilising because this only makes them grow faster and bigger — not desirable in a confined space. If you feel the need to add anything, a few drops of liquid fertiliser can be put into the water. If a plant becomes too big, remove it with a length of wire bent round to form a hook. Scrape off surplus soil and pull the plant out roots first or the foliage will stick in the neck of the bottle.

Bottle gardening is fun and will give a new lease of gardening life to people in units or people who can't get outdoors.

Flowering Pots

Nurseries are now well stocked with long-flowering potted plants to gladden the hearts of unit gardeners. Polyanthus, *Primula abconica* and *P. sinensis* bought in bloom will brighten balconies and window ledges or make a table decoration, and new flowers will develop for several weeks. Cyclamen too are at their best now and make wonderful indoor plants provided they are not watered too much. Water from below – never over the bulb.

It seems hard to believe but Cyclamen was once grown for medicinal purposes rather than for its exquisite flowers. One of its uses was to cure baldness. The roots were powdered and put into the nostrils. I wouldn't advise you to try it — our modern hybrids have lost their punch.

Another flowering indoor plant in good supply is Calceolaria. Calceolaria has clusters of flowers that resemble speckled purses. They come in bright colours — sulphur yellow with orange speckles is the most common combination. They aren't really pretty flowers but quaint and colourful with the flower stems rising from a rosette of soft green spring foliage.

Calceolarias — bright orange and yellow blooms for indoor colour.

CHECKLIST

September means spring and gardens will be at their best during the next few weeks. Take time out to enjoy the results of your work in the garden and take the opportunity to visit parks and gardens open for inspection. Wildflowers are in bloom for spring too and can be enjoyed in bushland and reserves.

Flowering Now

Trees and Shrubs:
Agonis,
Azalea,
Bauhinia,
Beloperone,
Camellia,
Catalpa,
Cersis,
Coleonema (Diosma),
Cornus (Dogwood),
Datura,
Eupatorium,
Fuchsia (some species),
Jasminum mesneyi,
Lavender (French),
Magnolia,
Malus,
Philadelphus (Mock Orange),
Pieris,
Prunus,
Rhododendron,
Robinia
Rondeletia,
Roses,
Spiraea,
Syringa,
Viburnum,
Virgilia.

Perennials and Annuals:
Alyssum,
Antirrhinum (Snapdragon),
Aubrieta,
Bellis perennis,
Campanula,
Centaurea (Cornflower),
Cheiranthus,
Cineraria,
Daisy (Marguerite),
Delphinium,
Eschscholtzia,
Forget-me-not,
Gazania,
Gerbera,
Gypsophila,
Linaria,
Lobelia,
Mignonette,
Nemesia,
Nigella,
Penstemon,
Polyanthus Primrose,
Poppy,
Primula,
Schizanthus,
Statice,
Stock,
Vinca.

Bulbs:
Anemone,
Babiana,
Clivia,
Crocus,
Daffodil,
Freesia,
Hyacinth,
Iris (Bearded and Dutch),
Ixia,
Lachenalia,
Narcissus,
Ranunculus,
Scilla (Bluebells),
Sparaxis,
Tulips,
Watsonia.

Climbers:
Bougainvillea,
Clematis,
Doxanthus,
Gelsemium (Carolina Jasmine),
Jasminum polyanthum,
Wistaria.

Natives:
Acacia,
Actinotis (Flannel Flower),
Anigozanthus (Kangaroo Paw),
Banksia,
Bauera,
Boronia,
Callistemon (Bottlebrush),
Dendrobium (Rocklily),
Epacris,
Eriostemon,
Grevillea,
Hakea,
Hardenbergia,
Hovea,
Isopogon,
Leptospermum,
Leschenaultia,
Pittosporum,
Prostanthera (Mint Bush),
Pultenaea (Bacon and Eggs),
Tetratheca,
Thryptomene,
Westringia (Coast Rosemary).

SEPTEMBER

Plant

Trees, Shrubs and Climbers:
Plant out all container-grown plants now including citrus,
Azalea,
Hibiscus,
Passionfruit,
Rhododendron,
Wistaria and native plants.

Climbers from seed:
Antigonon,
Cobaea scandens,
Dutchman's Pipe (Aristolochia),
gourds,
Mina lobata,
Thunbergia gibsonii.

Annuals:
Ageratum,
Alyssum,
Amaranthus,
Antirrhinum,
Aster,
Balsam,
Carnation,
Celosia,
Chrysanthemum,
Cleome,
Cosmos,
Globe Amaranth,
Kochia,
Marigold,
Mexican Poppy,
Mignonette,
Nasturtium,
Painted Daisy,
Penstemon,
Petunia,
Phlox,
Rudbeckia,
Salpiglossis,
Salvia,
Snow-on-the-mountain
(Euphorbia variegata),
Statice,
Swan River Daisy (Brachycome),
Verbena,
Viscaria,
Zinnia.
(See also p. 169.)

Bulbs:
Agapanthus,
Beladonna (Amaryllis),
Canna,
Crinum,
Dahlia,
Eucharis,
Gladiolus,
Gloriosa Lily,
Hemerocallis (Day Lily),
Lycoris,
Sprekelia,
Valotta.

Vegetables:
Beans (dwarf or climbing),
beetroot,
cabbage,
carrot,
celery,
choko,
cucumber,
egg plant,
garlic cloves,
herbs,
leek,
lettuce,
marrow,
melon,
potato,
pumpkin,
radish,
salsify,
silver beet,
squash,
sweet corn,
sweet potato,
tomato.

Cool-temperate areas only:
Peas,
spinach.
(See also p. 173.)

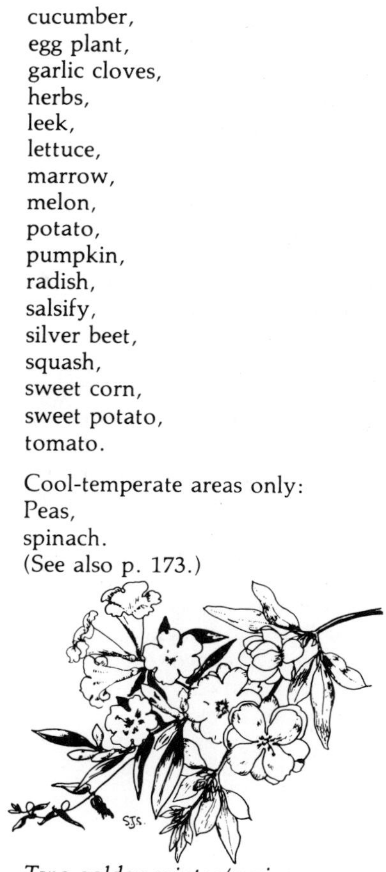

Two golden winter/spring flowers: climber Carolina Jasmine, left, and shrubby climber Primrose Jasmine.

Fertilise

For Camellias, Daphne and Azaleas that have finished blooming, use one of the special fertilisers formulated for these acid-loving plants or water on one of the foliar fertilisers such as Aquasol. Water before and after fertilising to avoid root burn.

Spring-flowering annuals can be kept going with an all-over spraying with a foliar fertiliser. This also applies to bulbs as they finish flowering. Bulbs can also be given a little all-purpose fertiliser watered in well. Don't allow granular fertiliser to touch the bulb.

Feed Agapanthus, Hydrangea, Hibiscus, Abelia and other summer-flowering plants using complete fertiliser watered in well.

Citrus should be watered well and fed with complete citrus food or sulphate of ammonia if not previously attended to.

Feed lawns with lawn food or sulphate of ammonia.

Apply blueing compound to Hydrangeas and water it in.

Prune

Hibiscus should be pruned now to develop bushy plants. Shorten branches by about one-third of their length and remove any damaged wood.

Poinsettia that have finished flowering need pruning back to two or three eyes.

Cut back Oleander fairly hard.

Flowering Peach must be pruned immediately after flowering to develop new flowering wood for next season and to prevent fruit developing because this will encourage fruit fly.

Japonica (Chaenomeles) can be pruned after flowering.

Camellias can be trimmed as soon as flowering is finished and before new growth commences.

Cut back Cotoneaster as soon as berries are spent.

Plumbago can be trimmed to keep it under control and Reinwardtia can be cut to the ground when finished.

Fuchsias and Geraniums can be tip pruned to produce bushy growth.

Diosma should be clipped all over when flowering is finished.

Native shrubs such as Mint Bush should be trimmed to just behind the spent flowering sprays to encourage bushiness.

Bouvardia humboldtii — *a small shrub with scented white flowers — often hard to buy but available this month in flower.*

Pests and Diseases

Azaleas and Rhododendrons must be sprayed every ten to fourteen days while in bloom to protect flowers from the fungus disease petal blight. Use Bayleton, or any other fungicide that is recommended for this disease, following the directions on the label.

Leaf gall is also a fungus disease of Azaleas and sometimes appears on Camellias causing distorted growth on new leaves which appear swollen, pale yellow-green tinged with red, and twisted. Pick off the worst infected leaves and burn. Spray foliage as directed for petal blight.

Red spider and lace bug attack new growth on Azaleas. Red spider also attacks other ornamentals such as Fuchsia and *Viburnum tinus*. Symptoms are red specks on the backs of leaves and, later in season, silvering of foliage. Spray with Malathion or Rogor for lace bug and Kelthane for red spider.

Spray Gladiolus regularly from two-leaf stage to protect from thrips, using Malathion.

Use snail bait round young vegetable and flower seedlings, and Clivea while in flower.

Aphids attack new growth on Roses, Pansies and other plants. Spray with Malathion or a pyrethrum spray.

Cabbage white butterfly becomes active on members of the cabbage family including flowers such as Stocks and Wallflowers. Mignonette and Nasturtiums are also attacked. Spray caterpillars with Malathion or dust with Derris. Vegetables are best kept dusted.

Watch for leaf spot on berry fruits and spray with Bordeaux. Shot hole on Plum, Almond, Cherry, Apricot needs spraying with Bordeaux at pink bud stage.

When they come into leaf check grape vines — fruiting and ornamental types — for vine moth caterpillars. Spray with Dipel or insecticide such as Malathion. Fuchsias are also attacked.

Garden Care

It is important to keep gardens watered now. Spring-flowering plants use a lot of water while in full bloom; young seedlings and newly planted shrubs need regular watering to prevent drying out that will check growth. Windy days dry out gardens quickly so check soil and water when necessary. Try to keep water off Azalea and Rhododendron blooms because this spreads petal blight. These plants are best watered from below the foliage.

Spray lawns to rid them of summer weeds etc. (See also p. 162.)

Watch Gardenias for signs of soil deficiency and disease and keep regularly fed and watered in preparation for summer flowering. (See also p. 161.)

THE SEPTEMBER GARDEN

Do you reach for tissues and anti-histamine or are you enjoying the scents of spring — especially at dusk when the perfume of many flowering plants is released into the evening air (usually to attract night-flying pollinators rather than human beings).

If your garden is short on the sweet smells of spring, here are a few suggestions for flowers that will scent the air. Choose the ones which will suit your climate. Freesias, Stocks and Violets will grow in most gardens so try to have one or more of these. *Daphne odora* is a fragrant little shrub for temperate climates which flowers right through winter into spring, making it really good value. Brown Boronia (*B. megastigma*) is an Australian native which has the most piercingly sweet scent of all flowers. It is usually on sale at nurseries when it is in flower and, though difficult to grow unless you have the perfect conditions for it, it is well worth buying a pot to enjoy the fragrance even if it only lasts for a couple of seasons.

The perfume which floods the air on September evenings right along the east coast comes from the Pittosporums that grow (often uninvited) in bushland and gardens. *P. undulatum* is very attractive in spring with its lime-green spring leaf and clusters of small, scented cream flowers which give it its common name of Native Daphne. On the east coast of the United States, Japanese Pittosporum (*P. tobira*) is grown frequently as a hedge plant. It is very similar to our *Pittosporum undulatum* with sweet scented flowers and shining leaves, but is a much better garden plant. If you can buy it anywhere it is well worth using — the flowers almost hide the foliage in spring.

Viburnum carlesii repays a gentle sniff — it is the sweetest of all Viburnums. Not as showy as *V. opulus* (the Guelder Rose or common Snowball Bush) but worth a place in the temperate garden for discerning flower-sniffers. Don't overlook the value of Orange Blossom in the garden — it's marvellously fragrant. And of course that vigorous climber Jasmine (*Jasminum polyanthum*) will provide perfume galore.

I can't write about the scented flowers of spring without mentioning the Port Wine Magnolia (*Michelia figo*) with its heady perfume — like port wine, bananas or tangy chewing gum, according to your nose. The flowers are small, insignificant and an uninspiring brownish-cream flushed with purple. But the perfume is intoxicating. Apart from its fragrance, the Port Wine Magnolia is a shrub which makes a good, dense privacy planting. It will grow in filtered sunlight and will do well in the shade of trees where more sun-loving shrubs will not prosper — and it grows in warm climates such as Brisbane, as well as cooler areas. Several other *Michelia* species which will also grow well in warm areas — such as *M. doltsopa* — are well worth planting.

Tree Tulip (Liriodendron tulipifera) *— a tall stately tree with interesting flowers in spring.*

GARDENKEEPING

Gardenia Care

Gardenias often worry their owners at this time by developing a number of yellow leaves. Some yellowing may simply be the natural dying of old leaves but if widespread it can be caused by several different things. Gardenias prefer rich, well-drained, lime-free soil with a 6.0 pH. If plants are growing in limey soil, the yellow leaves indicate a deficiency of magnesium. The addition of decayed animal manure will help, as will watering the soil and plant with a bucket of water in which one tablespoonful of Epsom salts has been dissolved.

Another cause of yellowing leaves is attack by the eelworm or root nematode. This is particularly a problem in sandy soils. Infected plants have knots or lumps along the roots. Nematode infection can cause the death of plants, but nematodes can be controlled by watering the soil with a nematode spray such as Nemagon or Nemacur or similar specific. One of the best ways to rid soil of nematodes is to plant Marigolds (Tagetes). This is not a folk cure but a legitimate method of controlling nematodes which has been used commercially on a considerable scale. Nematodes survive by invading the root tissues of a plant and forcing the plant to supply food to the nematode rather than to itself. Marigolds are attacked by nematodes in the same way as other plants but Marigolds ignore the message from the nematodes and continue to supply themselves with food. The nematodes are starved out and die without laying eggs so that after a time they disappear.

Keep your Gardenias growing strongly with regular fertilising, watering and mulching so that their growth is not checked and they will reward you with masses of sweetly-scented blooms all summer.

The Perils of Digging

No matter how carefully a garden is planned for year-round effect there is no doubt it will reach a spring peak that cannot be surpassed for the rest of the year. Nature is heavily programmed to respond to the rites of spring — rebirth after the dormancy of winter. In Australia we don't get the full drama of the return of the sun and renewal of life that is experienced in northern hemisphere countries. However, most of us respond to that feeling of spring in the air as warmer weather brings out a rush of spring flowers.

My own garden manages to clothe itself in carpets of Freesias and Forget-me-nots, Iris and Ixias, Daffodils and Daisies and Bluebells. All wonderful plants that, once planted, grow themselves each year with very little help from me.

My garden is rather like a modern supermarket — it's all self-help — and this sort of garden only works if the gardener doesn't. It is not at all the garden for someone who feels the need to be constantly digging. Digging in my garden is usually fatal because various bulbs, corms, rhizomes and other underground roots stocks are busy colonising every centimetre of soil, leaving no room for garden forks and very little space for weeds.

It is not only these plants that resent being stabbed with a fork — many shrubs and trees bitterly resent having their roots disturbed and the soil level changed by enthusiastic digging, and this is the cause of a great many plant losses in gardens. If you regularly lose shrubs and trees — particularly Azaleas and natives — it may be because digging has broken and exposed roots or piled soil against the trunk of the plant, causing rotting of the bark.

The best time for digging in any garden is before planting. If the soil is prepared well by digging in plenty of humus in the form of leaf mould, peat moss, manure or compost to create a good friable soil that won't cake or set hard, there will be no need to dig.

Weeds are another reason for digging but if the ground is well mulched with bark chips or leaf mould the weeds will be surpressed and any that do appear can be easily hand-weeded. The mulch should be spread over the whole root area, taking care to keep it out of direct contact with the trunk or main stem of your plant.

Weeding Lawns

If you want to get the grass growing under your feet, it is time to start looking after your lawn. Weeds usually grow freely in lawns in spring before the grass is in active growth, and a clean-up of weeds is often the first step to improving the lawn.

Bindii is a menace in summer lawns and can make life a misery to anyone who walks on the lawn in bare feet — including children and pets. Spray now for this pest — if it has been a problem in the past summer — with a specific weedicide such as Weedoben. Don't delay if you intend to spray for this pest because once the plant has set seed they will be there for the whole summer.

Many weeds can be killed off easily by sprinkling them with straight sulphate of ammonia. Do this when the lawn is dry and during the hottest time of the day. Choose a day when there is no likelihood of rain. Make sure the fertiliser is put right into the centre of the plant for most effective results. The weeds will burn and shrivel after about twenty-four hours and then the lawn can be watered. Some burning of surrounding grass may occur but it will soon green up.

If the grass looks thin, oversow with grass seed. This is effective with a couch lawn which is dormant during the cold weather. Oversowing now with bent or a lawn mixture containing bent will thicken up the lawn quickly. Spread top-dressing thinly over the lawn first and rub it in with the back of a rake. Spread the seed and rake it in and water well. Keep the lawn moist for one to two weeks until the grass has germinated. The denser the grass cover the harder it will be for weeds to find a foothold.

If starting a new lawn remember that time spent in preparation is worthwhile. Once down, a lawn should last a lifetime and improvement to drainage, soil, digging and levelling of the site are all good investments. Home gardeners often neglect drainage and as a result have problems with moss, reedy weeds and soggy spots. Flexible agricultural piping now available is light and easy to handle. Most hardware stores stock one or more brands.

The soil around new homes has often been churned up during the building process so that sub-soil or heavy clay is brought up to the surface. Soils should be treated before planting with gypsum or dolomite — it is simple and inexpensive and works wonders with the soil structure. Some complete fertiliser should also be added to the soil and watered in before planting. Next, spend some time levelling and raking the lawn site to get rid of all the bumps. The top 25 mm (1 in) of soil shoud be fine and smooth with no lumps or clods. A lawn seed-starter should now be raked into the surface to help the germination. When sowing seed by hand you can get a more even spread if you shake it through an ordinary kitchen colander.

For quicker results you might prefer using turf or rolls of instant lawn. If possible buy from someone who has been recommended as supplying good, weed-free turf. Sometimes perennial weeds in turf can give you a lifetime problem.

Established lawns can be watered and fertilised with a special lawn fertiliser.

TREES AND SHRUBS

Great Oaks . . .

I have been admiring a huge Oak tree in a friend's garden. This month it provides a dramatic burst of bright, lime-green spring leaf which looks marvellous against the blue Australian sky. This vivid colour combination would never be seen in its native England, where the colours are softer and the newly-leafed trees shimmer in the moist air, creating quite a different visual effect. When you consider that many of the English Oaks and other deciduous trees traditional to the landscape of Britain and other European countries were planted for sentimental reasons — particularly in the early days — this dramatic effect must have come as something of a surprise to homesick eyes.

If you have a yen to grow an Oak tree there are better ones to grow than the English Oak. The Scarlet Oak (*Quercus coccinea*) has intense scarlet autumn foliage in cool climates and the Pin Oak (*Q. palustris*) from the US has a lovely pyramidal shape and marvellous red to scarlet foliage in autumn — also in cool climates. And before you plant an Oak (or even an acorn) remember that old adage "Great Oaks from little acorns grow". They do, and in Australia they grow much faster than in countries with colder winters than we have here, so don't plant one unless you have a large garden or an unimpeded footpath. Be content to admire other people's — or grow one in a tub or as a bonsai.

Incidentally, not all Oaks are deciduous. Some, like *Q. ilex* (the Holly Oak or Holm Oak) and *Q. virginiana* (the Live Oak from the US) are dense, round-headed and handsome trees, good for shade and shelter trees in country areas in temperate regions.

Oaks have been relatively pest-free until recently when a pest called oak blotch miner arrived here. This pest, the larvae of a tiny moth, mines the leaves and they appear brown and burnt by February. Small trees can be sprayed with a systemic insecticide and large trees will be protected by a tree injection treatment given during November/December when the pest is first seen.

Trees in Bloom

The blossoming fruit trees add a great deal to spring gardens. These are the flowering Prunus (Peach, Plum, Cherry, Apricot and Almond) and Malus (Apple, Crabapple) and Pyrus (Pear), all bred for flowers rather than fruit. They are small trees which usually grow to around 7 m (about 20 ft) and are ideal for small suburban gardens. Though some, like the Flowering Cherries, are only suitable for temperate climates, most of the flowering Prunus grow and flower well over a wide area. *Prunus cerasifera* (the Cherry Plum) will grow in climates as warm as Brisbane and *P. persica* (the Flowering Peach) flowers as far north as Rockhampton.

The popular purple-leafed Cherry Plums with their shell-pink single flowers and richly coloured foliage show up well planted against pale foliaged plants such as the Golden Elm — a striking combination used a lot round Sydney. The Flowering Peach has two different types — winter-flowering and spring-flowering. Both have double white, pink and red varieties and the spring flowers include a striped variety as well as one which bears all three colours on the same tree.

The best time to buy flowering trees like these is while they are in bloom so that you can choose the varieties you like best. They are always on sale in containers at nurseries during the flowering season and can be planted out immediately or enjoyed as a potted plant until the blooms have fallen.

*Tree Gardenia (*Rothmannia globosa*). The white bells with pink-spotted throats are sweetly scented.*

The Tree Gardenia

The Tree Gardenia (*Rothmannia globosa*) always attracts a lot of comment when it is in flower. It is a small, erect tree which grows to about 3 or 4 m (10 or 12 ft) and covers itself with bunches of white bells in spring. Apart from the Gardenia-like perfume, it does not bear much resemblance to a Gardenia but is well worth growing, particularly if you have a narrow space where more spreading plants won't fit. Rothmannia has the added advantage of being suitable for a wide range of climates from Melbourne to Rockhampton. Like Gardenia, the Rothmannia requires an acid soil.

One of its distinctive features is the fruit which follows the flowers. Each one is about the size of a walnut and turns sooty black, hanging on the tree through summer.

Rondeletia and Viburnum

Among all the more glamorous spring flowers, two old-fashioned shrubs tend to be overlooked — *Rondeletia amoena* and *Viburnum tinus*, which are marvellous in the garden. Rondeletia is a warm-climate shrub which does well in temperate areas in a warm northerly aspect where it is sheltered from frosts. The dense flower heads are made up of dozens of tiny pink flowers with yellow throats. It is more fragrant in warmer climates. The lesser known species *R. strigosa* is quite different with long arching canes bearing clusters of bright crimson flowers in summer.

Viburnum tinus is a somewhat similar shrub. It also has heads of slightly scented blossom made up of many tiny flowers (white with red buds). The shrub has attractive foliage and a dense rounded shape. Both shrubs are very attractive in the bud stage.

Both Rondeletia and *Viburnum tinus* are very good for privacy planting being evergreen and fairly fast-growing. They can be used with other shrubs in an informal hedge-type planting, or *Viburnum tinus* can be grown alone as a clipped hedge, making a much more attractive hedge than the popular red-leafed Photinia.

Rondeletia will be improved by regular pruning after flowering. Cut back the flowering wood to within 15-20 cm (6-9 in) of the past season's growth.

Both shrubs are relatively pest free though *V. tinus* does sometimes suffer from red spider attack and should be sprayed in late spring/early summer with Kelthane to control this mite which may disfigure the foliage.

If you like Weigela it could be mingled with a planting of Rondeletia and *V. tinus*. It looks rather shabby in late winter — but the other two are looking their best and distract the eye from the temporary sad look of the Weigela.

Viburnum tomentosum, *a shrub with pure white flowers on horizontal branches.*

Browallia and Brunfelsia

If you get a bit tired of all the pretty pastel pinks of spring, try growing an orange Browallia (*Streptosolen jamesonii*). It is at its peak of flowering in spring but bears clusters of orange marmalade-coloured flowers all year. It is easily grown in a sunny, frost-free garden and can be pinched back to keep it compact and shrubby or trained up walls or over banks — and it's just great in a warm climate.

Another spring-flowering shrub that's not pink is Brunfelsia with the long common name of Yesterday, Today and Tomorrow from its striking habit of changing flower colour from lavender blue to white as the flowers age. It's sweetly perfumed, likes a warm climate and is sure to arouse comment from visitors who do not know it.

Orange Browallia (Streptosolen jamesonii). *Two-tone heads of yellow and orange bells are in flower throughout the year.*

Azaleas

Azaleas make a major contribution to the spring garden in many parts of Australia. No other shrub is so generous with its flower display — Azaleas in full bloom are so smothered in flowers that the foliage is practically invisible.

The most popular Azaleas grown in our gardens are the evergreen hybrids which include the Indica and Kurume varieties, and vary from the tall growing singles such as "Alba Magna" to the small flowered Kurumes like "Hexe" and dwarf-growing Gumpo Azaleas which grow only about 40 cm (16 in) high.

The evergreen varieties grow in all temperate to warm areas and can be found in gardens from Melbourne to Brisbane, giving an indication of their tolerance of climate. In the cool to cold areas the deciduous Azalea takes over. Commonly lumped together as Mollis Azaleas, there are really many different deciduous Azaleas, some heavily perfumed and differing from the evergreen varieties by including rich yellows and oranges in their colour range.

Azalea "Only One Earth" — a spectacular bloom with large heads of cerise hose-in-hose flowers in bloom now.

Azaleas are actually Rhododendrons, something that many people do not realise, and many of the handsome Rhododendron varieties can be grown in gardens where Azaleas flourish. Members of the Rhododendron family need acid soil, containing plenty of humus, and filtered sunlight. Azaleas will grow in full sun, particularly the tall-growing singles which are sometimes used as hedge plants. However, the flowers will burn off quickly on hot days. There is also more chance of Azaleas drying out on hot dry days because the root system is very shallow and once it dries out the plant is likely to die.

In spite of the disease petal blight that has struck Azaleas in coastal regions during the past few years, Azaleas are still easily-grown, low maintenance shrubs for the garden. They need little attention except for watering and spraying in summer to control red spider and lace bug, both of which attack the leaves. Use Kelthane against the red spider mite and a systemic such as Rogor or Malathion against lace bug.

There are so many varieties available that it is best to choose the ones you like best when they are in bloom in spring. Choose semi-doubles or doubles for containers or for shady areas and put the singles where they can grow up tall and free. Filtered sunlight is the ideal. Rhododendrons make good privacy shrubs and thrive under the cover of taller trees. Don't put them into too heavy shade though — the effect can be depressing when they are not in flower because the foliage is large and dark.

Grow other acid-loving plants in an Azalea garden — Camellias, Pieris, Liliums, Daphne — and shade-loving plants like Bluebells, Forget-Me-Nots and Snowflakes. Don't dig round your Azaleas — they don't like having their roots disturbed. Hand weed if necessary and renew the leaf or pebble mulch when necessary. Water the roots not the flowers when they are in bloom — wetting the blooms will spread petal blight.

Azaleas also make good bonsai subjects and can be used in containers indoors while they are in flower. They will drop their leaves very rapidly if they are not getting enough light indoors so if this happens move them to a better lit situation or back outdoors. They also make great cut flowers, lasting well in flower arrangements.

If you have unsuitable soil for Azaleas grow them in tubs or pots. They make charming container plants and are ideal for partly shaded balconies, patios and courtyard gardens. Azaleas also need a layer of mulch spread round their root area — taking care that it does not touch the main stem where it can cause rot. Composted autumn leaves make excellent mulch but garden compost and pebbles can also be used. A pebble mulch is ideal for potted plants and will help keep the roots cool in the hot weather.

Petal blight infects only the flowers and causes them to develop wet-looking spots which spread rapidly until the flower collapses in a sticky heap. Infected flowers cling to the bush instead of dropping cleanly to the ground and a bad infection will leave the bushes covered in dry brown flower heads which cling for months if not removed. Petal blight is often not recognised by gardeners who think their flowers have wilted because the day is hot. Don't think you don't have this disease in your garden. Everyone who grows Azaleas will have trouble with it and it is even seen in the cool mountain gardens at times. However, it doesn't kill or even weaken the plant itself and we usually can enjoy the flower display for a few weeks before they are spoiled.

When the shrubs are in bloom it is worth taking some trouble to pick off and burn the flowers that show signs of petal blight. This will help to keep the disease under control though it won't cure the trouble — just slow it up so that you can enjoy the display a little longer. In a dry spring petal blight will be less of a problem because this fungus disease spreads quickly in warm, moist weather. Gardeners in climates drier than the humid coastal areas will have less trouble with this fungus. Spraying with a fungicide such as Bayleton early in the season, starting when the buds colour, will help control it, and spraying the bushes and the soil under the plants at the end of the flowering season will help get rid of overwintering spores.

Azaleas — hose-in-hose, single and double-flowering types give massed flowers in spring.

If you are planting Azaleas don't put any lime into the soil because this can be fatal to these acid-loving plants. Also, in new gardens, don't plant them near new brick walls where lime from the mortar will be in the soil. Add plenty of humus in the form of home-made compost and leaf mould or peat moss to the soil before planting and if the soil is heavy build the level of the bed up at least 18 cm (7 in), so that the Azaleas are more or less growing on top of the heavier soil. These plants have shallow, fibrous roots that can't penetrate heavy soils, and they will also fail in badly drained soil though they do need regular watering.

If you can grow Azaleas try your hand at Rhododendrons too. There are many easily grown varieties which are very beautiful, particularly when mature. Rhododendrons do particularly well in many areas of Victoria, in the Adelaide Hills and in the mountain areas along the New South Wales coast. Mature rhododendrons can grow into bushy trees about 10 m (30 ft) tall and are a breathtaking sight in bloom.

Rhododendrons and Azaleas do not need any pruning though Azaleas can be trimmed lightly after the new leaf growth has developed in early summer to give them a more formal shape if this is desired (in a Japanese garden).

If you are thinking of planting Azaleas this season a visit to an Azalea nursery in the next couple of months will be pleasant. The single varieties will be easier to grow. The double-flowered plants tend to make the singles seem a bit ordinary but the doubles are generally not so vigorous, grow more slowly and need more protection than the singles. The lovely single Azalea "Jean Alexandra" is worth trying for. It is pale pink and has a long blooming period before it breaks into the main spring flush. I have a "Violacea", a deep violet double, which I love. This colour is one which people either love or hate, but planted alongside a glowing red and a clear pink, it produces a striking colour combination.

If you have an open sunny position you want to fill with an Azalea, the tall-growing single varieties are the ones most suited to the sun. It is also a good idea to pick early-flowering varieties so that they flower before the sun gets too hot and fades the blooms. A few further suggestions for single varieties are "Agnes Neale", "Mauve Schryderii", "Maves" and "Victoria".

In nurseries in temperate regions there is also a good supply of deciduous Azaleas (yellow or orange-flowered unnamed seedlings) — very fragrant — and Rhododendrons in bloom. These do quite well in cooler areas and are worth trying in a sheltered position. An interesting variety is the Exbury hybrid Azalea "Sand Dune" which has heads of large ruffled flowers in a glowing creamy yellow flushed pink — "Just the colour of desert dunes at sunset", its proud owner assured me. Cool-climate gardeners could keep it in mind when buying deciduous Azaleas.

Shrubs With Bells

Lily-of-the-valley (*Convallaria majalis*) is one of the romantic flowers which have a great attraction for gardeners. Part of its charm is the exquisite perfume but the dainty white bells also have a powerful emotive appeal. There are a number of other plants, trees and shrubs which have similar white bells which are almost as fascinating.

Like the Lily-of-the-valley, most of these prefer a cold winter climate. *Pieris japonica* (often called Lily-of-the-valley Shrub) enjoys soil and situation similar to Rhododendrons; it is a compact shrub with bronzy new growth turning light green with pearly fringes of small bells hanging in clusters all over it.

One form of *P. japonica*, "Bert Chandler", is an Australian-raised seedling with colourful new growth which turns from brilliant pink to pale pink, cream and finally green. It makes a good tub plant for a sheltered position. A variety from the US — "Flamingo" — has pink flowers opening from red buds. Pieris is an ideal companion plant for a garden where Azaleas, Camellias and other acid-loving plants are grown.

Clethra arborea (called Lily-of-the-valley Tree), is a delightful small tree that grows to 6 m (20 ft) and is evergreen with serrated leaves. New growth is an attractive rusty-copper changing to rich green and flowers appear in late spring. A double-flowered form (*C. arborea* "Flore-pleno") is also available.

When I saw a *Halesia carolina* in bloom for the first time (in Kew Gardens) I was thrilled with its beauty. Its common name was given there as Wedding Bell Tree but it is also known as Snowdrop Tree. Halesia is deciduous and the pure white bells hang in clusters in late spring.

Leucothoe is a small shrub with graceful arching branches. The leaves are reflexed to display the fringes of dainty blossom hanging from the branches. In cool climates it has a good autumn colour and, like Pieris, it likes an acid soil. One of its common names is Dog Hobble.

One of the most fascinating of these plants with Lily-of-the-valley-like flowers is *Stachyurus praecox* which has slender satiny brown branches fringed with greenish-cream bells with a brown calyx. Stachyurus is deciduous and flowers on the bare branches, the new growth appearing at the tips of the flowering wood. The leaves are at first small, light green and serrated but become quite large in full leaf. The flowers last well in water and become quite dry and papery after a couple of weeks. Stachyurus is not a showy plant but is an interesting and unusual shrub for gardeners looking for something different. A friend of mine who grows it in her Sydney garden picks the flowers and sells them to her local florist each year — they are very popular with florists and are in great demand.

One of our own native trees — the Blueberry Ash (Elaeocarpus) — covers itself in fringed sprays of Lily-of-the-valley-like flowers in November. This is a very attractive tree, very pretty in bloom and the blue berries last for months. If you're looking for a native tree suitable for a suburban garden, the Blueberry Ash has a lot to recommend it.

. . . and a Currawong in a Pear Tree

We all know about the Christmas partridge in a Pear tree — but a currawong in a Pear tree is definitely a spring thing. Walking home one sunny day I saw the biggest, blackest currawong, all his white hidden, sitting in a tall snow-white Siberian Pear tree. He looked like a portrait of spring in black and white. And he left that partridge for dead.

Pyrus ussuriensis is a handsome tree — shapely and showy in spring (covered in white blossom) and in autumn (when its leaves are a glossy bronze-red). It is best used as a specimen tree with plenty of room to be admired, and is best in cool climates.

PERENNIALS AND ANNUALS

Plant Now for Summer Colour

There are lots of annual and some perennial plants which can be put in now either from seed or advanced bedding plants to provide weeks and even months of summer flowers. Nothing gives as much bright colour as quickly as a bed or border of summer annuals, and you don't have to have a big garden to have a good display. Many are suitable for hanging baskets, window-boxes, troughs and other containers on patios or sunny balconies. Rockery gardens can be given a lift with annuals planted among the permanent rockery plants.

Petunias are among the most popular summer flowers and a range of popular Petunia varieties is available — "Avalanche", "Blue Mist", "Bobby Dazzler", "Bonanza", "Cascade Chiffon", "Cherry Tart", "Colour Parade", "Elegant Cascade", "El Toro", "Sundance", "Sonata", "Titan" and "Victorious Double". All are F.1 hybrids and each one has something different to offer. The Cascades are ideal spillover plants — "Sundance" is a coral salmon with good rain resistance; "Victorious Double" is the largest Petunia available and has a sweet scent; "Bobby Dazzler" and "Bonanza" are compact and with bright colour mixes. If you are planting to a colour scheme, "Avalanche" (white), "Blue Mist" (blue), "Cherry Tart" (rose and white), "El Toro" (brilliant red) and "Sundance" (coral salmon) will provide a good range of separate colours. The yellow petunia "Summer Sun" is a recent addition to the Thompson and Morgan seed packet range.

Really great for hot sunny spots are the Amaranthus, starting with the bright foliage of Joseph's Coat, which is available in a good variety called "Flying Colours" with a range of yellow, orange, bright red and green. Another of the family, Celosia (known as Prince of Wales Feathers and Cockscomb), now comes in several varieties such as "Fairy Fountains" (a mix of pink, salmon, scarlet, light pink, yellow and gold plumes) and Cockscomb "Jewel Box" and "Coral Gardens". Globe Amaranth or *Gomphrena* "Little Buddy" will be a mass of purple ball-like flowers for weeks on end and is resistant to hot, dry conditions. All these members of the Amaranthus family make great container plants for full sun too.

If you like colourful plants try growing some of the varieties with ornamental foliage such as Basil "Dark Opal", Ornamental Cabbage "Cherry Sundae Mixed" (large rosettes of carmine or cream fringed with green or bronze) or Snow-on-the-mountain (Euphorbia) variety "Summer Icicle" (pale green leaves edged with silvery white). Coleus are beautiful foliage plants for semi-shade; however they must be protected against caterpillars and snails. These plants will provide colour contrasts in the garden and also make showy container plants.

A collection of Paper Daisies from Western Australia.

Snapdragons (Antirrhinum) can be planted at almost any time but will grow well from spring plantings. Some of the new hybrids are hard to recognise as the old Snapdragon but make a colourful display. Look for bedding plants in varieties "Bright Butterflies" or "Tetraploid".

Marigolds are great value in the garden or in containers. They flower freely and come in a range of yellow, gold, orange and brown. Unlike most flowers, with Marigolds you can choose a variety that will grow to whatever height you need from 20 cm (8 in) petites to "Jubilee", which is almost 1 m (3 ft).

Zinnias also come in a range of sizes and are good cut flowers. Grow them in a sunny bed or, if you are a balcony

Golden Forsythia frames Flowering Cherry and Daffodils at NOOROO, the Valdars' garden at Mt Wilson, NSW.

Streptosolen, for frost-free gardens, flowers from spring into summer.

In cool-climate gardens rich yellows and golds are provided by deciduous Azaleas.

gardener, try dwarf varieties "Thumbelina", "Mini Pink" or "Persian Carpet" in a container. The Star Zinnia (Z. *linearis*) — available only in seed — is a particularly good rockery or border plant and well worth growing.

If you are looking for a flower that just blooms on and on plant the red Salvias "Bonfire", "Bonfire Compacta" and "Blaze of Fire" for compact, shrubby plants covered in brilliant red flowers for many months. For a touch of blue in the summer garden try the blue *Salvia farinacia*, available in seed.

Nasturtium "Alaska" with variegated foliage is interesting in a pot or border planting.

For those gardeners who like to raise their own plants from seed there are many lovely annuals which are never available as bedding plants — like the Californian Poppy (Eschscholtzia), Godetia and Viscaria which are rewarding to grow. Simply sow them where they are to grow and keep watered gently until established. They are a little extra trouble but very satisfying when you get a good result.

Everlasting Daisies (Acroclinium) are Australian natives which will give a good display of papery Daisy flowers in a variety of pinks to red and white. They can be gathered and dried by hanging in bunches — upside down, in a cool, shaded place — to provide dried flower arrangements when fresh flowers are in short supply. Everlasting Daisies should always be sown where they are to grow and thinned if necessary because they do not like to be transplanted. Some other annuals that can be raised in this way are Linaria, Gypsophila, Cosmos, Nasturtium, Mignonette and Cleome (Spider Flower). This last is a really handsome, tall summer annual with masses of spidery pink, lavender and white-toned flowers — it should be grown more often than it is. Plant Cleome seeds at the back of a flower border because they are fairly tall-growing annuals — and they are great for picking.

Good selections of bedding plants and seeds are in most nurseries this month. Finding space might be a problem if you have a good display of spring annuals but you can pot up seedlings into containers and grow them on until you are ready to plant them out in the garden.

CLIMBERS AND CREEPERS

Spring Climbers

Two of spring's most showy climbers — Jasmine (*Jasminum polyanthum*) and Wistaria — grow almost everywhere and can be used in many different ways. Recently I saw a fence which consisted simply of a length of chain supported by posts at intervals. Jasmine had been trained along the chain turning it into a garland of flowers encircling the garden. Wistaria and climbing Roses can also be used in this way — in fact many climbing plants could be trained along gracefully hanging chains.

Both Jasmine and Wistaria can be trained over old stumps or dead trees (provided they are sound and safe) that are too difficult or costly to remove. Both can be trained romantically round columns and verandah posts — if they are kept under control — and Jasmine is good for partly shaded places where a privacy planting is needed on a trellis.

Wistaria can also be grown most attractively as a small tree either in the garden or in a tub on a patio. To do this, choose a plant (or cutting) with a straight, upward-growing stem. Plant it beside a stake for support (tie it with plant ties or pieces of old stockings to keep it firm) and rub off any shoots appearing up the stem which is to form the "trunk" of your tree. When the Wistaria reaches the required height (up to 2m (6½ ft) is manageable), let it grow out from the tip to form a canopy. Trim canes when necessary to keep your tree a nice shape. After a while the trunk will become quite thick and able to support itself without a stake.

Wistaria is an ideal climber for a pergola. It is fast growing and will quickly provide summer shade for outdoor living or to cool the hot side of a house. As it is deciduous, it will let the sunshine through in winter and, in spring when it is in flower, the chains of purple flowers will hang down under the pergola.

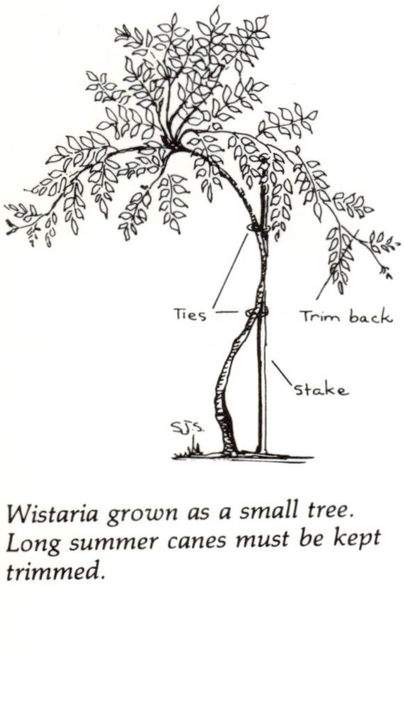

Wistaria grown as a small tree. Long summer canes must be kept trimmed.

There are a number of different varieties of Wistaria available besides the popular mauve one — not as easy to find, but worth looking for. There are some really choice double varieties and also pink and white ones.

There are also two different species grown. Japanese Wistaria (*W. floribunda*) has flowers in long pendulous racemes up to 1 m (3 ft) long in some cases, though more commonly half this length. The more common Chinese Wistaria (*W. sinensis*) has shorter racemes 30 cm (1 ft) long. *W. floribunda violacea plena* is the double violet-blue variety, variety *rosea* (pink) and *alba* white. I have seen white Japanese Wistaria used most charmingly over a pergola which covered the driveway in a Japanese-style garden. White Wistaria is not as spectacular and the flowers seem more fleeting than the more common mauve but it is delightful.

One of my favourite ways of using climbing plants is to grow them over an archway. Back in the thirties many gardens had a creeper-covered archway over the front gate. They looked pretty but were apt to be tricky to get furniture through if you moved, and they developed dry rot or termites got them and they fell down.

However, archways seem to be coming back — perhaps it is the interest in the fashions of the thirties and general nostalgia for that period. Whatever the cause, I think archways are great, and you don't need a fence or even a gate to have one at your entrance — it can simply be a frame to lead visitors along the garden path. You do need to build it wide enough and high enough to cope with moving days or fat visitors, and to make sure that the material you use is strong, durable and termite proof. A combination of stone or brick and timber is good. Timber supports should be set in concrete footings.

Finish your archway with a canopy of Jasmine, a yellow Banksia Rose, Wistaria or tropical Bougainvillea or Allamanda, or mingle two different climbers. Our archway has Wistaria on one side and a white Banksia Rose on the other. The Wistaria flowers first, followed by the Rose.

BULBS

A Scarlet Freesia

Spring bulbs are popular with most gardeners and there are some easily grown bulbs which are not well known but which are an asset in the low maintenance garden. One of these is the Scarlet Freesia (*Lapeirousia cruenta*) — a bright, salmon-pink flower with a scarlet blotch which does perhaps bear a passing resemblance to a Freesia. Both come from South Africa and both belong to the Iridaceae (Iris) family.

Like most South African bulbs, the Scarlet Freesia is a gift to gardeners in warmer climates where a lot of the choice spring-flowering bulbs won't flower well, or at all. It also likes woodland conditions, meaning that it will thrive in partial shade or filtered sunlight (good news for people like me with shade problems) and it doesn't object to being a bit on the dry side though it likes some regular water during the summer. Though it does well in places like Brisbane, it is also hardy to cold and is dormant in winter. It grows and flowers quickly from seed and looks most attractive naturalised under trees, among other bulbs and light ground-cover plants that enjoy similar conditions of filtered sunlight.

There are two local sources of seeds for the Scarlet Freesia — Thompson and Morgan (Australian agents: Erica Vale, Jannali, New South Wales) and a Victorian nursery called Bellevue Gardens, at Boronia.

L. cruenta is easily raised from seed and blooms a few months after sowing. They can be planted in spring for summer flowers or in autumn for spring blooming, and are good for naturalising under deciduous trees.

Good news for people north of Sydney — it will grow in warm climates.

No matter where you live in Australia you can have some spring-flowering bulbs — even the cool-climate daffodils — though in warm areas you will have to be prepared to buy fresh bulbs from a southern bulb nursery each year, or lift bulbs and chill them in the refrigerator or cool room (if you have access to one) for at least six weeks before planting. Nurserymen overseas (and to a lesser extent here) use the chilling method to induce early flowering of glasshouse-grown tulips and other florists' bulbs for the cut flower trade.

Solomon's Seal, one of the last of the spring-flowering bulbs. The flowers are white green-tipped bells among green leaves.

EDIBLES

Preparing Beds and Vegetables to Plant Now

Now that spring is officially here it is time to get enthusiastic about growing vegetables again. If the vegetable garden has been allowed to run to weed during the cold weather and football season you will need to start by digging out perennial weeds and forking the soil to break it up. Then add as much compost as you can, and fork it lightly through the topsoil. If you composted your autumn leaves and last summer's grass you should already have a good supply of compost. If not, buy spent mushroom compost, peat moss or animal manure and add that.

If you are starting a new garden choose a spot in the sun and mark out the shape with a string line. Drainage must be good for a vegetable garden and if it is less than perfect build up the bed rather than digging down. Heavy soil should be treated with dolomite or lime before planting. If the soil is sticky clay treat it with gypsum to help break it up and improve the crumb structure of the soil. Add as much humus as possible.

Time spent in soil preparation is well worth while and will return dividends in increased crops and save you from the struggle and frustration of trying to grow vegetables in unsuitable soil. Where soil is shallow and sandy it will need plenty of humus to improve its structure, plus mulch to help retain moisture after planting.

While you are preparing your vegetable beds for planting you can sow seed boxes to give them a head start. Otherwise most vegetables can be sown directly into the beds where they are to grow.

To supply all the needs of the average family you would need to devote almost the entire back garden to growing vegetables. Unless you are experienced, a vegetable garden this size is difficult to cope with and it is better to start off with a smaller garden and gradually increase it.

For the new grower an area of 10 × 6 m (30 × 18 ft) divided into three beds would be enough. Don't be tempted to plant things in a higgledy-piggledy fashion — it may be quicker initially but will mean hard work later. Use a string line to mark out straight planting rows with even spacing between. Weeding, fertilising and mulching between the rows will then be simpler and quicker.

Narrow paths between beds are important and they should have a surface which helps keep them free of mud and weeds. Permanent beds can have concrete or brick paving but a thick mulch of sawdust is effective and economical, particularly if there is a timber yard handy. Another suggestion is to use pieces of old carpet and underfelt on paths. They suppress weeds and provide firm footing.

Get rid of any existing weeds by watering with something like Weedex or Polyquat, which have a short residual life in the soil. Then add mulch.

When the beds have been prepared, sprinkle over some all-purpose complete fertiliser such as Gro Plus at the rate of one cup a square metre, and water well. Leave for a week, watering if the soil dries out. Then lightly scuff over the soil surface with a rake to disturb any weeds that have germinated and you are ready to start planting.

Choose plants with care. Take into account whether you and your family like the vegetable, how much room it will take up in the bed and if it will give you enough return to justify the space it will occupy. Where space is limited, quick crops of small growing plants that can be picked while young all give you a good return for space. Things like radishes, shallots, carrots, lettuces, tomatoes, silver beet and herbs don't occupy a lot of space and they grow quickly. Potatoes, melons and pumpkins need a lot of space for several months. However, if you are particularly fond of something like sweet corn it would be worth while devoting the entire space to it.

When you have decided on your crops, don't plant the whole seed packet at once. Make successive plantings every couple of weeks to stagger the crop so that everything won't mature in the same week.

Save space by growing climbing crops on a trellis against a fence, wall or carport (provided it is sunny enough). Climbing beans do well on a trellis or tripod (an arrangement of poles placed teepee fashion and laced round with some supporting wire or string). Cucumbers, "Telephone" peas, marrows, pumpkins and chokos also can be grown in this way. Tall tomatoes can be grown on a trellis or staked.

Alternatively, you can grow dwarf varieties of many of these plants. Look for "Patio Pik" cucumber, "Golden Nugget" pumpkins, "Black Jack" zucchini and "Pot Luck" cucumber. The new dwarf bean "Limelight" produces pods which can be picked young and pod and seeds cooked whole. Dwarf varieties are not just for people with gardens on balconies. Pots or tubs can be placed by a door, on a patio or in sunny spots round the garden and planted with decorative small crops of cherry tomatoes, ornamental chillis, ruby-stemmed silver beet, capsicum or herbs to get extra mileage out of your garden space.

When you have planted your vegetables, don't think you can sit back and wait for them to fall into your mouth. Vegetables need regular, even daily attention. Arrange your day so that you can spend at least half an hour checking your plants. Pull weeds out or scuff them out with a dutch hoe or rake as they appear; check for pests or diseases (aphids, snails, caterpillars, red spider and green grasshoppers are the most common pests while fungus diseases like mildew and leaf spots infect vegetables in warm humid weather). Water when the soil surface feels dry and after watering push your finger or a stick into the soil to check that the water has soaked down to the root area. Wetting the surface only will bring roots to the top of the soil where they can dry out.

Fertilise regularly with nitrogen-rich soluble fertilisers such as Aquasol, Thrive, Zest or Bloom — particularly good on leaf crops — plus side dressings of blood and bone or all-purpose fertiliser once or twice during the growing period. Animal manure can be used as a mulch if it is available. This will ensure that crops grow fast and are full of nourishment. Crops starved of fertiliser and water are tough, bitter and low in vitamins and minerals.

Pick your vegetables young. Don't wait for them to grow big and tough. Picking vegetables like beans while they are young will keep plants cropping longer. Lettuce, radishes, carrots and beetroot can be planted fairly close and thinned by pulling some of them as soon as they are bite-size and leaving others to mature in the space left.

CHECKLIST

Spring gardens in cool areas reach their peak this month and many are open for inspection. Cool-climate trees, shrubs and flowers not commonly grown in coastal gardens can be seen.

Flowering Now

Trees and Shrubs:
Azalea,
Bauhinia,
Beloperone,
Camellia,
Catalpa,
Coleonema,
Deutzia,
Eupatorium,
Fuchsia,
Jacaranda,
Jasmine,
Laburnum,
Lavender,
Malus (Crabapple),
Philadelphus (Mock Orange),
Pieris,
Prunus (Flowering Cherry),
Rhododendron,
Robinia,
Rondeletia,
Roses,
Spartium (Spanish Broom),
Spiraea,
Syringa (Lilac),
Viburnum,
Virgilia,
Weigela.

Annuals and Perennials:
Alyssum,
Antirrhinum,
Aquilegia,
Armeria (Thrift),
Aubrieta,
Bellis perennis,
Campanula,
Centaurea (Cornflower),
Cheiranthus (Wallflower),
Cineraria,
Daisy,
Delphinium,
Echium,
Eschscholtzia,
Forget-me-not,
Foxglove,
Gazania,
Geranium,
Gerbera,
Gypsophila,
Linaria,
Lobelia,
Nemesia,
Nigella,
Penstemon,
Peony,
Poppy,
Statice,
Stock,
Vinca.

Bulbs:
Arum Lily (Calla),
Babiana,
Bluebell (Scilla),
Dutch Iris,
Iris,
Ixia,
late Narcissus species,
Sparaxis,
Tulips.

Climbers:
Bougainvillea,
Clematis,
Doxantha,
Gelsemium (Carolina Jasmine),
Jasminum polyanthum,
Trachelospermum,
Wistaria.

Natives:
Banksia,
Bauera,
Boronia,
Brachychiton acerifolium,
Callistemon,
Ceratopetalum,
Chamaelaucium,
Chorizema,
Epacris,
Eriostemon,
Grevillea,
Hakea,
Hardenbergia,
Hovea,
Hymenosporum (native Frangipani),
Isopogon,
Lambertia,
Leptospermum,
Melia (white cedar),
Prostanthera (Mint Bush),
Sollya (Bluebell Creeper),
Telopea (Waratah),
Thryptomene,
Viola (native Violet),
Westringia (Coast Rosemary).

OCTOBER

Plant

Trees, Shrubs and Climbers:
Container-grown plants of all kinds can be planted out in all areas. Stake in windy positions and keep watered until established.

Annuals:
Ageratum,
Alyssum,
Amaranthus,
Aster,
Balsam,
Carnation,
Celosia,
Chrysanthemum,
Cleome,
Cosmos,
Globe Amaranth,
Kochia,
Marigold,
Mexican Poppy,
Mignonette,
Nasturtium,
Painted Daisy,
Penstemon,
Petunia,
Phlox,
Rudbeckia,
Salpiglossis,
Salvia,
Snapdragon,
Snow-on-the-mountain,
Statice,
Strawflower,
Swan River Daisy,
Verbena,
Viscaria,
Zinnia.
(See also p. 186.)

Bulbs:
Canna,
Crinum,
Dahlia (seed, seedlings or tubers),
Eucharis,
Eucomis (Pineapple Lily),
Gladiolus,
Gloriosa Lily,
Iris,
Lycoris,
Nerine,
Sprekelia,
Valotta,
Zephyranthes.

Vegetables:
Beans (dwarf or climbing),
beetroot,
capsicum,
carrot,
celery,
cucumber,
egg plant,
herbs (seed or bedding plants),
lettuce,
marrow,
melon,
parsnip,
pumpkin,
radish,
rhubarb crowns,
silver beet,
squash,
sweet corn,
sweet potato,
tomato (plants).

Cool-temperate areas only:
Cabbage,
leek,
peas,
potato,
spinach.

Bauhinia, a small tree with pink or white, scented orchid-like flowers blooming well now and good for garden or street planting.

Fertilise

For established fruit trees, sprinkle sulphate of ammonia over the soil to the line of outer foliage and water in well.

Bulbs that have finished flowering should be fertilised with complete fertiliser and kept well watered. Do not cut off foliage until it begins to yellow.

Apply foliar fertiliser to vegetables (except root vegetables) and annuals to keep them growing well.

Fertilise shrubs — Hibiscus, Abelia, Oleander, Hydrangea, etc. for good summer blooms. Hydrangea blueing compound can be applied now. Azaleas and Camellias require fertilising after flowering. (See also p. 182.)

Prune

Spring-flowering Peaches must be pruned immediately flowers are finished. Do not neglect this. (See also p. 183.)

Keep new vigorous growth on spring-flowering creepers like Jasmine and Wistaria under control. Tie up long canes or remove if unwanted.

Prune spring-flowering climbing Roses when blooming is over. Cut out old canes and shorten laterals.

Prune Bottlebrush as brushes fade. Light clipping after flowering will keep native shrubs compact. Trim back Diosma (Coleonema) after blooming.

Prune Hibiscus if not already dealt with.

Pests and Diseases

Azaleas and Rhododendrons should be sprayed for petal blight with fungicide as directed on the pack. (See also p. 182.) Check Azaleas also for leaf gall, a fungus disease that causes leaves to swell up into a cauliflower ear. Pick off infected leaves and burn.

Another fungus disease, grey mould, similar in effects to petal blight, often attacks Carnations, Stocks, Petunias, etc. If wilting and rotting of blossoms is noticed, spray as for Azaleas.

Spray Gladiolus from two leaf stage for thrips, using Malathion.

Aphids attack new growth, particularly on Roses. Black aphids attack Citrus and Cherry and Peach — spray with Malathion.

Pear and Cherry slug (tiny, black and slug-like) defoliates trees — spray with Carbaryl.

Vine moth caterpillar attacks grape vines, Fuchsias — spray with Dipel or Malathion.

False looper caterpillars are prevalent on vegetables, ornamentals and potted plants (including indoors). Pick off or spray with Malathion.

Web girdling stem borers are also about, particularly in Leptospermum (See p. 121.)

Garden Care

Adult vine moth and feeding caterpillar.

Keep plants watered on dry or windy days to maintain spring show. Remove spent heads. Keep vegetable beds weeded.

Some Hibiscus are showing yellow leaves and this can be corrected by spraying with iron chelates. Whether you prune or not, Hibiscus should be fertilised well now with a good, all-purpose plant food like Hortico's "Complete Garden Food" which includes trace elements in the formula. The perennial Hibiscus is beginning to shoot from the old root stock — guard the tender shoots from snails with some snail bait. They will grow quickly now for the summer flowering season.

Regular mowing of lawns will be needed to keep down annual weeds and stop them from seeding. If you're thinking of planting a new lawn, October is the month to do it. Grass seed is cheaper than turf and will establish well now.

The brilliantly flowered native, Chorizema, flowering now.

THE OCTOBER GARDEN

Wisteria provides clouds of lavender-coloured flowers that hang like bunches of grapes.

By now, many of you will have seen at least one of the beautiful gardens open for inspection during spring. It is not difficult to achieve the same spectacular result, because the flowering shrubs that are the backbone of many spring gardens are available from any nursery and are usually easily grown. If you are visiting gardens wear walking shoes — they are more comfortable and will not damage lawns. (Leave your toddlers and dogs at home if possible. Lovable as they are, they can be a menace in strange gardens — especially if there are ponds to fall into.)

Spectacular results can be obtained by using a few free-flowering shrubs such as Spiraea, usually called May in Australia, in one or all of its forms. *S. cantoniensis* with its arching canes of snow white, single flowers in dense clusters is one of the most easily grown plants available. The double-flowered variety *S. lanceata* is just as lovely.

Another species not seen so often is Bridal Wreath (*S. prunifolia* "Plena") with clusters of small, white, double flowers along the stems. Spiraea will grow in any normal garden soil in sun or partial shade. It makes a good shrub for a border but should be given enough room for the arching canes to develop.

One of the showiest plants in the spring garden is Wistaria, which can be grown as a creeper or trained into a small tree by staking and pruning. It grows quickly and provides clouds of lavender-coloured flowers. Trained over an archway, the flowers hang down like bunches of grapes.

The yellow Banksia Rose (*Rosa banksiae* "Lutea") — a fast-growing, thornless Rose with clusters of small, yellow Roses — provides an attractive colour combination beside Wistaria. Both the yellow and the white Banksia Roses lend themselves to training over windows or doorways. The white Rose is not as vigorous as the yellow but has a sweet perfume.

Jasminum polyanthum is another easily grown creeper which provides a good show with very little trouble. The flowers open white from pink buds and are sweetly perfumed. This climber is quite rampant and needs to be controlled by tying up long canes that tend to grow along the ground and root freely.

Another inhabitant of prize gardens is *Weigela florida.* This shrub looks particularly attractive in spring with its arching canes, decorative new leaves and rose-pink flowers. The variety, "Variegata", has golden margins and is a handsome plant, although not as free-flowering as the parent.

Weigela, for all its spring beauty, is a shrub often dug out by gardeners because of its one flaw — the leaves can become very tatty and persist on the shrub into winter before falling. If you can resist the temptation to prune it or chop it down in winter it will reward you in spring. Weigela does best in a temperate climate with protection from hot winds.

Coleonema pulchrum, commonly called Diosma, is another free-flowering small shrub which will provide a good contrast to the others I have mentioned. It has fine, scented foliage and tiny, pink, starry flowers, and responds well to occasional clipping to keep it bushy.

Crabapple (Malus) for cool climates only, is a shapely small tree, one of the most attractive and easily grown being *M. floribunda*, with pink buds opening to white. This tree can be grown as a specimen and will become rather broad, with branches weeping almost to the ground. These should never be pruned off so you can mow under the tree because this ruins its graceful appearance.

Add a few tall single-flowered Azaleas and you will have a good background planting for a show garden every spring. Then, if you want a really glamorous garden, you can set about collecting some expensive treasures like Orchids, unusual Maples, grafted Weeping Cherries, Blue Spruce or exotic dwarf shrubs.

Crabapple (Malus floribunda) — *a small tree for picturesque spring flowers.*

GARDENKEEPING

Azalea and Camellia Care

Azaleas which have finished flowering should be fertilised now. Several foods are available, but Azaleas respond well to liquid fertilisers and they are fool-proof.

The new leaf growth is also an invitation for lace bugs to lay eggs in the leaf tissue, from which the nymphs hatch and suck the sap from underneath the leaves. Leaves eventually develop a silvery look on top and the undersides look rusty. Lace bug is worse where Azaleas are grown in full sunlight, and once damaged the bushes look unsightly until the old leaves are replaced by new growth. Spray with Malathion, taking care to wet the undersides of the leaves. If you prefer not to use sprays, substitute a weak solution of Condy's Crystals or dust the plants with sulphur while they are still wet. Sulphur is easily distributed by putting it in a nylon stocking and shaking it into the bush.

Tall-growing single Azaleas make good privacy plantings

The red spider also damages Azaleas (also Camellias, Viburnum, Fuschias and beans, which are also favourites with Tetranychus species) but can be controlled by two or three sprays of Kelthane at 10 day intervals as directed on pack.

When you have finished spraying and fertilising, spread fresh mulch around Azalea beds. Leaf litter, bark chip and pine flake is available by the bag from nurseries.

A good layer of mulch will keep down weeds, keep the roots cool during summer and help prevent the plants from drying out on hot, windy days. Never allow mulch to touch the trunk or main stem of any plant or tree but spread it generously over the rest of the bed.

If you like your Azaleas to be shapely, they respond well to a light clipping across the new growth. This will induce a denser growth and a thicker mass of flowers next season. Otherwise Azaleas should be left unpruned unless they are being grown as a standard — when all side growths must be removed — or when an occasional branch grows more vigorously than the rest of the shrub.

Potted Azaleas are susceptible to burning from fertiliser, so always sprinkle it round the edge of the pot rather than over the whole area. You don't have this problem with a liquid fertiliser but better results will be obtained by making three weak applications over a three-week period.

Camellias are generally in full leaf growth now and these can be clipped to keep them from spreading too much. Camellias should also be given a good mulch for summer and a good handful of cottonseed meal over the root area. Daphne will appreciate mulch and fertiliser too but don't prune it.

Rhododendron Care

A friend of mine had a sick Rhododendron. When she noticed it was looking poorly she watered it and gave a "good strong dose of fertiliser". It is now on the seriously ill list — another victim of kindness.

Rhododendrons and Azaleas — their smaller brothers — are surface-rooting plants and should never be given large doses of fertiliser. It burns their roots and kills the plant.

If you have a peaky Rhododendron, first feel the soil — the long spell of dry weather has made some shallow-rooted plants dry out. For dry soil, give the plant a good soaking by leaving the hose dripping under it so the water soaks into the ground without washing soil away.

If the soil isn't dry, examine the plant for insect attack or disease. Check that it is firmly in the ground because Azaleas can easily be loosened by wind and rain. Badly drained soil may lead to root-rot — check round the base of the trunk to make sure the bark is healthy.

Yellowing leaves may mean a soil deficiency. This can be adjusted with a sprinkle of iron chelates or a tablespoon of Epsom salts in 4.5 L (1 gal) of water. Another reason for failure in members of the Rhododendron family is alkaline soil. Lime should never be used and they should not be planted near new concrete work. A sprinkle of sulphur will adjust the balance.

If you feel you must give your plant some nourishment, water it all over with a weak solution of liquid fertiliser like Aquasol — about half the recommended strength. Plants very rarely die from lack of fertiliser, but are often killed by too much.

I sometimes think the "good strong dose" is a hangover from Grandma's giving castor oil to any child who looked a bit off colour — and remember all the trouble that caused.

So if you don't want to have to call the tree surgeon in the middle of the night, stay your hand with the fertiliser on your peaky plants. This advice applies to all plants, not just Rhododendrons and Azaleas.

Pruning Prunus

The long wands of dwarf Prunus (*P. glandulosa*) have attracted a lot of attention from garden viewers. To get the mass of flowers right up the stem, prune severely immediately after flowering, cutting the stems almost to the ground. This encourages suckering and by next season should give you 1.5 m (5 ft) stems crowded with flowers. *P. albiplena* is the double white variety and *P. sinensis* is the rose pink.

Spring-flowering Peaches should be pruned as soon as they have finished flowering. There have been a number of complaints about peach leaf curl on new growth. Prune any branches with leaf distortion and burn them. Spray affected trees with copper oxychloride next year at bud-burst to prevent a further outbreak.

Flowering Cherry and Crabapple should not be pruned, but any damaged branches can be cut back.

Petal Blight

Petal blight is a fungus (*Ovulinia azaleae*) which only attacks Azaleas. They first show watery flecks which enlarge until the whole flower collapses in a soggy mass. If you remove these flowers they will feel sticky. It is this stickiness that causes them to cling to leaves and branches, and they cling there until they are brown and dry.

Although the flowers are dead, the fungus is not. It

continues with the next stage of its development, producing black, seed-like bodies — the sclerotia, or resting bodies of the fungus. These fall to the ground and remain dormant until the following spring, when the resting bodies produce tiny stalks, each with a terminal cup.

Spores develop in the cup, and when ripe are ejected upward with enough force to reach a host flower and the whole cycle starts again. The only way to break this vicious circle is to spray the plants thoroughly with a fungicide. Effective new fungicides are coming onto the market now. If you have Azaleas that have died in the way I have described, you should spray the bushes and the ground under them thoroughly.

When the Azaleas begin to come into bud next year, the ground and the bushes should be sprayed again, with most attention being paid to the soil surface where the sclerotia lie. A further spray about ten days later should protect the blooms. However, if you have a neighbour who hasn't sprayed for a time the spores will spread. Daily picking off of diseased flowers helps but they must be burned or put in the garbage bin not thrown on the garden. Once bushes are in full bloom this becomes impracticable.

TREES AND SHRUBS

Two Crabapples: top Malus spectabilis, *lower* M. floribunda *— good for cool-climate gardens.*

Trees in Spring Finery

I have seen several interesting trees in flower and you might care to look out for them. First, the Horse Chestnut (Aesculus) — a most beautiful cool-climate tree covered in candelabra-like spikes of pink and white blossom.

There is a rather unusual green-flowered small tree which intrigues people. This is *Prunus serrulata* "Ukon". The bunches of flowers are double, pale green with a flush of pink. Though not as spectacular as *P. serrulata* "Kanzan", the double pink, it is attractive and interesting.

Have you noticed how beautiful the Golden Elms are in October? Their bright yellowy-green leaves are very handsome in early summer, when they look so fresh and new. But they retain the bright fresh look right through summer and make a bright foil for darker-leaved trees, particularly the purplish ones like *Prunus pissardi.*

So many trees are blooming in spring that less spectacular trees pass unnoticed. Japanese Maple (*Acer palmatum*) is in delicate leaf (try growing the variety "Hisio") and another, *Acer negundo,* is covered in pale golden tassels.

Crabapples are at their peak. One of the prettiest — *Malus floribunda* — grows to about 4.5 m (15 ft) with clusters of red buds opening almost white.

Virgilia

Virgilia oroboides is one of the fastest-growing trees known and I have noticed a lot of these graceful trees laden with rosy-purple pea flowers. Virgilia is a good small tree for the garden and will provide a fast screen for a new garden, though it may be fairly short-lived. It also needs wind protection.

White-flowered Shrubs

White flowers are often unpopular. Many people shun white Roses with an almost superstitious shudder. Possibly this is because they still think of white flowers as funeral flowers — though the fashions in wreaths have long since swung away from this tradition.

It is a pity, though, if superstition prevents people from growing white flowers. Nothing so enlivens and lights up a garden as a snow-white flowering bush. We enjoy particularly two charming white-flowering shrubs which grace our garden at this time of year — Deutzia and Philadelphus.

Mock Orange (Philadelphus) which flowers in October and grows to 2 m (6 ft). It has white flowers on arching canes and tolerates partial shade.

The popular names of both these shrubs have bridal overtones — Philadelphus is called Mock Orange because of its orange-blossom perfume and the double form of Deutzia is called Wedding Bells. They both flower on arching canes, a habit of growth which is particularly graceful if your garden slopes (as ours does) so that you look up at them.

If you are searching for shrubs that don't require full sun, these are just the thing — both are deciduous and like some shade in hot areas. If you can shelter them from strong winds the flowers will last longer. Otherwise they are easily grown and don't seem troubled by pests or diseases. Both Deutzia and Philadelphus need to be cut back after flowering. Old canes should be cut right out from the base of the plant.

The scented white climber, Trachelospermum, is blooming now too. It can be planted with its roots in shade but so that it can climb up into the sun. Trachelospermum can also be grown as a tub plant. It will trail if you don't want it to climb. It is also well suited to growing over an ornamental arch because its dense growth of shining leaves will very quickly hide the supporting arch completely.

Echium and Eupatorium

I am always being asked the names of two blue-flowered shrubs, Echium and Eupatorium, which are both blooming at present. Echium forms a spreading mound of greyish foliage and sends up all blue flower spikes with a reddish fuzz round them caused by the extruded stamens. They are good seaside plants and grow well in poor, well-drained soil. Allow them room to spread and prune them back immediately after flowering. This striking plant is related to Patterson's Curse (*Echium vulgare*), and you know how easily that grows in Australia.

Eupatorium is like a giant Ageratum and makes a good background shrub for spring-flowering Prunus.

Star Jasmine (Trachelospermum) — a climber with white scented flowers suitable for tub or trellis.

PERENNIALS AND ANNUALS

Summer-flowering Annuals to Plant

October is a good time for summer planting. Everything will get away quickly in the warming soil. Summer annuals like Petunias, Phlox, Zinnia, Verbena, Torenia and Salvia can be planted out or raised from seed.

There are a number of F1 hybrid petunias to choose from which are all good. There are several "Cascades" on the market and the latest is "Elegant Cascade". These varieties are particularly useful in pots, baskets or garden beds where there is room for them to trail over a rock wall or rockery.

If you like Petunias, here's an idea you might like to copy. Last summer I saw an old brick house with a very small frontage and a dull brick porch with steps centre-front, which had been enlivened by large pots of white Cascade Petunias placed top and bottom and on either side of the steps. The effect was to lighten the appearance of the house so that it had a pleasant and inviting look, in a way that was in keeping with the old-fashioned style of the house itself.

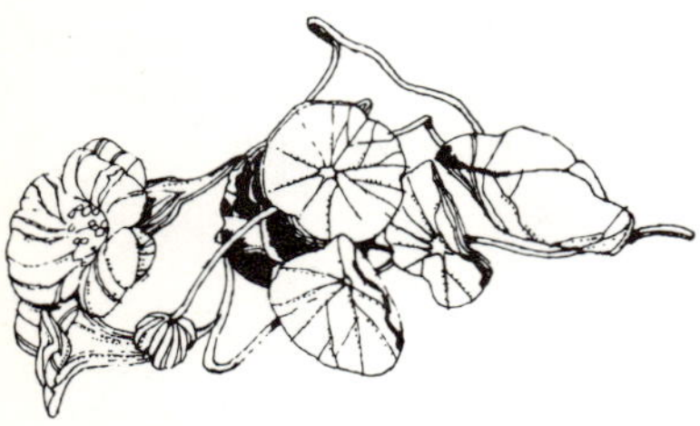

Jewel bright blooms of Nasturtium last from spring through to autumn.

Another new Petunia is "Sweetheart" which gives you a mixture of pink and blue plants in each punnet. There is also the new Salvia hybrid "Spangles" which introduces some new colours in a low, bushy plant.

Look for Hollyhocks — there will be some double-flowered varieties available soon. These plants are now rust-resistant and worth growing. For flower-arrangers, there are seedlings of the green Zinnia "Envy" — a must for summer flower arrangements.

The Dahlia "Hi Dolly" will give a mass of summer flowers and can be discarded when it has finished flowering, like other annuals — avoiding the bother of storing tubers as is usual with Dahlias.

A neglected summer plant is Cosmos. This is easily grown from seed and gives masses of colourful flowers which are good for cutting. Cosmos will grow almost anywhere and provide quick colour in a new garden. Gladioli planted now will have flowers by Christmas.

October Planting for March Blooming

Garden weddings always send me into a rosy glow of remembrance of my own garden wedding — a positive orgy of organdie, Roses and jellied trifle — at our family home.

A friend planning a garden wedding in early March had the interesting problem of arranging for plenty of flowers to be blooming then. Autumn Roses are the mainstay of the March garden, and although there are lots of Roses in this particular garden the autumn flush is never very good. This is probably because the deciduous trees in the garden have made a lot of growth through the summer and the Roses are rather shaded by March.

Cape Forget-me-nots, Rochia and other succulents fill a narrow space with vivid colour.

Nemesia "Blue Gem" in a Strawberry pot.

Pacific Coast hybrid Iris, with a background of Californian Poppy and Artemesia, in a corner of my own spring garden.

Columbines in an ideal semi-sun position.

Rosa senica alba—*a beautifully delicate climber that blooms only in spring.*

Judicious tree pruning would let the sun through — sometimes it is just one or two branches that block the sun from a particular flower bed and a little trim will work wonders without spoiling the symmetry of the trees.

Summer annuals planted at Christmas time will be blooming in March. Marigolds make a good splash of colour and Petunias can be planted in pots and grown on in a sunny corner. The day before the wedding the flowering pots can be arranged anywhere where colour is lacking.

Fuchsias are still blooming well in March and will thrive in partial sunlight. So will the delicate Japanese Anemones. These can be planted now and there are doubles as well as singles available. I like the delicate old-fashioned single white Windflower best, although the newer varieties are bigger and better.

Some of the early-flowering *Camellia sasanqua* varieties bloom in March and several advanced specimens could be planted now.

Potted Chrysanthemums in bloom will be available in March from nurseries where they are grown under hothouse conditions and brought into flower early. A few pots of these ordered in advance from a local nursery would guard against any flower failure in the garden.

When you are planning a party in the garden there is always the danger of rain or wind spoiling the flowers you have been cherishing for months. But the fairly new trend towards potted flowering plants provides a good standby in an emergency.

Chrysanthemums, Cyclamen and Poinsettias are the seasonal standbys. Where money is no object, there are plant hire people who will cater for flowers.

Rehmannia — an unusual perennial related to the Foxglove. Flowers are cream, pink and purple and bloom from spring through to autumn in warm climates.

Pelargoniums and Geraniums

Pelargoniums are at their best in October. The Regal Pelargoniums make a good display backed up by the more humble Ivy and Zonal Geraniums which are hard to beat for a good, bright splash of colour in the garden or containers. Though most people have a few Geraniums growing, not nearly enough use is made of the Regal Pelargoniums which will provide just as lavish a display of flowers as Azaleas do earlier in the season.

The regals grow easily and vigorously and modern hybrids have huge heads of frilled and blotched blooms — the big, dark velvety blotches are a real feature of these lovely flowers. They are not prone to disease or insect attack though the flowers may be damaged in humid weather by grey mould fungus, which has a similar effect to petal blight of Azaleas. This is usually fairly easy to control by picking off and burning infected blooms and spraying with Mancozeb. The only drawback that regals could be considered to have is that they only flower naturally in the spring though they will repeat flower in the summer if spent heads are pruned off after flowering. Geraniums can be counted on to flower throughout the year in warmer areas and even in winter there are occasional blooms.

This is the best time to buy Regal Pelargoniums. Most nurseries carry good stocks while they are in bloom. There are many strikingly named varieties but you might have to go to a Geranium nursery for these. Most of the flowering plants on sale in general nurseries seem to be unnamed and the only way to make sure you are buying a colour you like is to buy plants in flower. You will find regals that are everblooming like "Firebird", copper-rose colour, short and stocky and suitable for pot plants; "Silversheen", orchid pink and ruffled or tall and self-branching for the garden; "Opera House", magenta and rose-pink, ruffled flowers.

Some of the taller varieties make lovely standards and they are easy to grow this way, either in the garden or in a pot. The plant must be firmly staked at planting time and tied to the stake as it grows upwards. Side shoots must be rubbed off using your thumb to encourage upright growth and the plant should not be exposed to wind. You get the full effect of the beauty of the flowers when Pelargoniums are grown this way.

Cactus Geranium "Fire Chief" — an unusual variety flowering now.

Pelargoniums need full sun and very well-drained soil and a light hand with the fertiliser. Too much feeding will result in lush leaf growth at the expense of the flowers.

Ivy Geraniums appreciate a situation where they can trail down over a warm stone or brick wall in full sun. If Ivy Geraniums are pinched back they will be bushier and carry more flowers. Left to themselves they will have long trailers that flower on the ends only.

There is a large range of rich and pastel colours available in single and double-flowered varieties and a mixed planting of three or even four contrasting colours creates a very striking effect. One combination I like is "Firedragon", dark vermilion; "Amethyst", deep lavender; "Galilee", rose-pink double; and a scarlet double like "Sir Percy Blakeney", or the old-fashioned salmon-rose "Madam Mourrier".

If you have a sunny patio or balcony you should be able to grow Geraniums well in troughs or pots. The Zonal (upright type) Geraniums are also showy and easy to grow though unfortunately prone to rust on the leaves in the humid coastal area.

Some of the showiest of the zonals are the Irenes, with compact growth and very large heads of semi-double flowers. These are usually sold by nurseries though unusual types of zonals will only be found in specialist nurseries.

Rosebud Geraniums are worth looking for — they make good pot plants and there are several varieties including "Appleblossom Rosebud", greenish white, pink edges; "Rosebud Supreme", brilliant red; "Red Rambler", blood red, white reverse flushed crimson; "Rosebud", tyrian purple. These are distinctive with clusters of double flowers resembling tight rosebuds.

If you're lucky you may find some of the cactus type of Geranium with small, palmately-lobed leaves and ragged-edged petals. The late Mr Ted Both hybridised a number of Geraniums using the cactus type as a parent. Usually called Star Geraniums, many are miniatures and very distinctive with their star-like flowers and leaves.

There is a new Ivy Geranium called "Rouletta" which has two-tone white and red striped blooms and stocky growth and which would be suitable for baskets, window-boxes, etc. If you are looking for Ivy Geraniums for hanging baskets try "L'Elegante" with leaves edged white with pink tinges and dainty white single flowers, or the novelty Ivies: "Crocodile", with dark green leaves veined cream, pink single flowers and "Gay Baby", which is a miniature Ivy with small mauve flowers. These two are Australian hybrids and are showy basket or pot plants.

Massed Annuals in Baskets

My hanging baskets of Pansies are still blooming — I counted fifty flowers in one basket — and the double "Victorious" Petunia is in full bloom in a basket with white Alyssum.

Don't imagine I have any special hanging baskets to hold so many flowers — they are just ordinary wire hanging baskets lined with mulch mats filled with potting mix, and crammed full with a whole punnet of plants. They need to be watered twice a day (even three times on hot days) and are given a little soluble fertiliser every week. I also pick off any spent blooms every day. It is a little bit of extra work but very rewarding when you see fifty little Pansy faces smiling at you as they jostle for space and cascade over the edges of the basket. I smile back.

Something else that is doing very well in a hanging basket here is a variegated Vinca. This is an easily grown trailing plant with very pretty foliage, shiny green with cream edging. The flowers are quite large, flat and bright blue.

Variegated trailing or creeping plants are attractive when used in hanging baskets and look decorative even when they are not in flower. I discovered a variegated dwarf creeping fig which makes a very striking basket plant. This plant is available from nurseries and is well worth looking for if you are looking for good, hardy basket plants.

Regal pelargoniums — easily grown plants flowering now.

ROSES

Yellow Banksia Rose — suitable for a trellis.

Spring-time and Roses

I never cease to be delighted by the succession of flowers each season brings. Just as there is regret at the passing of the flowering Peach, Cherries and Spiraea, their place is taken by the pink and white of Bauhinias and the fragrant white Philadelphus (Mock Orange).

Azalea-flowered Pelargoniums are a happy substitute for spring-flowering Azaleas but Roses are no substitute for anything — they are just being rosy everywhere. At this time of the year the dozen Roses I have managed to squeeze into my garden just don't satisfy me. I yearn for a positive bower of Roses. It is only by muttering "black spot, thrips, mildew, die-back" that I can remain calm.

Fortunately for people like me it is now possible to buy Roses in containers almost any time. The nurseries and even chain stores carry stocks of Roses in bloom. I have seen some well-grown garden varieties as well as miniature types.

If you are planting container-grown Roses, plant them out in the cool of the afternoon and water them well. Established Roses may be suffering from some of the diseases or pests I mentioned earlier and which are now infesting Roses in humid coastal areas. Black spot and mildew can be controlled by spraying with fungicide, but if the plants are not badly infected pick off the diseased leaves and put them in the dustbin. (Remember, there could be a total fire ban at times if you are thinking of burning them.)

When you go round the garden take a plastic bag and collect any diseased leaves and flowers you see. Thrips can be partly controlled this way if they are spoiling your Roses. Cut off any Roses that are past their prime and put them into the plastic bag too. This will stop the thrips already in the Roses from migrating to new buds to spoil them.

Some die-back becomes apparent now because of bad pruning. Cut any dead branches off well below the damaged section and dab some bituminous paint on the cut to seal it. These little dead bits on Roses, called "hat-pegs", are usually only a few centimetres long but if they are not cut off the branch will continue to die back.

CLIMBERS AND CREEPERS

Wistaria

Wistaria is in full bloom at present and there are many interesting uses of it. For instance, a house on a corner with a high paling fence running the full length of the block on two sides — facing north and north-east — would normally look ugly and forbidding. However the top of this fence is draped along its full length with Wistaria which hangs like fringing on a shawl. Along the bottom of the fence is a narrow bed planted with pink and red Geraniums in full bloom. Instead of looking dull and ugly, the grey fence is banded with vivid colour and the scene is beautifully tidy and well cared for, making a definite attraction out of a liability.

Here is another simple use of Wistaria which could solve a lot of problems in new areas where home sites have been carved out of rock, leaving homeowners with raw rock faces to cover: just train Wistaria over it.

Wistaria grows quickly in summer, sending out long, snake-like canes almost overnight so that a Wistaria planted now could provide quite a satisfying expanse of flowers by next spring.

Often there is no soil at all in situations like this, where rock faces have been blasted or jack-hammered to make our sandstone hills conform to subdivision. However, a small bed can be built up with stones and a little cement, filled with soil to give the creeper a good start, and later its roots will find their way down through cracks in the rock. Two or three strategically placed wires stretched across the rock face will provide support for the growing plant. As the Wistaria grows it can be fastened to the wire with strips of old nylon stocking or plant ties from your nursery.

Wistaria will run riot if it is allowed to — running up trees and climbing on to roofs uninvited. This is not always very good for either the trees or the roof. However, there are two Jacarandas on a footpath which I look out for each spring. The trees are, of course, leafless, and delicately hung with the very dainty white *Wistaria floribunda* "Alba". The white form is not as spectacular as the mauve species *W. sinensis*, but is very dainty and graceful with the added attraction of being a little unusual.

Wistaria will grow readily almost anywhere but it likes a fairly acid soil and plenty of water during the flowering period. The root system has to supply perhaps 30 m (100 ft) of creeper laden with bloom and under dry conditions the flowers will very soon wilt and fall. So remember to give your Wistaria a good drink round the root area on dry, windy days to prolong the flowering period.

BULBS

Iris

Washing the dishes for our giant economy-size family gives me a marvellous opportunity for garden-watching. The garden outside the window was designed to be viewed from the kitchen sink. The washer-up can gloat over the blue Felicia tumbling over the rocks, the nodding blue Columbines (Aquilegia) and the tall neighbouring clump of blue and lilac Bearded Iris. Each Iris bloom only lasts for a short time. But they don't blush unseen while there's washing-up to be done.

The tall Bearded Iris is fairly familiar to most gardeners, but a number of species and hybrids can be grown just as easily in the home garden. Louisiana Irises, hybrids bred from Southern

Iris japonica — *lilac-fringed flowers that like semi-shade and a damp position.*

US species, are particularly well suited to the humid coastal climate.

They can be grown round pool margins, but adapt well to the garden if given plenty of water and rich soil containing humus in the form of compost, or well-rotted manure which will help the soil retain moisture. A layer of mulch will also help. Unlike the Bearded Iris, their rhizomes should not be exposed to the sun because they will dry up and die. Plant in semi-shade.

Louisianas — tall and well-branched — carry a number of flowers to a stem and stay open over several weeks. Dr G.B. Loveridge, an Iris enthusiast, told me that he has one which has borne sixteen blooms for a month. He has a wonderful variety of Irises in his Turramurra garden, and finds them free of pests and diseases.

Another charming group of Irises is the Pacific Coast hybrid — also from the US — which grow up to 60 cm (2 ft) with Orchid-like colours and the rather flattened flowers characteristic of the American hybrids. They like sun — with some shade from its full heat — acid soil, and plenty of water in winter for the spring flowering.

Irises are not often available at general nurseries but can be bought from specialist nurseries. The two I have been talking about can easily be raised from seed.

The gorgeous Japanese Iris (*I. kaempferi*) makes an attractive pool plant. It should be grown in containers and placed in the water in late spring and summer. But *I. kaempferi* will not grow permanently in water and the pots must be taken out after flowering to dry out.

I have some growing in a pot with a deep saucer which I keep filled with water during the flowering season. They can be grown in the garden, as long as you keep them well watered in summer. If you would like to grow Iris permanently in your pool, try *I. pseudacorus,* which is a golden yellow, or *I. laevigata,* a relative of *I. kaempferi,* with blue or purple flowers.

I. siberica is also suitable for the poolside and will die down in winter. It sends up vigorous spring leaves which will form a 1 m (3 ft) clump, and bears rich purple flowers.

I. spuria is recommended as suitable for humid coastal conditions. They grow in almost any soil and will withstand drought though they need moisture at flowering time. They thrive on a little Rose fertiliser. Pacific Coast hybrids respond well to fish fertiliser, while the *kaempferi* and *sibericas* like Camellia and Azalea food.

EDIBLES

Growing and Using Herbs

A herb luncheon I attended gave great pleasure and some beautiful recipe ideas. I sampled chicken cooked with Rosemary, pineapple with chopped Pineapple Mint and salad dishes spiced with Parsley, Chives,

Thyme and Basil. I also admired an unusual herb garden built from railway sleepers. Railway sleepers can be used in many ways in a garden, and their rustic look is particularly suited to a herb garden.

Most herbs like a well-drained situation and a raised bed of sleepers provides the right conditions — particularly if the existing soil is clayey. Herbs are attractive and useful plants. Many of them have decorative foliage, all are aromatic and some have flowers which are pretty enough to justify their place in the garden for their beauty alone. Borage has flowers of a bright, intense blue and Chicory (sometimes used as an additive to coffee) has a delicate flower like a lilac-blue Cosmos which unfortunately fades as soon as it is picked.

There were several of the old medicinal herbs in this garden as well as the usual culinary herbs, and "strewing herbs" like Tansy. In ancient castles, Tansy was strewn over the rushes to improve the smell and repel flies, fleas, ants and mosquitoes. Vacuum cleaners are a great improvement on strewing herbs, though not as interesting.

Lavender, Cotton Lavender (Santolina) and Rosemary were used to repel the clothes moth. Remember when your grandmother's linen cupboard smelled of Lavender? Those fragrant herbs can still be used in cupboards. Pick bunches when the dew has dried off them and hang them in an airy place to dry. They can then be used freely in cupboards to keep moths away from winter woollies or make your sheets fragrant.

Another good herb is Lemon Grass, which is an ingredient of oriental cooking and is used to make a medicinal tea. Lemon Grass forms quite a strong grassy clump — particularly in warm climates. It is the source of the lemon fragrance in many products, including soap powders.

Some herbs are difficult to get in Australia because of a seed shortage. The old herb seed gatherers in European countries are dying out and it is not profitable enough to attract young people. It sounds like a romantic rural occupation. If any one is thinking of dropping out of the rat race they might think of setting up as a gatherer of herbs and spices.

Herb pots, those tall earthenware jars with lipped holes around their sides, are useful but should be planted in a special way. Begin with a handful of ordinary charcoal in the bottom of the pot, then fill to the first layer of holes with a good potting mix. Put your plant down into the pot and thread it through the hole. Firm it down well into the soil and work up to the next layer, planting each hole from the inside out. A little blood and bone once a year will provide nourishment.

Herbs are easy to grow. The ones I have mentioned, and many others, are available from nurseries and chain stores. Most herbs like plenty of sun, though Mint and Parsley appreciate a little bit of shade.

If you are planting a herb garden, put taller-growing plants at the back where they won't smother the low growers like Thyme and Marjoram. Tansy and Fennel will grow to 1 m (3 ft) in the

Lovage — a celery-flavoured perennial herb for use in soups, stews and salads.

garden. If you want to include Lavenders and Rosemary you can keep them small by picking, or, if you want them purely for interest, by regular trimming.

Don't be too kind to herbs — they don't like too much water or fertiliser. They prefer slightly alkaline conditions, so if you have acid soil a little lime will help. Don't ever spray herbs with insecticides or fungicides. Because of their aromatic oils they are not particularly palatable to pests. But if you do find a caterpillar or a snail enjoying your Parsley, just pull it off or dust with Derris.

INDOORS

Using the Right Soil Mix

As the popularity of indoor plants continues to grow it is becoming easier to care for them. There are all sorts of special products available to help plants survive indoors, ranging from specially formulated indoor plant soil and food to special containers and lighting systems.

When you begin to grow plants in containers it is important to use the right potting mix. Don't try to economise by digging up some soil from the garden — garden soil is unsuitable for pots and baskets because it will cake or set hard as well as being full of weed seeds, fungus disease, etc. If you visit your nursery or garden centre you will find a whole range of potting mixes designed for different types of plants — orchid compost for Orchids, African violet compost for Gesneriads, bulb fibre, etc. It is well worth investing in one of these composts if you are trying to grow special plants which need specific soil conditions, though the ordinary potting mix is suitable for most plants.

Fertiliser packs formulated for container-grown plants are also worth while because they have been designed for use by plants growing in a small amount of soil and, used to directions, will not burn or damage plants. They are usually in small, compact packs that won't cause storage problems in a small flat or unit. There are also sprays for pests and diseases which have been formulated for indoor plants, so that plants can be sprayed safely indoors. (I still recommend doing any necessary spraying outside wherever possible to avoid having spray in the house.)

Two of the most common reasons for the loss of indoor plants are faulty watering and insufficient light. The first can be overcome by using one of the special containers available which work by hydroponics — that is by having a built-in water supply which can be drawn into the soil when it becomes slightly dry. The fertiliser is usually added, in small amounts, to this water too so that the plants can draw up what is needed. There are several different systems available from nurseries, department stores or garden centres in various sizes and price ranges. One of these is the Luwasa Hydroculture system in which the roots are put into pebbles of expanded clay which provides a base to support the plant and to keep the root system moist by capillary action. A water level indicator lets you know how much water is in the pot and when it needs to be refilled. A special nutrient is added to the water so that the plants absorb water and food at the same time.

The advantages of this and other systems on the market at present are that plants only need watering once every few weeks, the soil substitute is clean and free of weeds, pests and soil parasites and cannot go sour or mouldy. There is also a range of self-watering planters available from Rite-Gro, called the Gardenair system, which are available from garden centres and some nurseries.

Planting Out Scraps

If you are on a tight budget and can't afford the luxury of buying lots of large potted plants, try looking around your kitchen for potential plants.

Search the vegetable basket for an old potato which has begun to sprout, and plant it in a pot. If it is very large it may have several shoots and can be cut into large sections to provide more plants, but small potatoes can be planted whole.

Sweet potatoes that have begun to shoot may be planted in a container with a stake. Sweet potatoes make attractive climbing plants or can be allowed to trail over a hanging basket. Pinch out the growing tips as the plant grows to make it more bushy.

Save the seeds from a lemon, orange or mandarin and plant them for small shrubby plants with shiny, aromatic foliage. Avocado seeds and loquats also grow into handsome potted plants.

Chokoes start shooting in spring and can be planted with a stake for climbing plants. Passionfruit seeds grow quickly and have deocrative foliage. The seeds from fresh dates can be planted and will grow into little date palms.

All of these plants can be used in containers on balconies, patios or verandahs and can be taken inside as temporary house plants when they are large enough. Start them in small containers and move them into larger pots as they grow.

Don't expect to harvest any crops from these seedling plants but if you give them regular fertiliser and water and pinch the growing tips sometimes to keep plants bushy and compact most of them will give you years of pleasure at absolutely no cost.

CHECKLIST

Roses fill gardens with scent and colour now and it is a pleasure to be out and working in such surroundings. With this in mind perhaps this is a good month to prepare for the inevitable rainy periods of summer. There are garden and storm-water drains to be cleared of leaves and beds will benefit from a mulch which will stop soil being washed away.

Flowering now

Trees and Shrubs:
Abutilon,
Bauhinia,
Berberis,
Brunfelsia,
Calliandra,
Calodendron (Cape Chestnut),
Catalpa,
Ceanothus,
Choisya,
Dais,
Deutzia,
Duranta,
Erythrina crista-galli (Cockspur Coral Tree),
Escallonia,
Felicia,
Fuchsia,
Gardenia,
Heliotrope,
Hibiscus,
Hypericum,
Jacaranda,
Kalmia,
Lantana hybrids,
Lavender,
Leonitis (Lion's Ear),
Liriodendron (Tulip Tree),
Magnolia grandiflora,
Metrosideros (New Zealand Xmas bush),
Philadelphus (Mock Orange),
Plumbago,
Prunus (Flowering Cherry),
Raphiolepis (Indian Hawthorn),
Rhododendron,
Russelia,
Spartium (Spanish Broom),
Spiraea bumalda (pink May),
Tamarix,
Virgilia.

Perennials and Annuals:
Ageratum,
Antirrhinum (Snapdragon),
Campanula,
Cerastium,
Delphinium,
Dianthus,
Gazania,
Gerbera,
Kentranthus,
Lobelia,
Nepeta,
Petunia,
Phlox sublata,
Phlox (annual),
Portulaca,
Salvia,
Tagetes (Marigold),
Tropaeolum (Nasturtium).

Bulbs:
Agapanthus,
Canna,
Gladiolus,
Hippeastrum,
Iris,
Lilium (Madonna and November Lily),
Watsonia,
Zanthedeschia (Arum and Calla Lilies).

Climbers:
Beaumontia,
Bougainvillea,
Campsis,
Clytostoma,
Cobaea,
Dolichos,
Doxantha (Cat's Claw),
Jasmine,
Lonicera (Honeysuckle),
Manettia,
Phaedranthus,
Stephanotis,
Thunbergia,
Trachelospermum (Star Jasmine).

Natives:
Acacia mollissima,
Agonis (Willow Myrtle),
Angophora cordifolia,
Boronia,
Brachychiton (Flame Tree),
Calicoma (Black Wattle),
Callistemon (Bottlebrush),
Castenospermum,
Ceratopetalum,
Chamaelaucium,
Grevillea robusta (Silky Oak),
Hymenosporum flavum
Kunzia,
Lagunaria,
Melaleuca,
Oreocallis wickhamii (Queensland Tree Waratah),
Sollya,
Wahlenbergia (native Bluebell).

NOVEMBER

Plant

Trees, Shrubs and Climbers:
Container-grown shrubs, trees and climbers of all kinds can be planted now. There are plenty of fruit trees around too, including grafted mulberries and a variety of fruiting grape.

Perennials and Annuals:
Seedling plants of all summer-flowering annuals (see October) can be planted now, together with Chrysanthemums.

Bulbs:
Bearded Iris,
Crinum,
Dahlia,
Nerine,
Waterlily.

Vegetables:
Plant from seed or seedlings:
Beans (French; climbing),
beetroot,
capsicum,
carrot,
celery,
cucumber,
egg plant,
endive,
herbs,
lettuce,
marrow,
parsnip,
pumpkin,
radish,
rockmelon,
squash,
sweet corn,
tomato,
zucchini,

Cool-temperate areas only:
Brussels sprouts,
cabbage,
cauliflower,
peas,
potato.

Prune

Diosma (Coleonema) can be trimmed lightly to shape.

Cut back unwanted growth on Jasmine (*Jasminum polyanthum*) to keep rampant growth under control.

Shorten back Deutzia, Choisya and Bottlebrush behind flowering heads when they have finished blooming.

Philadelphus is pruned after flowering by cutting out old branches to make room for new, vigorous wood.

Prune back Privet to prevent seeding.

Cut runners off strawberry plants.

Light prune flowering native shrubs such as Mint Bush, cutting behind spent flower heads.

Prune climbing Roses once the flowering has finished. (See also p.206.)

Cape Chestnut (Calodendron capense) — *in bloom this month.*

Frangipani (Plumeria) — a scented shrub for summer which tolerates city smog.

Fertilise

Vegetables and summer-flowering annuals require side dressings of blood and bone or an all-purpose fertiliser and water. Leafy vegetables, annuals and Azaleas will benefit from spraying with a foliar fertiliser such as Aquasol, Bloom, Zest, etc., best applied in the late afternoon.

Fertilise, water and mulch Camellias, Daphne, Rhododendrons and Azaleas using special acid formula fertiliser.

Hibiscus can be given a dressing of all-purpose fertiliser, also any spring-flowering shrubs that have finished flowering and Agapanthus, Fuchsias and Hydrangea.

Pests and Diseases

Insect invaders and diseases seem particularly prolific at this time of year.

Fruiting trees, shrubs and ripening vegetables should be sprayed for fruit fly using Rogor or Lebaycid (some fruit trees are sensitive to Rogor). Hang Dak Pots in fruit trees and start spray programme six weeks before fruit is due to ripen. Flowering Peaches that have not been pruned should be cut back to remove unwanted fruit that will harbour fruit fly.

Spray Azaleas for lace bug and red spider which disfigure and weaken foliage, using Malathion, Rogor and — for red spider mite — Kelthane. Spray Apple and Pear trees for Codling moth using Supracide (if available) or Carbaryl.

Pumpkin beetle attacks pumpkins, melons, cucumber, etc. Use either Malathion or Derris dust. Young plants are most susceptible to attack.

Gladiolus should be sprayed from two leaf stage with Malathion for thrips.

Watch for caterpillars on vegetables, vines, Fuchsias, Geraniums and annuals. Dust or spray with Dipel or pyrethrum.

Garden Care

Lawns are in good growth and should be mowed regularly without cutting them too short. Bare patches after close mowing will result in weed infestation. Oversow thin lawns with a mixed lawn seed and keep watered. Control annual weeds by regular mowing to prevent them from seeding. Fertilise by watering, applying sulphate of ammonia or special lawn food and water again. (See also p. 200.)

Plant out Dahlia tubers and stake. (See also p. 208.)

Keep watering and feeding vegetables and weed and mulch vegetable beds. (See also p. 222.)

Spring-flowering bulbs should be cared for until foliage begins to yellow. It can then be cut off and bulbs lifted if necessary. Most bulbs (except Tulips) can be left in the ground, provided it is well-drained, through summer, until they become overcrowded. If lifting, store in mesh bags and hang in a cool, dim place. (See also p. 208.)

THE NOVEMBER GARDEN

Like Picasso, gardens have a blue period — that time in early summer when the high tide of Hydrangeas reaches half-way up the walls of old houses, Agapanthus heads nod in summer breezes and Jacarandas tinge every view with a misty blue. I have a weakness for blue flowers in the garden and this is my favourite time of the year.

In summer most of us like to have the garden a blaze of colour. Nothing shows up a colourful garden to better advantage than a mass of white flowers. And in summer white flowers give a crisp, cool look to the garden.

White-flowering creepers — Trachelospermum, Mandevilla, Stephanotis and Beaumontia — can provide a white frame. White Oleander used on its own is insipid but combined with the clear pink variety "M. Belagieur" or the deep-pink double *splendens* it really glows.

The queen of white-flowering trees for summer is *Magnolia grandiflora* — strictly for the large garden but a lovely tree. In all but cold climates Frangipani provides creamy-white blooms all through the warm weather. In the more tropical areas grow the Singapore Frangipani with its deep green foliage and pure, white flowers which open flatter than other Frangipanis so that their petals curl back. And don't forget Gardenias and Angel's Trumpet (Datura).

Not nearly as romantic but practical in a small garden are the Shasta Daisies — there is a lovely frilly double which is worth growing and white Marguerites give a great mass of flowers for weeks on end and will grow anywhere in the sun. White Alyssum "Carpet of Snow" flowers most of the year and shows off the beauty of gaily coloured annuals. White "Cascade" Petunia planted now will give a good display through summer.

Plumbago capensis, *a shrub with clear blue, phlox-like flowers — makes a good hedge plant.*

GARDENKEEPING

Mow Gently, Sweet Gardener

Australian gardeners tend to be very lawn conscious and a great deal of gardening time is devoted to keeping up the ideal of a velvet sward. Unless you are aiming at a show garden, a lot of lawn work is not necessary. The primary purpose of a lawn is to provide a ground-cover which will give protection from dust or mud, provide a cool surround for the house and give you a smooth surface that is pleasant to play on, sit on and look at. It doesn't have to be perfect.

You can achieve a lawn that looks acceptable by following a few simple methods of maintenance which may mean changing your habits a little. In our summer climate, mowing the grass becomes a major chore and bad mowing habits cause a lot of lawn problems.

Many people try to cut down on mowing by cutting the lawns far too short, so that the entire leaf area of the lawn is shaved off, leaving bare stems and often bare sections of soil. With the leaf area gone, the grass roots are not being supplied with the food normally manufactured in the leaves and become weaker so that weeds move in. Vigorously growing grass will smother many weeds and to keep it growing strongly no more than half the leaf area should ever be removed at one mowing.

If you are mowing your lawn so that it looks brownish instead of green when you have finished, adjust your mower to give a higher cut. When the grass gets a bit long because you've been on holidays or the weather was too wet at the weekend, make two cuts several days apart rather than one severe cut.

When you mow regularly you are, in effect, harvesting a crop from the soil. Constantly cropping the same soil, whether vegetables or grass clippings, takes the nourishment out of the soil and it should be returned. The cheapest way to do this is to compost your grass clippings and spread them back on the lawn as a top-dressing. Burning grass clippings or taking them to the dump is wasting the main crop of your garden.

If you don't already compost your clippings, start right now so that you will have a good supply of rich soil to return to the lawn next season. In the meantime fertilise your lawn with sulphate of ammonia or a commercial lawn food to keep your lawn crop up to standard.

Regular mowing will control most annual weeds because they will be mowed off before they can seed. Perennial weeds can be dug out with an implement like an old chisel — very effective for Dandelion and curled Dock which have a single, strong deep root.

A lot of lawn weeds can be killed off by direct application of sulphate of ammonia sprinkled on to the weeds. Do this during the hottest part of the day. This will burn surrounding grass but not kill it. Water the lawn the next day. There are several effective commercial products which can be used on lawns, but read the directions on the packets before using, as some weedkillers will also kill certain grasses.

Persistent seasonal weeds like Bindii (a menace in lawns because of its sharp burrs) and winter grass can be effectively dealt with by regular annual use of pre-emergence spray at the time of seed germination.

A weed that gardeners worry unnecessarily about is white clover. This plant has nitrogen-fixing nodules on its root system and is actually a beneficial, soil improving plant rather than a weed, and mows well. If white clover has taken over your lawn give in and grow a clover lawn.

A recently released lawn seed mixture called "Stays Green & Hardy" contains clovers for a green, low maintenance lawn.

Coping with Hot Winds

In many parts of Australia hot, dry winds burn up the garden with the approach of summer. You can't stop the wind though wind-breaks — hedges, tree plantings or a creeper-covered trellis — will protect the garden. A fine spray of water that will turn the wind into a still hot but damp wind also helps.

On hot, windy days we put our sprinkler in the part of the garden where the wind will blow the spray over as big an area as possible. The jet of water is put on to the finest setting and directed as high as possible so that every gust of wind carries cooling water vapour over the garden instead of a hot furnace breath that turns plants into dried-up chips. Ideally, use a spray with an adjustable spray pattern so that a huge area can be covered without wasting water.

Plants transpire a tremendous amount of water under normal summer conditions but when high temperatures are accompanied by hot winds, the plants transpire water faster than they can draw it up. The result is first wilting and then collapse of cell tissue.

A shower of rain or watering will enable the plant to draw up more water and it will recover except for the permanently damaged scorched areas, but this is enough to spoil the appearance of the plant for the rest of the season. The new leaves on deciduous trees are susceptible to scorch damage which spoils their appearance until leaf fall in autumn.

If your garden has suffered from hot winds be ready for the next heat wave with your hose and sprinkler in good working condition. If you are away at work all day, I don't advise leaving hoses or sprinklers running unattended, but do the next best thing and check the weather forecast so that you can soak the garden in the evening or early morning when high temperatures are expected. A good layer of mulch over garden beds will help keep roots cool.

TREES AND SHRUBS

Jacaranda for superb summer colour.

The Jacaranda

The Jacaranda is one of the most beautiful trees in the garden. It is lovely when it is in bud — like lace against the sky, exotic in purple bloom with a pool of fallen petals beneath it, and finally it provides a pleasant dappled shade for summer. This is an ideal time to plant a Jacaranda. It will get away to a good start with plenty of good growing weather ahead.

As well as being beautiful it is easy to grow and not subject to pests and disease. In frosty areas it will need shelter until it has established itself, but will then grow successfully. As with all trees grown mainly from seed, there is quite a lot of variation among Jacarandas. If you look at several planted close together — down a street for instance — you may notice one that is very much paler or darker than its neighbours. There will always be some that flower very much better than others.

Not many people have room in a garden to plant a Jacaranda and a Flame Tree (*Brachychiton acerifolium*) to achieve the most spectacular of companion plantings. But as long as overhead wires are no problem, one tree could be planted in the garden and the other on the footpath. Or, if you have a friendly neighbour, you could have a joint planting with a Jacaranda on one side of the fence and a Flame Tree next door.

In mild climate areas the Jacarandas often begin coming into leaf at flowering time, encouraged by the warmth. In Melbourne they flower later when in full leaf. In warm climates many Jacarandas have a second, light blooming when they are in leaf. This long blooming period is another of the charms of the Jacaranda — it really gives you a run for your money.

Plants, like people and animals, are programmed to respond to an inner clock. They are sensitive to photo-periods (day-lengths and night-lengths) and to temperature changes. A long dry period will trigger a sort of panic button which causes them to flower magnificently and produce plenty of seed so that the species will survive even if the existing trees die of drought.

A period of warm weather in winter followed by rain will stimulate dormant trees into beginning to make spring growth. This particular instance of early-flowering Jacarandas is the result of a long dry period followed by a rainy spring.

In my student days in Brisbane we always watched the Jacarandas with a beady eye. Early flowering was supposed to mean that the examinations would be harder than usual.

Datura — a beautiful but poisonous plant common in home gardens.

Datura and Dais

A plant flowering now with an angelic name (though not a particularly angelic nature because it is poisonous) is *Datura suaveolens* (Angel's Trumpet). Judging by the number of requests I get each year for the name of this plant, people must find this flower attractive.

The enormous creamy trumpets that hang on the Datura are beautiful and sweetly scented, but the shrub itself is not very appealing when it is not in flower. Datura is a member of the tobacco family (Solanaceae) and has large, droopy leaves which make it rather top heavy and liable to wind damage. If you want to grow it, put it in a position where it is sheltered from wind. Datura will grow in any garden soil. But bear in mind that flowers and fruit are poisonous.

Still another shrub which always attracts a lot of inquiries at this time is *Dais cotinifolia*. This is a shrub which grows to about 3 m (10 ft) and is only noticed in gardens when it comes into flower.

The flowers are similar to those of Pimelea — a native plant, which belongs to the same family (Thymelaeaceae) and resembles pale pink pompoms, though the rather odd name, Dais, means a torch. Dais is available at some nurseries when it is in flower, and makes a satisfactory garden shrub.

Privet

I am a conservationist, but even the most devout conservationist must sometimes feel like exterminating something. And there are times when I wish I could exterminate Privet. Privet (*Ligustrum ovalifolium* and *L. lucidum* — shining leaves) is a menace to bushland and gardens alike.

It has its uses — as a fast-growing but unimaginative hedge plant, an understock for Lilac (though this practice is dying out) which belongs to the same family (Oleaceae) and as a plant for polluted areas where nothing else will grow. But it has invaded and choked bushland and gardens through lack of control.

Privet seeds freely and every time I go into my garden I pull up hundreds of seedlings spread by birds and rain from Privet in neighbouring gardens. Even pot plants are choked with them. This is the time to prune Privet to stop seeding and if there's Privet growing nearby, watch out for seedlings in your garden.

Some of the variegated forms of the small-leaved Privet are attractive and make good subjects for topiary, being more rapid growers than English Box which is the traditional topiary plant. The varieties *L. ovalifolium* "Aureo-marginatum" and "Aureum" look attractive clipped into a ball, and constant clipping prevents it flowering and seeding.

Privet can be used where soil has been polluted by factory waste. It has been planted in such areas along the Parramatta River. It is grown as a weeping standard and looks surprisingly attractive in flower when grown this way.

The large-leaved Privet *L. lucidum* grows into a small tree and the varegated forms "Tricolour" and "Aureo-variegatum" could be worth growing where conditions are too difficult for more desirable trees. The leaves are handsome and the tree grows quickly in the worst conditions.

Apart from its invasive habits, Privet is a menace because of its allergenic properties. The flowers cause a lot of asthma and hay fever and the sap from young growth can also cause allergic reactions. On the whole, Privet is something we can all do without.

PERENNIALS AND ANNUALS

Fuchsia gracilis — *delicate arching stems and drooping bells in pinky red and purple.*

Fuchsias

Fuchsias are delightful plants for the garden. They revel in a cool semi-shaded spot where more sun-loving plants will not thrive. There are many different varieties, some growing into tall garden shrubs, others suitable for tubs and low-growing plants with arching branches just right to droop elegantly from a basket. The Fuchsias in your gardens come from South America. They are found in Mexico, Peru, Chile and the Falkland Islands. There are also several New Zealand species, the best known probably being *F. procumbens.* It is a prostrate plant suitable for baskets or for trailing over rocks or stone walls.

Fuchsias like a rich, well-drained soil with a mulch of compost or manure. They are shallow-rooted and should not be dug round the root area. The brittle stems may need support from a stake or trellis.

Some of the tall, vigorous Fuchsias send out long, arching canes and lend themselves to trellis work. The stems must be tied in position like an espalier and this method of growing displays the flowers well. If left to themselves these long canes arch right over and the flowers are hidden. "Blue Lagoon", with pinky red sepals and huge, double lavender corolla, looks handsome grown this way.

If you have a problem fence along the shady side of the house, Fuchsias could be trained along it. Using Fuchsias this way is particularly good in terrace houses with their long, narrow back gardens with tall fences on either side. In fact, Fuchsias are invaluable in a small shady garden.

Fuchsias can be trained as standards and grown either in the open garden or in tubs. Choose a plant with upright growth, stake it and rub off all side growths. I have a Fuchsia growing as a small tree about 1 m (3 ft) high. It is growing with Azaleas and flowers in summer after the Azaleas have finished flowering. I prune it back each autumn to keep it the right size and tip-prune the new growth to get a dense flowery ball.

The best fertilisers for Fuchsias are the liquid types like Aquasol. They love fish fertilisers so if you don't mind a slight cod-liver oil smell, try one of those.

Pinks

Looking round the nurseries I have noticed scented Pinks in small pots. Each plant has at least one flower so you will know what you're buying.

Pinks make silvery borders or rockery plants and there is so much variation in the colours and markings on these flowers that you can get quite a collection. Colours are from white to pink and dark red in many shades and often have contrasting patterns on the petals. One of the pleasures of Pinks is their perfume — not all members of the Carnation family have that wonderful Carnation fragrance but you'll find it in the clove-scented Pinks.

Pinks can also be raised from seed planted in summer for flowers the following summer. A packet of Fairy Pinks will yield a selection of pink and white shades. All members of the Carnation family like plenty of sun and well-drained sandy loam with a dusting of lime.

In hot climates like Brisbane, members of the Carnation family are short lived and should be replaced after two or three years.

Blue-flowered Plants

Nierembergia is an attractive perennial which is useful as a summer-flowering border or rockery plant and is often available from nurseries.

Nierembergia or Blue Cup Flower comes in a range of blues to violet and is a native of Argentina. It can be grown from seed planted in autumn or early winter along the coast and spring in cooler areas. Because of its small size it is often mistaken for an annual and pulled out after its first flowering.

Nigella is another blue-flowered plant which could be grown more in summer gardens. This annual is popularly called Love-in-the-mist because of the way the sky blue flowers are fringed with ferny foliage. It grows readily from seed sown in autumn and likes a position where it is protected from hot winds and the hot afternoon sun.

As a substitute for Nierembergia you might try Torenia, a sturdy little blue-flowered annual for rockery or border which will flower all summer and stands up to heat and storms without turning a hair. Look for seedlings now or raise some seeds for flowers later in summer.

Love-in-the-mist (Nigella) — sky blue flowers are fringed with ferny foliage.

CLIMBERS AND CREEPERS

Seasonal Flowerers

There is an attractive mauve-pink creeper flowering now called Clytostoma, which hangs in a sheet of trumpet-shaped flowers backed by shiny green leaves.

This creeper was formerly called *Bignonia lindleyi*, a much easier name to remember than its present one of *Clytostoma callistegioides*. It looks spectacular while in flower and its glossy foliage is attractive all year round, making it an attractive cover for a wall. Another member of the Bignonia family also flowering now is the bright golden *Doxantha unguiscati* (Cat's Claw Creeper). This is a vigorous climber which looks very handsome climbing over the wire-netting walls round tennis courts. It can be used to cover ugly, high wire fences around factory sites and is useful for training over a dead tree stump. It can attach itself to fences or walls with its tiny cat's claws so that it is self-supporting.

Climbing plants will provide quick cover over raw or ugly surfaces and also will provide quick shade over pergolas and provide a privacy screen. Other climbers flowering now include *Thunbergia grandiflora*, the lovely twiner with clusters of blue trumpets; Star Jasmine (Trachelospermum), with clusters of sweetly perfumed white, starry flowers; and Honeysuckle.

I have several climbers growing in tubs including the blue

A native summer-flowering climber, Pandorea jasminoides rosea.

Thunbergia, Trachelospermum and the Australian native, *Pandorea jasminoides,* which has large pale pink or white bells with a red throat. They all grow well though Trachelospermum is probably most suited for tub planting, being a rather dainty plant with good, glossy foliage that is attractive even when the plant is not in flower. Also, there is a variegated type (*T. jasminoides variegatum*) which has cream and green foliage tinged with red. This makes a good tub plant although it does not flower as freely as the parent.

If you are thinking about planting a climber don't overlook passionfruit, either the fruiting ones or purely decorative varieties. All are quick growers and respond well to watering and feeding.

If you grow creepers, you should be tying up new growth to keep them under control. Spring-flowering Jasmine and Wistaria throw out long, vigorous canes now and will engulf the garden if you don't watch them. This is a good time for planting creepers and any put in now will get away well.

ROSES

Caring for Climbers

Climbing Roses are flowering well at present, and, though we are a long way from the next Rose planting season, this is the time to see them at their best and make a note of what to buy later. Many Rose nurseries now have good displays of climbers flowering and there are quite a few miniature Roses in pots on sale. The latter can be planted out now quite safely, and are a good addition to a rockery.

Most people like deep, velvety red Roses. I was given a bunch of "Josephine Bruce" recently — they looked as if they had been cut out of velvet. This is a strong grower and flowers profusely usually in clusters of three or four large flowers. It does not have a great deal of perfume and may have a tendency to mildew in coastal areas. A velvety red Rose with a wonderful perfume, "Typhoo Tea" is well worth growing.

Climbing Roses have to be treated differently at pruning time unless they are a climbing form of a garden variety like "Climbing Super Star", which would be pruned at the same time as other garden Roses. But many climbers are spring-flowering, and winter pruning would cut off all the flowering wood. Spring or summer blooming climbers can be pruned after flowering or in autumn. Lateral branches that have flowered can be cut back to two or three good eyes. Old canes or dead wood should be removed at the base.

Climbing Roses are not usually pruned during the first two years. The canes are simply tied down in a fan-shape and any spent blooms removed to a good eye to encourage future blooms. (Climbing Roses do not flower very much during their first year.) Canes obviously growing in the wrong direction which cannot be tied back on to the trellis or frame should be cut off at the base.

Weeping varieties, now in full bloom, need only the removal of spent flowering canes. "Mermaid" is a particularly strong-growing Rose which needs strong support. The canes can be kept securely tied, or tied to a certain height and then allowed to cascade freely. Quite spectacular effects can be achieved by growing "Mermaid" over to a tree and letting it run riot in the branches.

In my garden blooms a white Rose which was a mistake. Originally it was a white Banksia Rose which, soon after planting, was the centre of a dog fight. It recovered from this accident and grew rapidly, only to reveal itself at flowering time as the understock — *Rosa multiflora.* I should have taken it right out but it looked so attractive with its vigorous climbing canes (almost thornless), good foliage and cascades of tiny white scented flowers touched with pink that I left it and planted a new Banksia Rose nearby. Both now grow over an archway tangled with Wistaria and I am not sorry I spared the *multiflora.* It's growing in a difficult spot and is never troubled by any pests or diseases.

Rosa multiflora — *commonly used as an understock but occasionally escaping to flower in its own right.*

However, if the understock begins to shoot on your Roses, don't hesitate to cut out any briars flush with the trunk. On old Roses grafted on the understock known as *R. indica major* the briars often come from below the ground. In this case you will need to scrape the soil back a bit to find the source of the shoot and cut it off at its base. Just cutting at ground level will only result in more growth. The *indica major* understock has loose pink Roses and an untidy, sprawling habit — it's also very prickly. Sometimes old, neglected Rose beds are a mass of pink briar Roses at this time, indicating that the understock has overwhelmed the budded varieties completely. If you have inherited a garden full of briars from a previous owner take them out and start again with fresh Rose bushes. Check for survivors though. There may be some interesting and tough old Roses struggling among the briars.

Roses will need to be sprayed to protect them from the fungus diseases black spot and mildew which attack the foliage. Some Rose blooms may be showing signs of grey mould which resembles Azalea petal blight and thrives in humid weather. Use a complete Rose spray that will protect against insect pests as well.

BULBS

Hippeastrums

Those gorgeous big Lilies, Hippeastrums, which belong to the Amaryllis family, flower very well in summer and should be grown more in gardens or used as a container plant. There are some really striking modern hybrid varieties available now and if you have been admiring them flowering in other people's gardens, make a note to grow some yourself next season.

Bulbs are usually available during June, July and August and should be planted with their necks above soil level. Two or

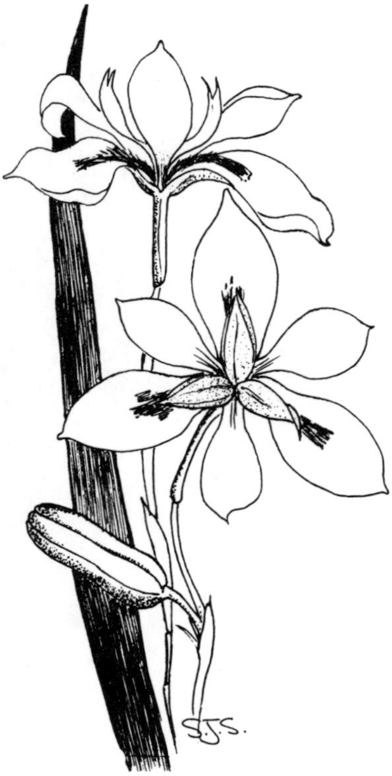

Dietes — the summer-flowering blooms are white marked with mauve and deep gold.

three can be planted in a 25 cm (10 in) pot with the bulb only half buried for a striking display in spring or early summer.

Bulb Care

Leaves on spring-flowering bulbs can be removed as they begin to yellow. They take up a lot of room in the garden at this stage but the leaves are providing food for the bulb and are essential if the bulb is to flower next year.

Summer flowering bulbs and bulb-like plants like Liliums should be kept watered and snail bait should be scattered around them. Gladiolus corms can still be planted for late summer flowers and any that have reached the four-leaf stage should be sprayed every ten days with Malathion or Supracide to combat thrips which are a serious pest of Gladiolus.

Dahlias

Dahlia tubers can be planted out all this month for a good display of flowers through summer-autumn. Dahlias take up a lot of space in the garden but even a few will be rewarding in length of flowering time. Dahlias should be staked at planting time and the plant should be fastened to the stake as it grows to prevent wind damage or toppling. Group plantings of Dahlias make a showy display if the colours of the flowers are chosen to blend or contrast. But don't let up on the snails for a minute — Dahlias are their favourite food.

Iris

There is a fairly unusual member of the Iris family flowering at present, *Dierama pulcherricum.* This plant has a number of common names such as Angel's Fishing Rod, Fairy Bells and Lady's Wand. It grows in a clump of narrow, tough, evergreen leaves and flowers on long thin stems which resemble wild oats before the flowers open.

The flowers are bell shaped and hang from thin wiry stems that look too fragile to support the flower. The stem sways alarmingly in the wind, but the plant is tougher than it looks and is surprisingly wind resistant. *Dierama* can be bought from specialist bulb nurseries and is an interesting plant to have for a sunny, well-drained position. If you grow Iris, add it to your collection for some colour after the rest of your Irises have finished flowering. Colours range from white to maroon, but the most common colour is a mauve pink.

NATIVES

Summer-flowering Natives

Native flowers are at their peak in spring, when they attract most interest. But plenty of summer-flowering natives are suitable for the garden — particularly a native garden. Some Wattles are summer-flowering. *Acacia elata* (the Cedar Wattle) is a tall, stately tree with bipinnate leaves, bronzy when new and green later. The flowers are large, pale cream balls, sweetly scented like all Wattle. *A. mollissima* has creamy yellow flowers and dark green, bipinnate leaves. This decorative tree is quick growing and useful as a temporary planting and for its summer flowers.

Hibiscus are also showy summer-flowering plants, and several interesting native Hibiscus make good additions to the garden. *Hibiscus splendens* is one of the best in the nurseries if you can find it, and *H. huegelii* is an interesting blue.

The red-flowered tree which is blooming now is *Erythrina crista-galli,* the Cockspur Coral Tree, a round-headed tree with masses of red pea flowers. It is the same family as the Coral Tree (*Erythrina indica*) which is such a familiar sight round Sydney through winter and spring. Like the Coral Tree, it is very popular with parrots and is usually full of these birds. The Cockspur Coral Tree is much smaller than its winter-flowering relative and more suitable for the home garden. It has rather a short, stout trunk and the flowering branches are herbaceous and die back after flowering until the tree is established.

Flame Trees (*Brachychiton acerifolium*) are also stunning, though these trees are unreliable flowerers at times. If you are lucky enough to own a good one, in a good year it will be a graceful column of scarlet bells carried on bare branches.

Flame Trees are among the most colourful and dramatic of our native flowering trees, but there are others flowering now which should not be overlooked, though their charms are more subtle. New South Wales Christmas Bush is a favourite with home gardeners but the Blueberry Ash should be grown more than it is. It is a small, graceful tree with a slender, upright habit of growth and grey bark. Leaves are a light green with rusty tips and at present the branches are hung with fringes of delicate flowers like those of Lily-of-the-Valley. The white or pale pink flowers are followed by blue berries which stay for some time.

There are quite a few flashes of blue in the native gardens too. Sollya, the native bluebell creeper, starts flowering now. Sollya is a shrubby climber with shiny, light green foliage and bright bluebell-like flowers. It flowers for a long time and has purple berries in winter. Wahlenbergia has been flowering in our native garden. Parahebe, a dainty spreading shrubby plant with bright blue flowers (Scaevola) and Brachycome Daisies with blue-mauve flowers are adding splashes of colour to the native garden.

All these flowering native plants are fairly easily found at nurseries. Any that are hard to come by will be found at specialist native nurseries.

If you are thinking of planting a native don't only consider a Gum-tree. They can be difficult to live with in small gardens. Alternatives, apart from the Blueberry Ash and New South Wales Christmas Bush, for home gardens are: the native Frangipani (*Hymenosporum flavum*), a slender upright tree with shiny green foliage and cream to yellow Frangipani-like flowers in October-November; Willow Peppermint (*Agonis flexuosa*); She Oak (*Casuarina stricta* or *C. torulosa*); and Black Wattle (*Callicoma serratifolia*), which is suitable for a moist shady spot.

Drumstick (Isopogon) — yellow flowers appear among the light-green anemone-like leaves in early summer.

Bottlebrush (Callistemon) breaking into pink leaf as blossoms fade.

EDIBLES

General Care

Keep watering vegetable beds, particularly on windy days, and give them a side dressing of all-purpose fertiliser to keep them moving. Vegetables should be grown quickly and eaten while they are young and tender.

Don't let weeds invade vegetable beds — they harbour pests and diseases as well as taking up water, fertiliser and sun that your plants need. Put down some mulch between the rows to suppress weeds and keep the soil from drying out. Use straw, mushroom compost, sawdust or seaweed, depending on what is available. Add a little extra nitrogen fertiliser to counteract nitrogen loss during decomposition of the mulch.

Pumpkins, cucumbers, melons and other members of this family are prone to mildew. If this is not controlled by regular spraying the plants become defoliated to the extent that developing fruit has no shade protection and becomes sun-scalded. Although fungus diseases that attack foliage don't usually kill plants directly, they do weaken them severely. Black spot mildews and rust on leaves cause them to wither and drop, leaving the plants with insufficient foliage to conduct photosynthesis. This weakens the plant and leaves it open to attack from other pests and diseases so that it will die. Untreated diseases spread to other plants and the problem increases so it is worthwhile protecting the plants from fungus diseases. Use a fungicide that is recommended for the particular disease, read the directions on the label carefully and spray according to directions.

Caterpillars can ruin home vegetable crops but there is a product on the market called Dipel, which is a bacterial control of caterpillars — the lepidoptera larvae like the cabbage white butterfly. Dipel is a biological control rather than an insecticide and kills the caterpillars by giving them a bacterial disease which only affects caterpillars.

If you have fruit ripening on trees now, take precautions against fruit fly. Dak Pots hung in trees are effective as long as you remember to hang fresh ones in the trees each season. Dak Pot is a chemical lure and should be used in combination with a spray programme. Rogor or Lebaycid are effective. Again, read the label before spraying — some fruit trees are susceptible to damage from Rogor. It is also important to gather up and burn all fallen fruit because this is a source of continued infestation. The larvae move into the soil to pupate and emerge as adults ready to start a new infestation.

Tomatoes

Home gardeners wring their hands over their tomato plants and urge them to ripen in time for Christmas when prices are always highest. A cool spring followed by a mainly cool summer slows down growth and ripening in the vegetable garden. Once tomato plants have begun to set fruit they can be helped along with side dressings of a complete fertiliser like Gro-plus, which should be watered in well.

Any well-developed fruit clusters can have their ripening process speeded if the cluster is tied loosely in a brown paper bag. The brown paper bag creates a warmer atmosphere and traps the very small quantities of ethylene gas the fruit releases. This is a ripening agent. This bag will also give tomatoes some protection against fruit fly.

If you want to try the brown paper bag idea, choose fruit clusters that are well-developed and ready for ripening. Do not be tempted to use plastic bags because they will make the tomatoes too hot and humid and they may develop fungus diseases. Wait for a nice fine day — it's no good going round your tomato plants with paper bags only to have them soaked by rain.

Nurseries are selling single tomato plants. This is a great idea. Usually if you plant a crop of tomatoes you get a glut all in one week, but by buying plants one or two at a time it is possible to have a succession of tomatoes ripening right through summer.

Help mature tomatoes ripen by tying them loosely in brown paper bags.

CHECKLIST

This is the holiday period and if you are going away make arrangements for your garden to be watered and lawns mowed so that your home won't look empty and an open invitation to burglars.

Flowering Now

Trees and Shrubs:
Abelia,
Abutilon,
Beloperone,
Buddlea davidii (summer Lilac),
Calodendron capense (Cape Chestnut),
Cistus,
Cuphea,
Delonix (Poinciana),
Duranta,
Escallonia,
Frangipani,
Fuchsia,
Gardenia,
Heliotrope,
Hibiscus,
Hydrangea,
Hypericum,
Jacaranda,
Lantana hybrids,
Lavender,
Nerium (Oleander),
Osmanthus,
Pentas,
Plumbago,
Protea,
Roses,
Russelia,
Salvia,
Spirea bumalda "Anthony Waterer",
Stenolobium.

Perennials and Annuals:
Acanthus,
Ageratum,
Alyssum,
Antirrhinum,
Aster,
Calceolaria,
Calendula,
Candytuft,
Canterbury Bells,
Carnation,
Centaurea,
Cerastium (Snow-in-summer),
Clarkia,
Cleome,
Daisy (Marguerite, Pyrethrum and Shasta),
Echium,
Erigeron,
Gazania,
Geranium,
Gerbera,
Globe Amaranth,
Godetia,
Hollyhocks,
Isoloma,
Linaria,
Lobelia,
Marigolds,
Nasturtium,
Nepeta,
Petunia,
Phlox,
Pinks,
Rudbeckia,
Stokesia (Stoke's Aster),
Sweet William,
Torenia,
Verbena,
Zinnia.

Bulbs:
Agapanthus,
Canna,
Dahlia,
Crinum,
Day Lily,
Dierama (Fairy Fishing Rods),
Dietes,
Gladiolus,
Gloxinia,
Hippeastrum,
Jacobean Lily,
Japanese Iris,
Liriope,
Tiger Lily,
Tigridia,
Tulbaghia.

Climbers:
Antigonon,
Aristolochia (Dutchman's Pipe),
Bougainvillea,
Campsis,
Convolvulus,
Lonicera (Honeysuckle),
Mandevilla,
Maurandia,
Pandorea,
Phaseolus (Snail Creeper),
Podranea ricasolina,
Quisqualis (Rangoon Creeper),

DECEMBER

Solandra,
Solanum,
Stephanotis,
Thunbergia,
Trachelospermum.

Natives:
Actinotis (Flannel Flower),
Angophora cordifolia (Gum Myrtle),
Backhousia,
Blandfordia (Christmas Bells),
Brachycome,
Ceratopetalum (New South Wales Xmas Bush),
Eucalpyts,
Grevillea robusta (Silky Oak),
Hibbertia,
Isopogon,
Kunzea,
Lambertia,
Leptospermum (some species),
Melaleuca leucadendra,
M. Linariifolia,
Oreocallis wickhamii,
Patersonia,
Sollya.

Plant

Trees, Shrubs and Climbers:
Container-grown trees and shrubs can be planted out. Many are being sold in flower at present and will add instant colour to the garden or go into tubs for patios. Climbers for colour or fast shade available for planting now are:
Antigonon,
Bougainvillea,
Mandevilla,
Ornamental Grape,
Passionfruit,
Phaedranthus,
Solanum,
Thunbergia,
Wistaria.
Provide a trellis or pergola on which to train them.

Perennials and Annuals:
Advanced herb, rockery and perennial plants are available, also flowering indoor plants such as Gloxinia, Tuberous Begonia, etc. Advanced bedding plants of summer annuals like:
Aster,
Marigolds,
Petunias,
Phlox,
Verbena,
Sweet William,
Zinnia are now available. *Zinnia linearis* can be raised from seed for rockery or border plantings.

Bulbs:
Bearded Iris,
Crinum,
Gladiolus,
Nerine.

Vegetables:
Vegetable seedlings or seed for late summer crops can be planted still. These are:
Beans,
beetroot,
carrot,
Chinese cabbage,
lettuce,
radish,
silver beet,
tomatoes.

Cool-temperate areas only:
Seed of broccoli,
Brussels sprouts,
cauliflower.

Pests and Diseases

Spray caterpillars on vegetables, herbs and all ornamentals with Dipel, Derris dust, pyrethrum-base or Malathion. (Don't use Malathion indoors.)

Rust, mildew, black spot and other fungus diseases on foliage and flowers on Roses, other ornamentals and vegetables should be sprayed with fungicide following instructions on label.

Spray beans, Azaleas, Fuchsias, etc. for red spider with Kelthane.

Codling moth in apples can be controlled with Carbaryl or similar spray.

Fruit fly in fruit and vegetable crops can be controlled by a combination of Dak Pots and sprays of Rogor or Lebaycid as directed on label. This is important. If you have fallen fruit under fruit trees, please rake it up and burn it. This is a big source of fruit fly infestation, and many gardens are literally crawling with the pests.

Snails are also prevalent and can be sprayed with garlic spray (see p. 219) or deterred with snail pellets.

Black spot of Roses — a fungus disease to watch out for in humid weather.

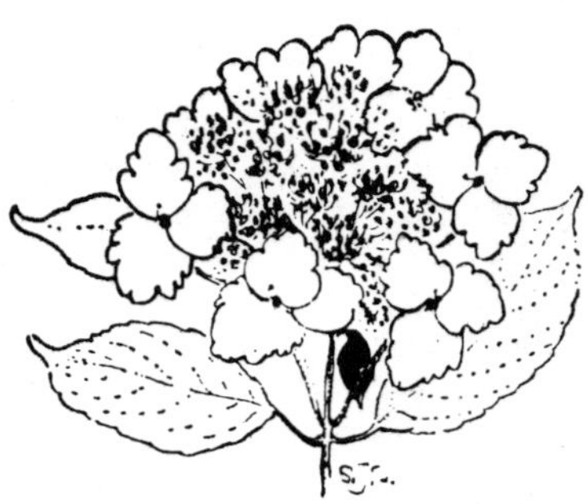

Hydrangea acuminata *(Lacecap) — flowering Hydrangeas need frequent watering.*

Garden Care

Mulching will reduce the need for watering of beds and shrubbery. Container and basket plants will need daily watering through hot weather.

Don't buy new plants or make new plantings if you intend going on holiday, though container-grown trees, shrubs and climbers will get away quickly now if given regular attention.

Sunburn can cause distress when gardening so if you plan to spend your holiday working in the garden remember to wear a hat and use sun cream. Protect skin from insect attack — bush flies and mosquitoes — with insect repellents and try planting Tansy, Rue and Pennyroyal around outdoor living areas.

Keep something on the feet when walking in bushland areas. The white-stemmed gum moth caterpillar moves between Eucalyptus and Brushbox trees when feeding and, if touched, irritant hairs break off in the skin.

Keep vegetables picked and eat them young. Arrange for a friend to water and pick them if you are going away.

Indoor plants can be kept damp over the holiday period by watering well and covering the plant and pot with a plastic bag tied firmly around the container.

THE DECEMBER GARDEN

We have the summer blues but it's not a case for sulphur and treacle — just the season for blue skies and a haze of mauve-blue Jacarandas, Hydrangeas and bold-blue Agapanthus. Why is the colour blue associated with sorrow and sordid jokes and movies, when it is the most desirable colour of all for the sky, sea, eyes and flowers? Summer's blues are definitely uplifting to the spirits and I hope you are all enjoying them.

The three blue, summer-flowering members of the plant family which contribute so much to December gardens are all very easy to grow, disease-free and need very little looking after. They can all be grown in association with one another too — the Hydrangeas grow well in the shade of Jacaranda trees and Agapanthus can be planted as a ground-cover round them where they should get enough sun to produce good flower heads while the tree is leafless.

Hydrangeas particularly are a real gift to the gardener who wants to hide unglamorous house foundations or fences. They really enjoy the sheltered position and — as long as they are not pruned too drastically, and are watered regularly — they will submerge posts and palings in a high tide of blues, mauves and pinks all summer. They also make good tub plants for shady patios and unit balconies. Hydrangeas flowering in small pots can be taken indoors for decoration and put out in the garden when they are past their prime. At this time of year they need nothing but regular watering, particularly on hot or windy days.

If you want to cut Hydrangeas for the house, get up early before the sun gets on them. Choose only mature heads, crush the ends of the stems with a hammer for several centimetres and plunge them into a bucket of cool water. Leave them for as long as possible before arranging them in a vase.

The big blue or white heads of Agapanthus are familiar to most people and, as familiarity very often breeds contempt, some gardeners may overlook the value of this bulbous plant in the garden. Agapanthus is an evergreen and its neat mounds of green, strap-like leaves are attractive all the year round. This makes it a valuable ground-cover or dwarf hedge and it is particularly useful as an edging along driveways and along fences on the footpath.

The thick, white roots are very good soil holders and a planting of Agapanthus on a bank or sloping footpath will prevent the soil from washing away and suppress weed growth.

They require no care other than a handful of snail bait tossed into them every now and then, a scattering of fertiliser when you are doing the rest of the garden and, of course, an occasional good soaking in hot or dry periods. The only other enemy of Agapanthus is children, who delight in breaking off the flat flower heads along the footpath when they walk home from school.

There are several other desirable blue-flowering summer plants out now. *Thunbergia grandiflora* is a creeper with large blue trumpet flowers which appear throughout the year, but the most heavy flowering is in summer. This plant is a member of a large family of vines and shrubs. The orange-flowered Black-eyed Susan (*T. alata*), the best known of this group, needs a warm, sunny and frost-free position.

Thunbergia grandiflora is not a rampant grower and won't become too big in the cooler areas though it grows more vigorously further north. The most difficult thing about growing it is finding a plant. However, there are a few around and it is worth asking for. Planted now it will be well established before next autumn. It can be trained up a sunny wall or used over a sunny rock ledge as a trailer.

Tweedia is an unusual little half shrublet, half twiner with greyish, downy leaves and starry flowers of a strangely intense light blue. Tweedia likes a well-drained position in filtered sun. It is a perennial and dies down in winter. It is easily lost at this time, so save a few of the downy seeds so that you will be able to keep growing it.

A touch of white will highlight the blues and there are plenty of white-flowered plants like Shasta Daisies, Queen Anne's Lace, Alyssum, the climber Trachelospermum and those prolific white Roses "Virgo" and "Iceberg" to put a sparkle in the garden. All are easy to grow, too, which is what you want in summer when it is too hot to bother with plants that need coddling.

Angel's Fishing Rod (Dierama) — a delicate bulb flowering now.

GARDENKEEPING

Gardens Don't Go on Holiday

If you are going away on holiday during the next few weeks, do not buy or plant out new plants unless you are sure they can be well looked after in your absence. New plantings just will not survive being left to their own resources during the height of summer. If you are anxious to acquire particular plants available now the best thing is to order them from your local nursery, and ask for them to be delivered after your holiday.

When you go away always try to arrange for someone to water your garden. If you are going to be away long, arrange for the lawns to be mowed (burglars are always on the lookout for unmowed lawns that tell them the owners are away).

If you cannot get anyone to water, deep-soak the garden and mulch with lawn clippings or partly composted leaves to keep the soil from drying out. You can even use a thick layer of newspaper to mulch the garden if you have no ready supply of leaf mould. Newspapers will need to be sprinkled with something — soil or pebbles, perhaps — to keep them from being blown away. A newspaper mulch will also suppress weeds, and I know one gardener who has used it successfully for years. Grass clippings are raked over the paper to keep it in place and improve the appearance.

Gardeners spending the holidays at home in the garden should be planting Nerines, sowing seeds of Aquilegias and Polyanthus and taking cuttings of Azaleas, Daphne, Camellias and native plants.

Azaleas will take root quite readily from tip cuttings taken from the new growth. It helps to use a hormone powder when you are trying to grow these cuttings — Camellias particularly will strike much more readily. Before the advent of the powder it was not worth while trying to raise them from cuttings, but rooting powder has changed all that. If you are trying to strike a Daphne cutting remember that it takes a long time, so do not despair.

Christmas is Coming

Lawns and nature strips should be mowed before Christmas to present a well-groomed look to visitors and also to stay kempt for a week or so if you are going away. Don't be tempted to set the mower blades extra low and "scalp" your lawns; they'll only go brown and develop bare patches that will become weedy. For a lush green look, keep the mower blades fairly high so that a good green cover is left, particularly if you hope to do some outdoor entertaining during the Christmas break.

Scented, summer-flowering plants near any outdoor entertaining area add an extra touch. Gardenias, summer-flowering Jasmines (*Jasminum azoricum, J. nitidum, J. officinale*) and Star Jasmine (Trachelospermum) are easily-grown plants which can be grown in the garden or in containers for summer scent.

Shaggy white stars of the summer-flowering Jasmine (Jasminum nitidum) *scent the garden.*

Garden Review

With the new year coming up now is a good time to review the garden and make resolutions to improve or change it. Once made, a garden doesn't have to stay that way. It can be redesigned or replanted, and a garden does not remain static — it continues to grow.

What might have been growing well last year may now be too big, so that the garden around is shaded or over-run with roots. When this happens, you have two alternatives. You can live with the large tree and replant the rest of the garden to fit in with it. That is, plant shade-loving things and, where surface roots are a problem, plant shrubs in large tubs. Or you can remove the tree or have it drastically pruned — a procedure that may spoil its beauty. It's your problem — you decide.

But the holiday period — while you are sitting round after turkey dinners — is a good time to think about it. Gardens should be full of colour now, and if yours is not, you should make a resolution to remedy it. Summer-flowering shrubs (Hibiscus, Oleander and Tibouchina) can give every colour of the rainbow, and are easily grown.

This is a good time to resolve to start a compost heap. If you compost lawn clippings and garden rubbish you will be saved the trouble of lighting smoky fires or making trips to the dump. And in a few months you will also have a supply of rich soil, absolutely free.

There's one new year's resolution everyone should make: Do not cover the trunks of your plants with soil or mulch. This causes stem rot that will kill the plant. Examine your trees and shrubs, and, if soil or mulch has been piled up against the trunks so that the plant is now deeper in the soil than before, scrape the offending material away and expose the stem back to the original ground level.

Christmas Beetles

Christmas beetles — those big iridescent things that come crashing through the windows on summer evenings — are numerous and some people have realised that they do more than blunder into you when you're watching television. They also chew up Gum-leaves, Tea-tree leaves and, for a change of diet, Pepper Trees (*Schinus molle*), Plum trees and other ornamentals in the garden.

They are leaf-eating scarabs (*Anoplagnathus* spp.) and are unusual in that it is the adult form that does the damage, rather than the larva. The adult scarabs lay their eggs in the soil where they grow into soft white curled grubs with well-developed legs and yellow-brown heads. They feed on decaying organic matter and plant roots until they reach the pupal stage when they build earth cells in the soil. Gardeners frequently turn these grubs and grub cases up in the course of gardening, and usually call them witchetty grubs.

By the time you realise that the Christmas beetles are damaging the leaves on your trees it is too late to do much about them. However, if you have a very bad infestation you could have the trees injected with a systemic poison by a trained operator. The insecticides used against beetles — Lindane and BHC — are very toxic to bees and, in any case, spraying a fully grown Gum-tree is just not practicable.

One gardener told me she had sprayed her trees with Chlordane (mostly used against grasshoppers and ants) in the hope of killing Christmas beetles. Chlordane is a chlorinated hydrocarbon — very nasty stuff which should be handled with care. Anyone spraying with these poisons should wear a mask, gloves and long sleeves. In any case, Chlordane should not be used as a spray in the garden because it is far too dangerous.

Keeping Ahead of the Munchers

The warmer December weather encourages lots of garden pests that have been either absent or present in very small numbers up to now. The vine moth caterpillar is one of these. Usually this handsome black-and-red-striped fellow is busy defoliating grapevines and Fuchsias in spring as soon as new growth is well established, but some seasons ornamental grapes particularly remain ornamental. You might try spraying them with the biological control spray Dipel.

Wet weather encourages an outbreak of mildew and black spot on roses. Spray with fungicide.

Green grasshoppers are quietly chewing up flowers. They are green and leaf-shaped, with very fine legs, and are hard to spot. Spray with Malathion, or, if you only spot the odd one, sneak up and catch it.

Gladioli opening will be damaged by thrips if the flowers haven't been sprayed. The flowers open with withered edges and are quite spoiled.

Look for red spider on new growth of Azaleas. You will recognise it by the spotting on the underside of the leaves. Spray with Kelthane.

Keep annual weeds in lawns from seeding by regular mowing through summer. If you have Bindii in your lawn it is too late to do anything about it because the prickly seeds have developed. This is a weed that takes all the pleasure out of running barefoot through the grass. Next spring, spray early with a pre-emergence spray and treat any young plants with Bind-di. Most weeds can be pulled out by hand.

Weeds

You always knew it was true, but now there is some scientific proof — weeds are stronger, more vigorous and more successful than the more desirable plants in your garden.

Research at the CSIRO's division of plant industry has shown that some of the world's worst weed pests have a different system of photosynthesis. Called a C4 photosynthesis pathway, it is the basis of the extraordinary vigour of the C4 weeds. However, the good news is that, having found out how they do it, the next step for the scientists is to work out a method of attacking them through this unique photosynthesis pathway.

In the meantime, it's easier to grow weeds than plants and in the US people are doing just that. A company there called Unlikely Products Inc has produced a line called Weed Seed, which includes a planter box, a packet of potting soil and a packet of fast-growing weed seeds! The company claims that with only a minimum of water and neglect, the weeds will sprout in several days. Not only that, for your money you don't get just any old weeds, but a carefully selected mixture. I wonder if they are C4s?

If you are having weed problems, the best way of getting rid of them is still by digging them out. Annual weeds in lawns can be controlled reasonably well by mowing them regularly to stop seed heads from forming. Annual weeds in vegetable beds can be cultivated out by scuffing the soil surface lightly with a dutch hoe or similar implement at regular intervals. This is simple if you have planted in straight rows. Some mulch run in between the rows will prevent weed re-growth.

Weeding is good exercise too and isn't the subject of controversy like jogging. But do it in the cool of the morning or evening when you can sit and contemplate nature in comfort while you're pulling or digging at the pesky things.

TREES AND SHRUBS

Hydrangeas

Flowering Hydrangeas are on sale in nurseries and stores in a wide range of tempting reds, pinks and blues. Many gardeners are disappointed to find that they often lose their distinctive colour when planted out and become the same colour as the other Hydrangeas in the garden.

This is because the colour is not bred in the plant, but only the result of the type of soil it is growing in. Acid soil with a pH value of 5-5.5 will produce blue flowers and an alkaline soil (pH value 6.5-7.5) will give pinks and reds. However, you will be perfectly safe with a white Hydrangea. The white ones are truly white and will not be affected by the soil.

White Hydrangea is a perfect foil for the rich pinks, blues and reds Hydrangeas come in. It needs a fairly sheltered position because too much sun and wind will brown the flowers and spoil the whole effect.

"Sheltered" is a word which is freely used in gardening books and in nursery catalogues and should be interpreted as a situation which will give the plant shelter from full sun and strong wind. It does not mean that the plant should go in the shade. Some plants will grow quite well exposed to sun and wind, but will have a longer flowering season if the blooms have some protection. Deciduous trees are invaluable in a garden for this reason — the garden can receive full sun in winter and in summer the leaves give shelter.

Hydrangea quercifolia — *the Oak Leaf Hydrangea.*

Though Hydrangeas are so popular with gardeners in most parts of Australia there are some special varieties which are not well-known and could be grown more. *Hydrangea quercifolia* is called the Oak Leaf Hydrangea because of its huge and very handsome Oak-like leaves (which is exactly what *quercifolia* means).

The flowers are also interesting. They form a pyramidal pinnacle with large sterile white flowers on the outside and masses of tiny fertile flowers clustering up the stems. They have a strong meadowy fragrance like a field of clover. The leaves go a brilliant red in autumn in cool climates. Another interesting one is *H. paniculata*, which also has creamy white flowers growing in a pyramidal form. It flowers in summer and looks rather like an out-of-season *Viburnum opulas* (the Snowball Bush).

The climbing Hydrangea *H. petiolaris* is not commonly grown. *H. petiolaris* really does climb, rather like an exotic Ivy, and clings to walls or rocks with aerial roots. I have a Lace-cap Hydrangea with a variegated leaf, which is very decorative. The flower head has an outer ring of large, white, sterile flowers, while tiny fertile flowers cluster in the centre like blue beads. There is also a Lace-cap in two shades of blue with a plain green leaf. None of these unusual Hydrangeas is easy to buy, but they are easy to propagate and the best way to acquire them is to ask people who grow them to give you some cuttings when the plants have finished flowering.

Proteas

I often get inquiries about where to buy Proteas, those fascinating South African flowers so popular with florists and flower arrangers. There is a nursery in Victoria which specialises in Proteas, called Proteaflora.

Proteas are becoming easier to buy and you may find your local nursery sometimes has a batch of plants. If you live in an area where Proteas grow well, try to get your nurseryman to order some plants for you. They need full sun and acid, well-drained sandy soil.

Gardenias

Gardenias are a joy while they are in flower and there are several varieties of the popular garden Gardenia which are different sizes so that it is easy to choose one suitable for the situation you have in mind. The smallest one is the variety *G. radicans* which is a perfect rockery plant with low growth, slightly trailing branches, glossy foliage and masses of small flowers which are miniatures of the larger types.

G. florida is a shrub which grows to about 1 m (3 ft) with double flowers 7 to 8 cm (3 to 3½ in) across and "Professor Pucci" has really showy flowers up to 12 cm (5 in) across. All can be grown in containers, the little variety *G. radicans* looking most attractive in a bonsai-style glazed pot while the larger Gardenias would eventually need a tub for a permanent home.

Gardenias don't thrive in a windy, exposed position but will do well in either full sun or partial shade, provided they have well-drained soil. Nematodes are the main problem with Gardenias, particularly in sandy soils. Fortunately Nemacur, the new treatment from Bayer, has improved our ability to combat the nematode problem a great deal.

Gardenias with glossy foliage and scented white flowers are good shrubs for the garden or sheltered courtyard.

Other plants that could benefit from a sprinkling of Nemacur granules are Chrysanthemums and members of the same family showing signs of leaf nematode — brown, blackened and shrivelled leaves moving progressively up the stems.

Lantana

Australia has a long and unfortunate history of introduced plants and animals which have become pests — Prickly Pear and rabbits to name a couple of the best known. An effective way of controlling these pests is by biological control and a lot of work has been done in this area for many years. The search for suitable predators is slow and even when successful predators are found it is often a long time before any results are evident. It is not often that success is as spectactular as the release of the Cactoblastus moth to control Prickly Pear.

A stem gall fly was released many years ago to control Crofton weed. Anyone who has this pest in the garden will probably have noticed that it is often heavily infested with galls but they don't really seem to slow it down very much.

Lantana camara is another of our introduced pests which has been the subject of a lot of research in quest of satisfactory predators. *L. camara* is an aggressive plant and can rapidly engulf large areas in the coastal districts of Queensland and New South Wales. In New South Wales there are more than 200 000 ha of forest land in the coastal area occupied by Lantana. Lantana is a native of tropical America and was brought here as an ornamental garden plant, rapidly adapting to the climate and soon becoming a pest.

The most successful predator has been the Hispine leaf mining beetle *Octotoma scrabripennis,* which was released in New South Wales in 1968. This beetle is small, about 6 mm (¼ in) long with a dark brown, oblong body. The adult feeds on the leaves and lays eggs in slits in the leaf. When the larvae hatch they tunnel through the leaf, eating the cell sap. The leaves develop large dead patches and fall so that a heavily infested plant becomes defoliated. This weakens the plants and though it does not seem to kill them, they grow much more slowly so that they spend all their energy in staying alive rather than spreading.

I visited Brooklyn with an entomologist with the Forestry Commission to look at the progress of beetles which were released in the area in 1973. There are two species of Hispine beetles — one that lives in warm sunny places and another which stays in shaded areas — so that plants in both situations are attacked. The damage is not spectacular but will become more noticeable after a few years when the beetles have become well-established and built up a big population. However, even in winter, when the beetles are not very active, the defoliation of many Lantana bushes was obvious.

The beetles have been even more successful in Queensland where the warmer weather produces three generations a year and they have really been attacking the Lantana. In New South Wales they have spread down the coast from Murwillumbah to Byron Bay.

However, when one pest is removed another often moves in to take its place and around the Brooklyn area it seems that it will be Camphor Laurel. There are vigorous young plants growing up in the scrubby margins along the foreshores already.

It seems to me that one reason why so many plants become pests here is that no one notices and no one cares. Home gardeners don't even bother to get rid of Camphor Laurels that grow up in their gardens — or Privet or Pampas Grass. Home gardeners are, in fact, responsible for the introduction and spread of most plant pests like Lantana, Privet and Cactus.

The infestation of thousands of hectares in Queensland with the dreadful Harrisia Cactus was spread from just one pot-plant. I often see Prickly Pear growing in home gardens though it is not supposed to be grown as an ornamental at all and recently I was told that a weed called St John's Wort (*Hypericum perforatum*) is being sold by some herb nurseries in New South Wales. Its leaves and stems are poisonous to cattle.

Although the damage to wild Lantana is good news, no doubt you are wondering what will happen to the garden forms of Lantana. The small-leaved lavender-flowered species (*L. montevidensis*) is apparently not attacked by the beetle because of the small size of the leaves. However, the *L. camara* hybrids — which are good garden plants — will undoubtedly suffer. The beetle is very host-specific and is not likely to spread to other garden plants.

BULBS

Jockey's Caps and Day Lilies

It seems a wicked waste of beautiful material on the part of nature — to spend eons evolving flowers with exquisite patterns and colours only to have them fade in a few hours.

Tigridia (Jockey's Cap) is one of these fast-fading flowers. The bright red petals with their gaudy yellow and red spotted "jockey's cap" in the centre have faded by afternoon. But like other members of the Iris family, a succession of flowers open day after day. It is well worth having a clump of them in the garden in a sunny position.

Another summer-flowering bulbous plant blooming now is the Day Lily (Hemerocallis). Again the flowers last only one day, but there are so many blooms in a flower head that they flower for weeks. Day Lilies bloom well in sun or partial shade. They are perennial, dying right down in winter and producing bright-green clumps of new leaves in early summer. It is a plant which can be put in and left alone. Every year it will provide masses of bloom and will not need to be touched unless the clump becomes too big. Many new hybrids on the market are well worth growing. The colours are lovely, and the plants just as tough as the old varieties. The correct time to move Day Lilies is during winter when they are dormant, but I have moved a clump in full bloom in an emergency without ill effect.

Day Lily (Hemerocallis) — bright coloured perennials for any climate or type of soil.

Water Hyacinth

Water Hyacinth is a declared noxious weed and anyone growing or selling it can be heavily fined. This water plant is spectacular in flower — the floating, amethyst flowers are exquisitely beautiful. But the plant multiplies at a frightening rate and will quickly choke a pond or watercourse. There is currently considerable concern about Water Hyacinth being washed into the Murray-Darling basin by floodwaters. Water Hyacinth would create tremendous problems if it got into this area, choking rivers and irrigation ditches.

If you are sheltering an illegal Water Hyacinth in your garden pool, please destroy it — and not by flushing it down the toilet or throwing it into the river: imagine the sewerage system of Sydney choked with plants. Burning would be safest.

Actually, with a little imagination Water Hyacinth could solve a lot of city problems. Planted on sewage ponds it will purify the water, solving the sewage disposal problem without polluting the oceans and rivers and without wasting vast quantities of water. The fast growing Water Hyacinth can then be harvested daily and put into a digester tank where it will produce methane gas — an energy source that will save fossil fuels.

NATIVES

The Cuddlepie Gum

An unusual request for the name of the "Snugglepot and Cuddlepie" Gum-tree had me somewhat baffled. I consulted the late May Gibb's book *Snugglepot and Cuddlepie,* both volumes of Stan Kelly's *Eucalypts,* talked to Betty Maloney (who draws beautiful Banksias and wrote those valuable books *Bush Gardens* and *More About Bush Gardens* with her sister, Jean Walker) and the people at the Herbarium. The consensus was that the drawings in the book are possibly a composite, rather than a specific species. Possible trees are *Eucalyptus calophylla* (*marri*), with large urn-like Gum-nuts and fluffy, cream flowers, and *E. ficifolia,* the red-flowering Gum.

Several people felt that *E. leucoxylon rosea,* the pink-flowered whitewood, was a suitable tree for the Gum-nut babies and some called it their "Bib and Bub tree". This is a most attractive Gum which grows to about 10 m (30 ft) and carries bunches of pink blossom and, of course, Gum-nuts. *E. leucoxylon rosea* is suitable for street plantings as well as for the garden and it stands both frost and drought. If you want a Gum-tree with colourful flowers it is a better choice in warmer climates than the lovely, but difficult, *E. ficifolia.*

Banksia serrata — *the inspiration for May Gibbs' creation, the bad Banksia men.*

Little Ragged Blossom seems to belong to *E. globulus,* the Tasmanian Blue Gum and the Bad Banksia Men come from *Banksia serrata.* The editor of the *Daily Bark* wrote his leading article on the Scribbly Gum (*E. haemastoma*) and the Gum-nut babies' sleeping bags were casemoth shelters — presumably minus the caterpillars. I believe May Gibbs used a lot of the trees and plants in her own garden in her drawings.

On the subject of native trees, the lovely native *Backhousia citriodora* is flowering now. This handsome tree is commonly called Lemon-scented Verbena tree and has the most gloriously lemony leaves and attractive clusters of creamy flowers. Backhousia is a member of the Eucalyptus family (Myrtaceae) from the eastern coastal gullies and rainforests. It makes a handsome garden or footpath planting.

Backhousia may not be easy to get but should be available from specialist native nurseries. It is an upright growing tree with a shapely round head which always looks neat and tidy — a habit not shared with many members of this family.

New South Wales Christmas Bush

The spectacular New South Wales Christmas Bush is usually on sale at nurseries and garden centres at this time of the year and can be planted out now from a container or tube. Christmas Bush (*Ceratopetalum gummiferum*) is easily grown in sandy loam but it does not do well in clay. It also needs good drainage and will do better in a position where it has some protection from the wind. It is quite conspicuous in the bush now, growing in the shelter of other trees so it is protected and develops into tall, shapely and slender trees rather than the shrubby bushes they usually become in the home garden.

Not all Christmas Bushes colour as vividly as others and the advantage of buying one in colour (not in flower because it is the calyx that ripens and colours so brightly) is that you can choose one that promises to have good colour. Sulphate of iron (100 g — 3½ oz a plant) scattered round the tree and watered in may improve the colour next season if you are disappointed with your tree.

Christmas Bush is one native that responds well to light pruning and large sprays can be cut for indoor decoration with no harm to the plant. When the display is past its best the bush can be pruned, cutting the young green wood only, to keep a good dense habit. After pruning mulch with compost or rotten manure, plus a dressing of blood and bone, and water well.

Native plants grow well and fast when they are planted out from tube stock. Of course, you won't be able to tell whether or not you have a plant that will colour well, but tube stock can establish itself more readily than larger container-grown plants which may have become pot-bound or be slow to adjust from pot life to outdoors.

New South Wales Christmas Bush makes a good shrubby tree for the garden.

EDIBLES

Hearts and Flowers

Christmas holidays come at the worst possible time of the year for home vegetable growers. Just as the vegetables are ready to pick, everyone goes away on holidays. Many vegetables have a tendancy to "bolt" (run to seed quickly) at this time of year and even if you are only away for a few days things like lettuce will have run to seed and presented you with flowers instead of a heart.

Beans and peas left unpicked will have developed mature pods suitable to use as seed but not for the pot. As soon as this happens the plants begin to dry off, having completed their life cycle. Just to add to the discouragement, weeds like summer grass will have spread through the beds and vegetable prices will have fallen dramatically.

No wonder so many home gardeners put "abandon vegetable growing" at the top of their list of new year resolutions. However, it all points up one thing about growing vegetables that tends to escape the home grower. Picking the crop is as important to success as watering and caring for the plants at the earlier stages of their development.

Vegetables should be picked young while they are tender and at their peak of nutrition. Constant picking encourages more development of the crop because you are preventing the plant from completing its sexual cycle by producing seed.

Home gardeners are always reluctant to pick their crop while it is young and small. Having raised a crop of beans, for instance, they want to see them grow big and fat (and consequently tough) before picking them. In some cases this is the result of the show exhibit syndrome — like the late Gracie Fields who had the biggest Aspidistra in the world, they get carried away with size and forget about quality. Often it is because vegetable growers also tend to be parents, who extend their child-raising feelings to their vegetables. They get the same satisfaction out of raising large vegetables as they do out of raising large children.

Whatever the cause, the message is — keep picking. After all, the longer the vegetable stays on the plant the more likely it is that some insect or disease will get it before you do.

INDOORS

Christmas Trees

Christmas is really breathing down our necks now and it is time to think of Christmas trees and things to go under them. I remain a firm advocate of the live Christmas tree, in a tub to be brought indoors, or growing in the garden where it can be festooned with coloured lights.

Picea (Spruce) makes the most traditional-looking tree and will stay indefinitely in a tub if it is cared for — though it is not suitable for warm humid areas. But almost any Conifer will make a splendid Christmas tree. Our own native Conifer *Callitris columellaris* makes a good dense tree to decorate and even Norfolk Island Pines can be grown in tubs for at least five years (and longer if they are root-pruned in bonsai style).

Take a look round your local nursery and pick out a tree which has the right Christmas tree shape. I suggest you steer clear of prickly ones like Junipers and Sabinas but almost anything else will serve.

Potted Plants and Books for Giving

Potted plants can be enjoyed by elderly people even if their active gardening days are over. Indoor plants — ferns, Ivy or succulents — just need light and water to flourish long after the Christmas pudding has been eaten. Nurserymen offer a wonderful selection of potted, flowering plants that will go a long way to solving your Christmas gift problem.

A flowering potted plant will make a happy gift for anyone. It can be used as indoor decoration for a while before being transferred to a balcony, patio or garden. Poinsettias have long been a Christmas flower in the US and now that they are available all year round in Australia the bright red bracts make a good substitute for the red-berried Holly of European Christmas decoration.

Hydrangeas make a showy gift and you will find them in white and every shade of pink mauve and blue. They make wonderful tub plants for a shady patio or unit balcony and you can control the colour very easily if the Hydrangea is grown as a tub plant.

Pure white and perfumed *Gardenia radicans* is a dwarf Gardenia which can be grown as a potted plant or planted in a rockery. There are plenty of Fuchsias around in pots or hanging baskets. Buy early, though, or there will be nothing much left to choose from.

Mini-Roses are charming and you will find them in flower and also mini-standards; potted Petunias are colourful and make a good gift for a friend in a flat who enjoys flowers without the problems of permanent plants.

Other suggestions for indoor or balcony plants are ferns, palms, Begonias, Crotons, Coleus, Philodendron and Hoya. Crotons are tropical shrubs with vivid leaf colour. They are easily the most colourful of all coloured-leaf shrubs and make splendid indoor plants, provided they are in a well-lighted position. They make an exotic gift. There are some very good Coleus available. They are also grown for their fascinating coloured leaves and are good gift material.

Men are difficult to buy gifts for but any man who works in the garden (even if he doesn't really like it) will appreciate a gift of sharp new secateurs, edging tools, shears or a sprayer that will reach to the top of trees.

A flowering plant might seem a bit sissy if you're buying for a bronzed Aussie type but what about a Bay tree or potted herbs for the man who enjoys barbecuing or running up the odd coq-au-vin. Then there are the many gardening books available from book shops and newsagents. If you aren't absolutely certain that the person you are buying for doesn't have a particular book, it is safest to choose a book which has been recently published.

Gloxinias

Gloxinias are gorgeous flowering plants for indoor use and the shops and nurseries are full of them now. I find them irresistible. The flowers are huge, bell-shaped and in dark rich colours, shown off by the large brittle surrounding leaves.

Like Tuberous and Elatior Begonias, Gloxinias must be placed in a well-lit position sheltered from direct sun and draughts. You will notice that they are grown in quite small pots for the size of the flowers and leaves and that the mixture is very peaty. Watering is very important in keeping these plants growing well. They should be kept moist but not over-wet and it is important to make sure that the soil mix is thoroughly moistened. Don't just dribble a bit on the surface.

The best method of watering is to stand the pot in a dish of water for about ten or fifteen minutes so that it can take up all the water it needs. Then, stand the pot on the draining board of the sink to allow any surplus to drain before returning it to its position. Don't leave pots standing in water because this will cause plants to rot. On no account allow Gloxinia flowers to get wet because this will spoil the blooms.

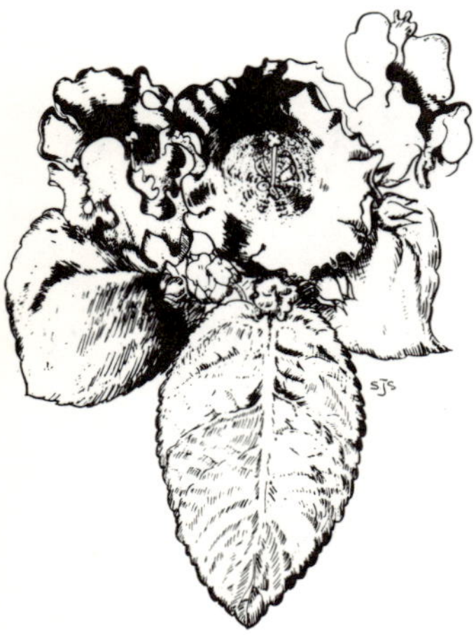

Gloxinia — an exotic flowering plant for indoor use available now.

INDEX

Major references are indicated in bold type
References to illustrations are in italics

C.

M.

N.